Straight Talk

Written Communication
for Career Success

Straight Talk: Written Communication for Career Success is a fresh new approach that gives tools needed to communicate with confidence. This text provides a thorough overview and hands-on practice in the written communication skills essential for life and work success. Whether writing person to person, or to a group, plenty of practical applications give hands-on experience in: practicing effective writing, handling professional memos, participating in teams, and gaining confidence in delivering formal and informal professional documents. This book also helps students prepare for competitive events and includes a 5-Step Strategic Communication tactic which students can immediately apply and practice.

Paul R. Timm, Ph.D. is Professor of Organizational Leadership and Strategy at Brigham Young University.

Sherron Bienvenu, Ph.D. has taught for 22 years at Emory University's Goizueta School of Business in Atlanta. In addition, she has been a Visiting Professor of Management Communication in the International MBA Program at the Helsinki School of Economics (Finland).

Straight Talk

Written Communication for Career Success

PAUL R. TIMM, PH.D.
AND
SHERRON BIENVENU, PH.D.

Routledge
Taylor & Francis Group
NEW YORK AND LONDON

First published 2011
by Routledge
270 Madison Avenue, New York, NY 10016

Simultaneously published in the UK
by Routledge
2 Park Square, Milton Park, Abingdon, Oxon OX14 4RN

Routledge is an imprint of the Taylor & Francis Group, an informa business

© 2011 Taylor & Francis

Typeset in Garamond by Wearset Ltd, Boldon, Tyne and Wear
Printed and bound in the United States of America on acid-free paper by
Walsworth Publishing Company, Marceline, MO

Library of Congress Cataloging in Publication Data
Timm, Paul R.
Straight talk : written communication for career success / by Paul R. Timm
and Sherron Bienvenu.
p. cm.
1. Business writing. 2. Business communication. I. Bienvenu, Sherron.
II. Title.
HF5718.3.T56 2010
651.7'4–dc22   2010011550

ISBN13: 978-0-415-80231-4 (hbk)
ISBN13: 978-0-415-80196-6 (pbk)
ISBN13: 978-0-203-84290-4 (ebk)

SUSTAINABLE
FORESTRY
INITIATIVE
Certified Chain of Custody
Promoting Sustainable
Forest Management

Contents

About the Authors

Paul R. Timm, Ph.D. is a Professor in the Marriott School of Management, Brigham Young University in Utah. He has written and trained extensively on management, communication, and customer loyalty topics. He also teaches in the MBA program at Aalto University (formerly the Helsinki School of Economics) in Finland.

Sherron Bienvenu, Ph.D. taught for 22 years at Emory University's Goizueta School of Business in Atlanta. In addition, she is a visiting professor of Management Communication in the International MBA Program at the (Helsinki School of Economics) in Finland. Dr. Bienvenu has extensive consulting experience in organizations throughout the US and in Europe.

one

Introduction to Straight Talk Writing

Discovering a Strategic Approach

Vigorous writing is concise. A sentence should contain no unnecessary words, a paragraph no unnecessary sentences, for the same reason that a drawing should have no unnecessary lines and a machine no unnecessary parts.

(E.B. White)

Discovering the Foundations of Message Planning and Writing

While business people often feel comfortable in their ability to communicate orally, that level of self-confidence often diminishes when the medium of communication is writing. Transferring ideas into the written word poses challenges for even the most articulate leader. An unfocused purpose, poor organization, grammatical, or syntactical misstep can ruin even a potentially powerful message full of excellent ideas.

This chapter overviews some characteristics of effective writing. It will also introduce you to a five-step strategic approach to professional communication. We call it the Straight Talk Writing Model, which forms the blueprint for better communication, especially in the workplace. As you read, keep in mind that this chapter presents a very broad overview of the model. We will provide additional elaboration in future chapters.

Awareness of these characteristics and strategic approach can dramatically impact your writing effectiveness—your ability to prosper with Straight Talk Writing.

Performance Competencies

When you have completed this chapter, you should be able to:

- Understand the *functional* nature of workplace writing and recognize the importance of focusing on a particular result.
- Describe key elements of the Straight Talk Writing model to adjust your message and writing style as dictated by the situation, the audiences (and their needs), media, sources, and timing options, message content and organization, delivery of the message, and use of feedback.
- Write strong introductions that include clear content preview, create appropriate expectations in the minds of the readers, grab attention, and establish reader benefit.
- Understand the principle of accessing—the use of verbal, psychological, and visual emphasis to help your reader understand key ideas.
- Write with efficiency through economy of language, simple conversational wording, and mostly active voice.
- Obtain and utilize feedback for ongoing writing skill improvement.

Writing is easy

"Writing is easy. All you do is stare at a blank sheet of paper until drops of blood form on your forehead," said American writer Gene Fowler in the early twentieth century. But that, of course, has changed. We now stare at a computer screen! The task of writing is nevertheless still daunting to many people. It just seems like such hard work.

Of the four basic communication skills (talking, listening, reading, and writing), writing is, for many, seen as the trickiest. Conveying ideas with the written word is not a spontaneous, natural way of communicating. And, for some reason, our words on paper seldom sound much like the way we normally talk. We feel the need to make writing somehow more formal or stilted or just plain difficult—to produce and to read.

Writing, however, need not be difficult. In fact the written medium allows some clear advantages over oral communication. You can check your work before you blurt it out. You can analyze your message for consistency, logic, clarity, and emphasis. You can add visual effects and provide verbal nuance. In short, building strong writing skills can give you a formidable advantage in the workplace as well as in your personal life.

Workplace Writing is Functional Writing

Writing can take many forms. Sometimes people write to capture and record their thoughts, or "think on paper." Sometimes people write in the hope that they will entertain or enlighten or amuse readers. Some writing is concise, some verbose. Some contains literary or poetic qualities. Some is eloquent; some conveys deep feelings and builds relationships between writer and reader. All writing can have value. This book, however, focuses on a specific type of writing: the kind of writing that serves the needs of people at work. This books deals with *functional* writing, writing that seeks to accomplish specific tasks, usually within or among people in organizations.

> **Workplace writing, in particular, is functional in nature. It seeks to accomplish specific tasks.**

Because of this special emphasis, workplace writing is different from other types of writing, such as personal letters, poetry, memoirs, or fiction. The difference between literature and workplace writing is like the difference between culture and agriculture. At work, writers are concerned with the *yield*. This is not to say that your writing should be so utilitarian as to be abrupt, abrasive, or overly blunt. Such writing could damage your credibility. When using writing in your career, your challenge is to be functional—accomplish a specific task—while also projecting favorable credibility. If you fail to keep this functional perspective in mind, fail to consider precisely what you are trying to accomplish, your reader will not know what to do with your message.

Since your task is *functional* writing, your challenge is to get readers to *do* something or to *think* in some way they would not had they not received your message.

One way to assure that your writing is indeed functional is to apply the Straight Talk Writing Model. Each step in the model supports the process of maintaining a functional focus in your writing by having you answer some important questions.

Build Your Writing Around a Straight Talk Writing Model

Perhaps the term "model" sounds a bit academic or long-winded to you. Why should we need a model? Doesn't this just further complicate the act of writing? Actually, a model doesn't complicate the process. A good model is a tool that clarifies and simplifies a complex task. The Straight Talk Writing Model we describe throughout this book is a tool and, as a tool, it helps writers to avoid the major pitfalls of ineffective writing. By applying the model, you will add impact and power to your writing. Your writing will be far more functional.

We have found that a key difference between successful and less successful communicators is the degree to which they effectively apply a model. The less successful communicators typically jump ahead of the process to the actual writing. In doing so, they risk the written version of "engaging mouth before brain is in gear." More effective communicators spend effort on planning the message in light of the context and considering various media options before putting pen to paper (or fingers to keyboard). The model serves as a reminder to apply good communication principles.

The Straight Talk Writing Model boosts communication effectiveness.

Let's overview the steps of the Straight Talk Writing Model. Below is a brief description of each step and some related questions that can help you accomplish them. There may be other questions you'll need to address in various situations, but these identify some that must be considered. In the rest of the chapter we will expand on how to use the model. Indeed, the rest of the book elaborates on the model and its implications for Straight Talk Writing.

- **Step 1: Define the context (situation, audience, objectives with each audience).** Is this message necessary? Does it respond to a particular need or problem? Have you thought carefully about your target reader(s) and their needs? Do you have a clear idea of specifically what you want to accomplish? Is your big idea something you can realistically achieve? Is your message addressed to the right person(s)?
- **Step 2: Consider your media, source, and timing options (how, who, when).** Is this message best delivered via written media? Are you certain that you need to write this or should the message come from you or from someone else? Would other ways of communicating be more effective? Is this a good time to write and deliver the message?
- **Step 3: Select and organize your information (right words/right order/right "stuff").** Does this writing contain the right information and is it well organized for understanding? Have you prepared thoroughly in light of your readers? Have you covered all necessary points? Do you have a reasonable number of main ideas that can be arranged in ways the reader will comprehend? Does the writing focus on specifics and personal benefit to readers? Does it reflect your credibility?
- **Step 4: Deliver your message.** Is your planned message one that can be produced to look professional? Does your writing style reflect enthusiasm, sincerity, concern for your readers? Does your personality come through?
- **Step 5: Evaluate feedback for continued success.** Have you thought through reasons your message may not work? Have you polished and edited the message before it is sent? Did you seek input from others to be

sure the message is effective? Do you offer the reader an easy way to respond to you? Have you evaluated your message in terms of your credibility?

If you make the Straight Talk Writing Model an integral part of your message planning and delivery, these five steps will determine the functional quality of your writing—will determine whether it accomplishes its tasks or not.

Define the Context for Your Written Message

To determine whether your document is necessary and appropriate, you need to consider the specific situation, your target readers, and your objectives. Some key questions:

- Have you limited the message to the key issue?
- Have you evaluated your primary reader? Who should you send the message to in addition to the primary reader?
- Do you understand these audiences in terms of their professional and personal characteristics? Their attitudes toward what you will say? Toward you?
- Are your communication objectives clear? Are these objectives different with different readers? Do you fully understand what you are trying to accomplish?

This may seem like a lot of questions, but such questions can be important in determining your message's effectiveness. Less successful writers assume a lot without articulating these kinds of questions. And, in doing so, they often get off track.

An excellent starting point for any writing project is to list such questions—in writing—and answer them as best you can. You may not have definitive answers, but the simple act of considering these questions will help you focus your message by better defining the context.

Write the kinds of questions your readers are likely to ask before preparing the message.

> **Activity: How Well Did You Define the Context?**
>
> Identify a specific writing task you have recently completed. Perhaps it was a workplace memo, a personal letter, a report, an announcement, or a request. In the light of what you just read, how well did you define the context? What might you do differently in future writing?

Consider Media and Timing Options Before Writing

After you define the context, also consider the fact that some people prefer written documents over oral conversations, and vice versa. Management guru Peter F. Drucker[1] observes that people have preferences for either reading or listening. Very few people are both reading- and listening-oriented. Drucker says that quite a few great leaders have risen to the top because they were effective as writers but then failed because their new leadership positions required them to be listeners. When Dwight D. Eisenhower, for example, was a successful speechwriter for General Douglas MacArthur, he could "describe a situation or explain a policy in two or three beautifully polished and elegant sentences." However, Eisenhower as President "was held in open contempt by his former admirers" who considered him a buffoon because he rambled on endlessly with incoherent and ungrammatical sentences.

Reading-oriented people prefer to learn from reading and analyzing written material. The reader-type is more comfortable thinking through ideas and expressing arguments in writing. These types of people may lose arguments because they don't come back with the best response as quickly as the listener types. Listener types prefer to pick up information from listening and conversations. They often prefer spoken media. As you define the context for your message, you may want to look for cues that indicate such preferences in your message receiver.

Food for Thought: Visual Versus Auditory People[2]

A field in psychology called Neuro-linguistic Programming (NLP) studies people's information-receiving preferences. Although we all use a variety of senses to perceive and digest information, we each tend to have a preferred way of making sense of the world. At least 55 percent of business people prefer to receive information visually. These would be the *reading-oriented* people Peter Drucker refers to in his research, as well as today's video generation who digest enormous quantities of information via animation, movies, and the like. A slightly smaller percentage prefer to receive information through hearing—they have an auditory preference. These are Drucker's *listening-oriented* people.

Paying attention to what people say can give you tips to their preference. Comments such as "How do you think this will *look?*" "I *see* what you are getting at" or "The reports *show* me that ..." tend to indicate a visual preference. Comments like "I *hear* what you are saying,"

"That *sounds* like a good idea" or "I need someone to *talk* to me about this," may indicate an auditory preference for information.

If you want to evaluate your message receivers to find cues that can indicate their preferred ways of receiving information, conduct a search on the Internet to get more information about NLP.

On a related note, marketing and advertising people see a marked shift in message preferences among young adults, away from large quantities of text to fewer words and more visual images. Note today's advertising for products aimed at such audiences, such as Apple iPods and similar products. The ads use virtually no words—just images. Likewise, studies have found that few consumers of, for example, cell phones or home electronic products actually read the owner's manual. (A friend of ours at cell phone giant Nokia tells us that only 5 percent of purchasers read the documentation.)

Today's workplace communicator faces two dilemmas: (1) a substantial percentage of people prefer spoken rather than written messages, and (2) the up-and-coming leaders in today's world prefer writing with less text and more alternative forms of visual information.

If a communication situation deals with sensitive or personal issues—say, you need to express dissatisfaction with someone's behavior—or is likely to require an extensive two-way exchange of ideals or impressions, don't rely on writing alone—call or visit.

Select a carefully written document, however, if the situation needs to accomplish the following:

- Convey fairly complex but not highly emotional information (a list of costs and serial numbers of parts, for example).
- Retain a permanent record of what was said (a proposal for services with prices quoted, for example).
- Project a somewhat formal message (a proposal or a contractual agreement, for example).

Disadvantages of written media include potential high cost and the lack of immediate feedback. In most cases, writing a document is harder work—and more costly—than just talking (although a formal oral presentation can be costly and time-consuming to prepare). Nevertheless, when you need the advantages of the printed word and can live with the disadvantages, writing makes sense.

Food for Thought: The Expense of Memos[3]

The use of written, hard-copy memos has diminished in the age of email and other electronic communications. Nevertheless, companies still use them—often without fully considering the expense associated with this medium.

Writing memos has a high price tag, according to a recent study by IWCC Training in Communications, a Toronto consulting firm. Planning, composing, and editing a routine memo takes an average of 54 minutes. This means that writing a memo costs almost $82, based on an annual employee salary of $35,000. And the annual cost of writing one memo per week? $4,258.60.

Select and Organize Your Information

Once you have decided that writing is the best medium for your message, you need to decide the most effective method for organizing and formatting your document. In this chapter, as we look at writing basics, we will consider a generic introduction, body, and conclusion.

Write Introductions That Get Attention, Preview Content, and Suggest Reader Benefit

When you are clear about your main point, put yourself in the shoes of your reader, who may be very busy and is probably being bombarded with many different messages. How can you motivate that person to pay attention to and digest your message? How can you make it easy for the reader to get your message? The answer lies in *reader expectations*.

When readers pick up a memo, letter, or other paper document, or receive an email, they immediately begin to *anticipate*—to form expectations—about the message. These expectations are guesses about the message even before they read it. They also make guesses about the credibility, motives, and intentions of the person writing the message. Psychologists tell us that expectations can have a strong influence on what we hear or read. What we expect is often what we "get"—even when we have to change our perception of the real message to fit our preconceived ideas. In other words, we may psychologically distort or misunderstand a message that says something we did not expect to read. Such distortion kills communication effectiveness.

Expectations triggered in the first words can help reader comprehension.

Expectations, however, can also work in a positive way for the communicator. If what a reader anticipates is confirmed, he or she will better understand the message. It makes sense, then, for the writer to create the most appropriate and positive expectations early in the communication. One of the most effective ways to set the right expectations is simply to tell the reader what the message (or the next section of the message) is about. We do this with *content preview*. Content preview can be general or specific. In either case, it sets the stage for what will follow. The following is an example of general content preview:

- This memo/email is to provide you with some background ideas on how various industries recruit employees.

A more specific content preview gives more details. For example:

- This memo/email describes your team's product-by-product sales results for last month and the year to date.

In both cases, content preview helps readers focus on what the message will be about and alludes to the value of that information. Readers who have a preview of what the message is about and why it may be valuable to them are more likely to read the message.

In longer documents, the last paragraph of a section can be used to create content preview for the section to follow. This description of the specific items that will be coming up links the parts of the document and helps the overall message flow better. Here is an example:

This report on our Hi-Tech Business Leader's Association recruiting results will give you an idea of the major challenges we face. The next section of this report will identify the three most significant problems and provides several recommendations for changing our approach to member recruiting.

As these examples show, the easiest way to create content preview is by simply telling the reader what's coming up next. This can be easily done when the message is direct and to the point—when the main point of the message is presented early. However, if your message would work better if written in an indirect arrangement (such as when conveying bad news or trying to sell the reader), use only general content preview. For example, you would not want to start a sales message by directly saying, "I want to sell you some insurance." That certainly previews the content but may also turn off the reader before you can offer your reasoning. But, for most other messages, you can use direct content preview.

Direct content preview works best unless you seek to de-emphasize the big idea.

Here are some more examples of direct content preview statements:

- The following report recommends renting the warehouse in the Westside Industrial Park.

- This performance review cites three incidents of substandard performance.

- In response to your request for a transfer, here are the procedures you'll need to follow.

- This business plan shows how an investment of only $5,000 can create a viable vending route that will produce monthly income of at least $600.

In many cases, the subject line serves as the content preview. Email has a standard template that includes a subject line. Memos and some letters also use subject lines. A typical memo format with a subject line is shown in Figure 1.1.

To get the most benefit from a subject line, make its wording *informative* rather than simply *topical*. An informative subject line conveys a complete thought; a topical subject line does not. In some cases, a topical subject line is no more than a category for filing the memo. Notice the difference between topical and informative subject lines:

Topical Subject Line	Informative Subject Line
Guest Speaker	Sen. Haley Barbour to be guest speaker at November luncheon
Advanced Management Program	You have been selected for the Advanced Management Program on May 28
Policy on Rental Car Insurance	Do not buy the $15 per-day insurance when renting a car
Staff Meeting	April 26 staff meeting at 2 p.m. in room 37

In each case above, the informative subject line conveys a complete thought. It need not be a complete sentence, but should be an independent clause; that is, a clause that can stand alone in conveying an idea. Using an informative subject line creates clear content preview for the reader.

Informative subject lines convey more information than topical subject lines.

MEMORANDUM

To: All sales representatives

From: Harrison Ford

Subject: New training in relationship selling to be offered in April

Date: March 1, 2010

[BODY OF THE MESSAGE]

FIGURE 1.1. Typical Memo Format

In cases where you choose to place the main point of your message later (such as in bad-news messages), you can still use informative subject lines. They will not explicitly reveal the main purpose of the message, but still create content preview. For example:

- Policy change will affect sales compensation.
- Update on new pricing schedule effective January 2012.
- Further details on last week's benefits briefing.

Presenting clear content preview is one of the simplest ways for a writer to create realistic expectations in the reader's mind. By doing this, you reduce misconceptions and improve the accuracy of your communication.

Content preview creates expectations for readers.

A final but equally important function of the introduction is to motivate the reader to read the rest of the document. You can best get readers' attention by appealing to their *needs*—establishing some *personal benefit* the reader will get from reading your message. Phrasing your opening remarks in terms of what the reader will gain from this message is often a good strategy. Statements such as, "This memo will give you the data needed for your performance review" or "Here are three proven sales tips for handling customer objections about our new model #223" establish why reading the message will be beneficial to the reader.

Then use their expectations to move them toward accomplishing your specific purpose.

Access Key Information in the Body of the Message

In the body of any message, certain ideas or bits of information are more important than others. Certain phrases convey crucial information while others are "word packaging"—words or phrases that clarify, qualify, or further define the key information. One common mistake made in functional writing is the failure to point out which bits of information are, in fact, more important. The following sections explain how you can avoid that mistake.

Give Important Information a Position of Prominence

The more the reader will need to understand that information, the more *accessible* you should make it. In literary writing, a reader is expected to read through the whole story to find the important material. The author doesn't normally help the reader to do that efficiently. In business communication, you need to make the key ideas more obvious. Ideally, a report, letter, or memo should be written so that it need not be read word for word but can be skimmed. The key bits of information should jump out at the reader.

You can signal to the reader which information is most important with good accessing.

As we said earlier, virtually any message will include key pieces of information needed for accurate communication and also additional verbiage or "word-packaging." Accessing is the process by which a writer points to certain bits of information, helping the reader easily identify the most important parts of a message. Your written message can use three types of accessing: *verbal*, *psychological*, and *visual*. Each of these will point to the key ideas of the message. Some are subtler than others, and, of course, you can use a variety of accessing techniques within the same document. Let's look at each.

Verbal accessing is the use of *word cues* to indicate that a key idea is coming up or has been stated. One way of doing this is to say such things as:

- The most important aspect is …
- This last part is particularly important …
- Please read these instructions carefully …
- Of all the options suggested, one stands out …

Psychological accessing entails deciding how to arrange information in the message. Three ways to achieve psychological emphasis are order, space, and freshness.

The *order of information*—when clearly pointed out to the reader—can help the reader anticipate what is coming next and to remember what has been said. This form of psychological emphasis helps separate the key ideas from the extraneous. The following is an example of ordering information:

> This report will give you a chronological look at the history of the problem from 1998 to present. (*This sentence provides content preview*)
> (*The following are headings the report might use*)
> 2010 to 2012 Gradual Reduction in Market Share
> 2009 Premature Introduction of the Abacus Product Line
> 2010 Resources Spent to Solve Abacus
> 2011 Loss of Key Management Personnel

Other orders of arrangement that are readily recognized by your reader will be to compare places ("Districts in the Midwest Region are compared ...") or cause and effect.

When we talk about *space* in terms of psychological emphasis, we are referring to the relative amount of space devoted to a particular topic. If, for example, a sales letter for a piece of machinery spends several paragraphs describing reliability and only one short line indicating something about its ease of operation, we psychologically determine that reliability is more important than ease of operation.

Finally, psychological emphasis can be achieved through *freshness* by suggesting that the message is a new approach, a catchy idea, or a particularly innovative notion. Imaginative wording such as identifying a problem by a clever phrase can give psychological emphasis to it.

Visual accessing includes the use of lists, icons, spacing, etc., to allow the reader to skim through the message and gather its important ideas. The following list offers suggestions on visual techniques you can use. Visual accessing techniques can include:

- Enumeration: 1, 2, 3, or I, II, III, or a, b, c.
- Listing: such lists are put in columns and can have these notations:
  1 Numerals.
  A Letters.
  - Bullets.
- "Wingdings" (such as ", ⊠, ☺).
- CAPITALIZING or **bolding.**
- Headings and captions.
- <u>Underlining</u> or *italics*

Borders around paragraphs, pages, or other sections

- Typeface variations using different **FONTS**, *styles*, and SIZES
- Icons, clip art, and simple illustrations.

- Colored paper and design borders (which can be purchased at office supply stores ready for your computer printer or photocopier).
- Graphics.
- Varied margins and line justifications to "frame" the message.
- Use of white space to provide contrast and give your audience a break.

Today's word-processing software gives anyone a wide variety of accessing capabilities once available only to artists and designers. Take the time to learn about such capabilities and you'll give added professionalism to your documents while providing better access for your reader. However, be careful not to use too many different visual techniques in the same document. Too much variety gives a busy, cluttered look.

Limit Your Main Points

Be sure to keep the number of main points in your message to a manageable number. People can seldom digest more than five main points. Messages with three to five points should be the norm. Some audiences can deal with more complexity, of course, but it is best to strive for the fewest number of main points possible to convey your specific purpose.

Most readers cannot comfortably handle too many main points. Three to five seem to work best.

Write Strong, Action-Oriented Conclusions

The third part of any business message is the conclusion. Business writing almost always requires a conclusion. The most common functions of concluding remarks are to:

- **Summarize.** A summary of main ideas provides a good review for readers. Don't repeat the whole document, of course, but an abbreviated recap can be very helpful.

- **Motivate action.** Since business writing seeks to get readers to do something, you should also motivate them to act. Make the requested action easy for the reader. Say what you want them to do or think in the conclusion of your message. Often, adding a few words about the urgency to act now can get readers to avoid procrastinating.

- **Leave the reader with something to remember.** The end of the document is a strong emphasis position and you should take advantage of that fact. Add a final comment that may recap your theme, add additional motivation or otherwise reinforce your big idea. Common examples of this are found in many sales letters that include "P.S." comments designed to reinforce or further motivate the reader. For example, a sales letter may close by saying "If you call within a week, you will receive an additional ...," or an instructional memo may recap the three steps needed to accomplish the specific purpose.

The last words of a message hold an emphasis position and can reinforce or trigger action.

Writing and Overload

Some people argue that today's technology (especially word processing) has virtually eliminated the physical drudgery of creating text. It is easier now than ever before to type, to insert, to delete, to cut-and-paste, to edit, and to format text.

The result of this revolution is an exponential increase—an explosion, really—in the total volume of new text being created. All this has intensified the competition for each reader's time and attention. Because there is so much to read and too little time in which to read all of it, readers are being forced to become more selective.

Consider all the written documents (mail, flyers, advertisements, emails) you receive on a particular day. Now think about and jot down your first-impression answers to these questions:

- How do you sort the important from the trivial?
- What causes you to pay attention to some materials and ignore or discard others?
- What criteria are most likely to grab your attention—to win the competition for your time and attention?
- What characteristics would cause you to immediately discard or ignore a piece of writing?

Deliver Your Message with an Appropriate Writing Style

Unless you have a boss or an organizational culture that dictates something else, the vast majority of your business writing is likely to use efficient sentence structure and vigorous, economical language. As always, it is important to use good judgment and to keep in mind your audience when writing any message. The following sections provide useful suggestions and discuss important elements of writing style.

Use Efficient Sentence Structure and Short Paragraphs

Long, complex, or compound sentences can damage message efficiency. They slow down both reader and writer. Therefore, use efficient sentence structure in the body of your message.

Sentences should convey bite-size pieces of information that can be digested by your reader, one piece at a time. The rule of thumb is that, for most adult readers, sentences should average about 16 to 18 words in length. Of course, some sentences may have only two or three words while others can run to 30 or so. This guideline is not intended to be a hard-and-fast formula, but for general readability—and functional communication—short sentences work better than long ones.

Another consideration in dealing with sentence length is that different lengths have different effects on readers. Short sentences have punch. They emphasize. They hit hard. However, the potential disadvantage of using only exceptionally short sentences is that they may sound like you are talking down to the reader. Too many very short sentences can create a dogtrot rhythm and sound like a children's book.

Longer sentences, on the other hand, can be useful in de-emphasizing information that may be objectionable or unpleasant for your reader. Such information can get "buried" in a longer sentence, which is a good place to put information that you do not want to dwell upon, but which may be necessary for understanding. The following is an example of a sentence attempting to hide information:

> The company is well aware of the unique requirements of this job, which, unfortunately, you have not yet had the opportunity to attain thoroughly, despite your admirable willingness to learn.

The essence of this sentence is "you are not qualified," but the longer construction tries to de-emphasize that harsh reality.

Longer sentences can be useful in hiding or de-emphasizing information.

Finally, in workplace writing, paragraphs are often shorter than you'd expect to find in literature, unless you are trying to de-emphasize a bit of information. People prefer to read information presented in manageable bits. When people receive a written message with long, heavy-looking paragraphs, they are likely to conclude that the message is going to be hard to read. No one wants to face a page covered with a huge mass of words.

Grammatically, a paragraph should develop one theme, but we have considerable flexibility in choosing when to break to a new paragraph. For functional writing, paragraphs should rarely exceed six lines.

How Do People Read, Especially Non-Fiction?[4]

People read in short bursts. To an observer, the reader seems to "scan" through an article, but what they are doing is reading small parts. If they "buy" into that small part, they read a longer part, which leads them into another section, and so on, until they reach the end.

The funny thing is that they have a very strong comprehension on those parts that "buy" their time.

If they don't "buy" a segment, then they skim through the rest, at least until they find something else that catches their attention. However, the chances are that, if they have skimmed through the piece, their retention of the article's facts is extremely small; often they remember practically nothing, except that the writer did not tell them anything and reading was a waste of time.

On average, reading speed is between 200 and 300 words per minute. Therefore, one second is approximately three to five words, and two seconds are seven to ten words.

Readers will gladly give you those two seconds, so use them well. Hone your words down to as few as you can. Do not be cute or misdirect your readers; they do not appreciate finding that you are playing tricks with words.

If you do this well, you will buy between 10 and 15 seconds more of the reader's time. Using the same yardstick for converting time into words, they will read 50 to 75 more words of your masterpiece. This is where you outline the gist of your article. You tell them what you are going to tell them and why they should read further. As with the headline, use as few words as possible. Make it a "teaser," if you can, but make sure that it really does tell them what you will have in the main body.

Do it right and you have bought a whole minute of their time— between 200 and 300 of your words!

These words are where you get across your basic message. Once they finish reading these words, they will have the most concise version of the information you want to give them. They will start to remember what you have written!

You might use a narrative approach at this point, something that "disturbs" or that fits with the reader's likely experience in the area, but keep it all within those 200 to 300 words.

The reader is still not committed to reading your whole piece, but they are much more open to let you buy another two minutes of their time—that's 400 to 600 words more!

When the reader finishes with these two minutes, he or she should have a very good understanding of your message. Not only that, the reader will be able to tell others the main content of what you have written. From there, readers are effectively hooked. They have the main meaning, and they want the detail to go with it. They are willing to give you as much of their time as you need to make your mark in their minds: you have "bought" (and earned!) that time.

Surprisingly, the "body" of the article does not need to be as rigorous in purchasing time as those first three minutes and 17 seconds. It does need to be reasonably well written, and it does have to deliver what you promised. It has to be worth the investment you have gained. Nevertheless, in essence, your reader has accepted what you have written.

Use Vigorous and Economical Language

Look carefully at your writing to be certain that each word or phrase carries its weight. Some phrases that show up in poorly thought-out business writing are there because people think that's the way business writing should sound. When inexperienced writers check the correspondence files to see how others have written in the past, they perpetuate what is often poor writing. They may end up using antiquated business phrases like:

- Herewith enclosed are the prices we quoted ...
- Attached you will find, as per your request ...
- Regarding the matter ...
- Due to the fact ...
- The aforementioned ...
- We beg to remain, yours very truly ...
- Enclosed, please find ...

A writer can sap the vitality out of a message by burying it under these kinds of expressions. In fairness, we should point out that many of these phrases have evolved over time from what was once considered business etiquette. Commerce was rich with formal and excessively polite and flowery phrases in years past. In some cultures, it continues to be so. We recently received a letter from a consulting client in Brazil ended with this sentence: "Staying at your disposal, we look forward to hearing from you." In the American business culture, we seldom use such expressions, preferring more economical, conversational language. In fact, led by the expansion of email, business writing is getting increasingly direct, concise, and virtually absent of ornate or flowery expressions.

To achieve economy of language, also work to reduce unneeded repetition and cluttered phrasing. The following sections present some ideas for boosting the vitality of your writing.

Unnecessary repetition or cluttered phrasing distracts and hurts communication effectiveness.

Avoid Unnecessary Repetition

Although repeating an idea can be an effective teaching device (especially in oral communication) and a useful form of verbal accessing, unnecessary repetition distracts the reader. Here are some examples:

Needless Repetition	Repetition Eliminated
The general rules for internship participants *will be enforced equally for each and every person.*	The rules will apply to all interns.
In my opinion I think the plan presents a reasonable picture.	I think the plan is reasonable.
Although not requiring *a significant paradigm shift*, we should adjust to changing realities.	We should change our approach without altering our basic plan.

Use Economical Wording

Drop any surplus words and cluttered phrases that add nothing to the meaning of the sentence. Change phrases that can be replaced by a single word or shorter expression. Remember that the objective is functional writing, and that often means direct expression. Here are some examples of un-cluttering:

Cluttered	More Concise
In the event that payment is not received ...	If payment is not received ...
The report is *in regard to the matter of* our long-term obligations ...	The report is about our long-term obligations ...
I have just received your letter and wanted to respond quickly.	I wanted to respond quickly to your letter.
The quality of his work is so good that *it permitted us to* offer him a long-term contract.	His work was so good that we offered him a long-term contract.
In this letter we have attempted to answer any possible questions you may have, but if you have further questions, please *do not hesitate to contact us.*	If you have additional questions, please call us.

To achieve a lively and economical language tone, write the way you would talk in a planned, purposeful conversation. For example, if you hand a document to a co-worker in your office, you wouldn't say, "Enclosed herewith please find the report I've written." In conversation you would be more likely to say, "Here's the report I prepared on ..." So why not write that way? Conversational language gets to the point and conveys your message efficiently.

Conversational tone, absent of unneeded verbiage, communicates best in business situations.

Use Clear, Concrete Wording
You improve language efficiency by using clear, specific words rather than vague or abstract ones. Clear wording creates vivid, specific mental images in the mind of your reader. Here are some examples:

Vague, Abstract Wording	Clear, Specific Wording
A leading candidate	Top candidate of 80 applicants
Most of our people	87 percent of our employees
In the near future	By noon Wednesday
Lower cost than …	$4,300 less than …
Low energy consumption	Uses no more power than a 60-watt light bulb
The cost would be significant	Every customer will pay $286 per year

Use Active Voice
You improve language efficiency by using active voice. The grammatical term "voice" refers to whether the sentence is constructed such that the subject of a sentence *acts* or is *acted upon*. If the sentence is written so that the subject *does the acting*, you are writing in the active voice. If the subject of the sentence is *acted upon* (or receives the action), passive voice is being used. (Can you hear the difference in the last two sentences? The first is active, the second passive.) Here are some additional examples:

Passive Voice	Active Voice
Each tire *was inspected* by a mechanic.	A mechanic *inspected* each tire.
A gain of 41 percent *was recorded* for paper product sales.	Paper product sales *gained* 41 percent.
A full report *will be sent* to you by the supervisor.	The supervisor *will send* … or You *will receive* a full report from the supervisor.
All figures in the report *are checked* by the accounting department.	The accounting department *checks* all figures in the report.

Active voice tends to be more efficient because it makes your sentences more *explicit, personal, concise*, and *emphatic*:

- **Explicit.** "The Board of Directors decided" is more explicit than "A decision has been made." With active voice, you know who did what.
- **Personal.** "You will receive our decision" is both personal and specific; "The decision will be mailed" is impersonal.
- **Concise.** The passive requires more words and thus slows down both the writing and reading. Compare: "Exhibit 2 shows" with "It is shown by Exhibit 2."

- **Emphatic.** Passive verbs dull action. Compare "An analysis was prepared by the intern" with "The intern analyzed ..."

The clearer relationship between subject and verb in active voice adds force and momentum to your writing. You help your reader visualize more clearly what is happening by closely associating the *actor* (noun or pronoun) and the *action* (verb). In some cases, of course, you may intentionally want to de-emphasize this association (or remove the actor entirely) by using passive voice. For example, which would you rather report?

I just deleted your report. (*Active*)
or
Your report has been deleted. (*Passive*)

"We have not passed that subtle line between childhood and adulthood until we move from the passive voice to the active voice—that is, until we stop saying 'It got lost,' and say 'I lost it.'" (Sidney J. Harris)

Use Simple, Everyday Wording

Often, a common word can do the job of a multi-syllable jawbreaker. Readers will sense a clear correlation between how many syllables are in a word and how difficult it is to read and understand. Using many big words slows down both the writer and the reader. In addition, long words usually don't communicate any more effectively than shorter ones, despite the increased effort. In the following examples, listen to the differences:

Long and Heavy Wording	Everyday Wording
Polysyllabic verbiage obfuscates comprehension.	Big words block clarity.
Our *analysis* of the *situation* suggests needed *experiential* training to *optimize* the job performance of our employees.	We think our people need more job training.
John *acceded* to the demands for *additional compensation*.	John agreed to pay them more.
My investment recommendations were *predicated* on the *anticipation* of additional *monetary funds* being made available.	My investment recommendations were based on an expected increase in money available.
Ramifications of our *performance shortfall* included *program discontinuation*.	Since we didn't reach our goal, management discontinued the program.

Some business writers feel they must use technical or formal language to convey the appropriate *image*. You serve only your *illusions* of status with language so technical and stilted that it loses meaning for your reader. Talk in terms that your reader is sure to understand. Nothing impresses so significantly as the ability to communicate clearly using terms your reader knows.

Obscure, technical language only impresses if the reader knows what it means.

Beware, too, of jargon—specialized language. Every organization has specialized terms understood by its members but foreign to outsiders. If you are certain that your readers understand the jargon, using it may be efficient. But, if you have any doubt about reader understanding, either eliminate the jargon or define it. Often writers define the term the first time they use it, and then repeat it throughout the document. This is especially true for acronyms or "initialisms" (words made up from the first letters of a phrase). For example, a company may measure "business office accessibility"—how easy it is for customers to reach a service rep. This may be referred to as BOA in a memo or report. But, to insure that the writer knows what BOA is, spell it out the first time you use it.

Every organization uses jargon. This can be okay so long as everyone knows what it means.

Incomprehensible Instructions[5]

The following instructions have been found on actual products. Obviously, these writers did not use the Straight Talk Writing Model in preparing their messages.

On a Sears hairdryer: "Do not operate while sleeping."
On a bag of Fritos: "You could be a winner! No purchase necessary. Details inside."
On some Swanson frozen dinners: "Serving suggestion: Defrost."
On packaging for a Rowenta iron: "Do not iron clothes on body."
On Boot's Children's Cough Medicine: "Do not drive car or operate machinery."
On Nytol sleep aid: "Warning: may cause drowsiness."
On a Korean kitchen knife: "Warning keep out of children."
On Sainsbury's peanuts: "Warning: contains nuts."
On Tesco's tiramisu dessert (printed on bottom of box): "Do not turn upside down."

Evaluate Your Feedback for Continued Success

The final step in the Straight Talk Writing Model deals with feedback—giving, soliciting, and receiving it. This feedback will help you evaluate your credibility and, as such, has a bearing on your continuous communication improvement

When writing, you can get two kinds of feedback: that received *before* you send the message and that received *as a result of* sending the message. Before sending a letter, memo, or report, re-read it and keep in mind the writing suggestions we discussed in this chapter. Double-check to be certain that:

- You wrote to the appropriate audience and used the appropriate medium of communication.
- Your message is well-organized.
- You included a strong, "what's-in-it-for-you" introduction, a clear body, and a solid conclusion.
- You used vigorous and economical wording.
- You used the best word in every instance (and clarified any jargon or specialized terms the reader may not understand).
- Your sentences are not too long or overly complicated and that they avoid passive voice in most cases.
- You avoided unnecessary repetition or wordiness.

After you have finished looking over your own writing, ask someone else to read your important messages.[6] The best way to do this is to volunteer to review or proofread other people's documents so that you create a team. Other readers will almost always see something you missed. Typos, missing words, grammar errors, unintended tone problems, or simply confusing language will jump out at another reader while you may miss them. Accept such criticism objectively and use it to help you write better messages. Writing can be a team sport.

Input from others can provide needed feedback even before the message is delivered.

Keep in mind also that it is never a good idea to rely only on your word-processing program to catch all your spelling or grammar errors. While these features are very helpful, they do not catch every mistake, so don't let them substitute for careful proofreading. And remember, even important email messages can also benefit from a quick review by a fresh pair of eyes.

Electronic Editing Tools

Word-processing programs such as Microsoft Word allow another person to edit your document and type in their suggested changes in red or another color. Using Microsoft's Track Changes tool, you can then look at the changes and decide which changes to accept and which to reject. If a third (or fourth, or fifth, and so on) person wants to add his or her edits, these edits will appear in another color, making it clear who is giving what feedback. Readers can also use the Insert Comment tool to communicate with you. Both of these tools are extremely helpful and can save you time.

The second kind of feedback is the results you get from your message. If you write a request for information and get no responses, you are receiving feedback! Something isn't working, and you may want to revisit your message. The ultimate feedback in functional communication is whether your readers do what you want them to do.

One final comment about writing and feedback: no one writes letter-perfect prose the first time around. Writing is a process of drafting and revising, often several times. Plan to revise, revise, and revise some more. Don't make the mistake of "pride in authorship" where you feel that because you wrote it and it sounds good to you, it must be perfect. Be open to suggestions and be willing to re-write, perhaps several times.

You can re-write and improve virtually anything you have ever written—even that "perfect" document you slaved over last week. Developing writing skills is an iterative and ongoing process. We have published more than 40 commercially successful books and countless shorter documents, and we firmly believe that anything we have written could be edited and improved today. *All writing is draft writing!*

Consider all writing as draft writing. It can always be improved.

Performance Checklist

After completing this chapter, you should be better prepared to recognize the role of the Straight Talk Strategic Model as it applies to functional business writing. Specifically, you should now understand that:

- Workplace writing is *functional* writing. It should always focus on a particular result.
- Good writers learn to adjust their message and writing style as dictated by the situation, the audiences, and their objectives with each audience.

They should carefully consider their overall goal, specific purpose, organizational environment, and the nature and characteristics of readers (primary, secondary, and hidden) when preparing their communication.

- A strong introduction should include clear content preview that creates appropriate expectations in the minds of the readers, grabs their attention, and establishes reader benefit. A what's-in-it-for-you focus is critical to holding reader interest amid competing messages.

- The body of a message should be limited to main points that are relevant to the audience and that can be remembered. Typically, three-to-five main points are ideal.

- The conclusion of most business documents should summarize, include a clear action step, motivate action, and provide a memorable close.

- Accessing adds verbal, psychological, and visual emphasis to important ideas in a message, thus helping your reader understand the main point.

- Most of today's workplace writing calls for an efficient, conversational style using mostly simple sentence structure. Message efficiency is achieved through economy of language, simple conversational wording, and mostly active voice.

- Feedback for the writer takes two forms: that received when proofing the draft message and that received after the message is sent. All writing is draft writing. We can constantly massage and edit a document to make it better.

What Do You Know?

Activity 1.1: Applying Information Sharing and Image Building

Every document does two jobs: (1) it *conveys a message* and (2) it *projects an image* of its writer. Writers should normally be concerned with both information sharing and image building in their documents. Going back to our discussion of word choices, people who insist upon using professional jargon in an attempt to feed their sense of elitism may convey a learned image but will soon turn off readers who can't figure out what they are saying. Such "impressive-sounding" letters may stroke the writer's ego, but they only frustrate the reader.

Conversely, the writer who spits out cold, heartless, but fact-filled sentences with great precision may seem like a well-programmed android. Good business letters are more than pure information transfer; they also involve impressions and expressions of humanity. Even when mass-printed by a computer, professional letters can sound like chat over the back fence with your neighbor. Letter effectiveness arises from both the informational and the "human" content of the message. With these thoughts in mind, complete the two steps in the following assignment:

1   Three sample letters are shown below (pp. 27–28). We have deleted the addresses and present only the body of the messages. Review these three letters.

2   In light of what we have discussed in this chapter, describe your impressions of the relative clarity and image projected by these letters. Look for writing that reinforces or varies from what we have discussed. Suggest how you could improve each letter. Pay special attention to the quality of the letter's attention-grabber, benefit for reader, content preview (or lack of it), accessing, closing remarks, and language use.

Activity 1.2: Searching for the Message's Critical Information

Review the three sample letters again. Look for the words or phrases that communicate the most essential information—that is, the information without which the message would not work. Identify these words or phrases using a highlighter. Where does the writer position these? Are these key bits of information well accessed? Is this the way you would write the letters? If not, what would you do differently? Why?

Activity 1.3: Completing Letter Re-Writes

Select one of the sample letters and re-write it based on the ideas discussed in this chapter. Be prepared to explain why you re-wrote it as you did.

Activity 1.4: Making a Case for Accessing

1   Write a short report (two-to-three pages) discussing why accessing is important in business communication. Include examples of each type of accessing.

2   Address your report to your peers who you assume have not read this book or taken a business communication class.

3   Include your thoughts on when a writer may want to *avoid* accessing key ideas. Describe some examples that will be relevant to your primary audience.

Sample Letter 1: To a Recently Lost Customer

Was it something we said? Or didn't say?

You've been one of our most valued customers, and we've been committed to serving you well. If we haven't completely satisfied you, please let me know what we might have done differently. I can assure you that when an important customer like you hasn't called on us recently, we take a fresh look at the way we do business.

If it wasn't something we said, did one of our competitors woo you away? If so, I'm certain we can provide you with a level of service that no one else can match. Your satisfaction is our goal, and we have expanded our staff and broadened our product selection to better meet your needs. This illustrates our undying commitment to preserve our most valued business relationships.

We miss you. So tell me—what can we do to regain your business? Please call me or visit soon.

Sincerely,
[signature]

Sample Letter 2: To a Job Applicant

Thank you for your interest in ZelCo Manufacturing. We appreciate your letting us know of your availability, and we're glad you think ZelCo is worth it.

The problem is, we don't have a position open right now that matches your background and experience. We are a fast-growing company offering tremendous employment benefits, as you know. But for now we don't see a fit for your qualifications. But we have started a file in your name for future reference. We will call you for an interview should our needs change within the next year.

We are pleased to expand our pool of potential employees with someone as well qualified as you are. Good luck in your current job search.

Sincerely,
[signature]

Sample Letter 3: To a Sales Manager Within the Company

You were chosen to be part of the Bama Software Shops team partly because of your willingness to strive for excellence in performing your job. So far, you are not totally succeeding, as indicated by dropping sales volume.

Our customers can get similar software from any one of hundreds of other companies. Some of them are closer to home and may offer more attractive pricing. Some are just a few keystrokes away on the Internet. How do we compete? By offering the best, most consistently pleasant and professional service available in our area. Service is what sets us apart and distinguishes us from the competition.

Customers must believe they're getting value for their money here at Bama. As we grow, it becomes increasingly difficult to give all customers the level of personalized service they expect from us. And yet, it's ever more critical that customers perceive our service to be superior.

To accomplish this, it will take every employee making the effort every day. It will take our unified dedication to finding ways to improve, even when that means changing old ways. I'm asking you to seek out those things that may inhibit our ability to deliver quality service—together we can change them for the better.

Let's get together next week after our Tuesday staff meeting and do some brainstorming about ways we can give customers better service.

Let's make quality a priority!

Sincerely,
[signature]

Activity 1.5: Ferreting Out the Passive

Select a sample of workplace writing. This could be something you wrote or something written by someone else. Do a hunt for passive voice. Look carefully at each sentence to determine if the subject is doing the action or being acted upon. For each instance of passive voice, try rephrasing the sentence in active voice.

Also note if you find examples of passive that are appropriate to the message; that is, situations where the writer is intentionally de-emphasizing the link between the actor and the action.

Reinforce With These Review Questions

1 Workplace writing differs from some other types of writing in that it is almost always _____ in nature—it seeks specific results from readers.

2 True/False Context analysis requires writers to think carefully about their reader(s), the organizational culture, and the writer's objectives.

3 Telling a reader up front what a document is about is called creating _____.

4 True/False Accessing is a process whereby the writer helps the reader separate the most critical information from the "word packaging."

5 The three types of accessing describes in this chapter are (1) _____ _____, (2) _____, and (3) _____.

6 True/False A critical but often overlooked element of an effective introduction is the statement of reader benefit.

7 True/False It is often important for writers to impress their readers with expansive vocabulary and use of sophisticated language.

8 True/False Writers may effectively use jargon or specialized language if they define it or are absolutely certain their readers understand the meaning.

9 For the vast majority of workplace writing (circle one) passive/active voice is most appropriate.

10 True/False Getting feedback on draft writing is critical when producing an important message.

two
Define Context
Before Writing

It is insight into human nature that is the key to the communicator's skill. For whereas the writer is concerned with what he puts into his writings, the communicator is concerned with what the reader gets out of it. He therefore becomes a student of how people read or listen.

(William Bernbach)

Analyzing Situation, Readership, Objectives with Each Reader, and Organizational Culture for Straight Talk Writing

Effective workplace writing requires understanding your target audiences. The more specific that understanding is, the more likely you will succeed. The Straight Talk Writing Model stresses the importance of defining the context for your messages, including the needs and wants of your target audiences. Many communicators use a shotgun approach, shooting in the general direction of the target and hoping to hit something. Professional, successful communicators must use a narrow, targeted focus—a rifle approach.

Too many writers fail to analyze the context effectively, instead giving lip service to the notion of understanding their readers. When a message is important enough to merit preparation, defining the context must precede the other steps in the communication process. This chapter discusses the steps necessary to do a thorough, in-depth context analysis. Think carefully about the context as described in this chapter and you will greatly enhance your Straight Talk Writing.

Performance Competencies

When you have completed this chapter, you should be able to:

- Describe and recognize the importance of the factors that comprise the communication context.
- Limit the topic of a written message to make it more effective.
- Identify key elements in the external business environment and internal organizational culture that may affect your message.
- Name seven characteristics of organizational culture that can have an impact on how a message is perceived in that organization.
- Distinguish among three groups of target audiences and explain why each audience may have different needs and wants.
- Use listening skills, observation techniques, and secondary sources to gather information.
- Define the overall objective, specific purpose, and hidden agenda of any message.
- Use the Context Analysis Worksheet to guide your thinking for message preparation.

Writing Without a Strategy: CEO's Email Blunder[1]

A classic case of miscommunication took place at Cerner Corporation, a Kansas City-based software provider that markets healthcare information systems. Doctors, hospitals, insurance firms, and others rely on these high-tech solutions for the myriad record-keeping and information distribution functions associated with healthcare.

From its earliest days as a company, Chairman and CEO Neal Patterson has stressed the importance of an organizational culture that supports creative, high energy, bright employees. Referring to employees at all levels as "associates" was one way to reinforce that culture of mutual respect.

The company's website says that Cerner associates are bright, talented individuals with diverse sets of backgrounds and experiences. Perpetuating the company's mission means working together with cross-organizational teams on a daily basis. Associates work in an open environment using an uninhibited communication style to foster knowledge-sharing. This is a critical component of Cerner's culture.

Another distinguishing feature of Cerner Corporation is that it provides a variety of programs to help associates find balance in their lives and manage their many work/home/family/community responsibilities.

Quoting its website:

Work/Life Balance benefits efforts within our organization are continually evolving as the company responds to business changes, as well as fluctuations in workforce participation, associate demographics, and the work/life situation as a whole. Although each area of the company utilizes different resources and responds to different challenges, each area is diligently working to leverage work/life as a business strategy to retain intellectual capital and to position Cerner Corporation as an "employer of choice."

To support these work/life balance efforts, Cerner made a significant investment by establishing the Athletic Club and CernerKids Learning Center—on-site childcare center and state-of-the-art health and fitness facility. The company also offers an on-site café, banking services, dry cleaning services, and an array of additional special benefits at discounted pricing. Cerner works with the local Transportation Authority to provide metro bus access to its Kansas City campus. In addition, Cerner established private meditation and new-mother convenience rooms within its facilities for use by its associates. In all, Cerner provides an atmosphere that empowers associates to manage their professional and personal demands with increased efficiency.

In light of the company's obvious good intentions to sustain a positive and supportive corporate culture, CEO Patterson's March 13 action seems completely out of place. That was the day he sent a blunt, and not-very-tactful, email that sparked a firestorm in the company's headquarters and reverberated all the way to Wall Street.

In a blistering memo to managers, Patterson threatened a 5 percent staff reduction and the installation of time clocks because some Cerner employees in North Kansas City weren't working hard enough. After the memo became public, the company's stock dropped almost 20 percent in two days.

"We are getting less than 40 hours of work from a large number of our KC-based EMPLOYEES. The parking lot is sparsely used at 8 a.m.; likewise at 5 p.m.," Patterson wrote.

"As managers—you either do not know what you EMPLOYEES are doing; or YOU do not CARE. You have created expectations on the work effort which allowed this to happen inside Cerner, creating a very unhealthy environment."

Patterson said the health of the company depends on long hours and hard work. "The pizza man should show up at 7:30 p.m. to feed the starving teams working late," Patterson wrote. "The lot should be half-full on Saturday mornings. ... You have two weeks. Tick, tock."

Patterson's internal memo, however, did not remain internal. The memo was leaked from the company and posted on a computer bulletin board on the Yahoo website, contributing to a $7.85 drop in the stock's price in the next two days.

Cerner stock traded at a record pace, with more than four million shares changing hands, nearly four times the typical volume. Cerner closed at $34, down $6.13 for the day.

Company officials acknowledged that the memo had damaged stock prices, though some analysts said the pain would be short-lived. Patterson saw his net worth drop by about $28 million over two days. The company's market cap fell $270 million.

In a follow-up interview, Patterson didn't back off his basic message—that the once-small, entrepreneurial company is experiencing growing pains. As it has grown, the company's culture has changed, and the entrepreneurial spirit that drove the company has dropped. "I'm pretty well-known for making candid statements and being direct," Patterson said. "I probably wouldn't have done it if I'd known all this would happen. But do I regret it? I'd hate to change."

Effective workplace writing requires understanding your readers. The more specific your understanding, the more likely you will succeed. The Straight Talk Writing Model, around which this book is designed, stresses the importance of defining the context for your messages, including the needs and wants of your readers, the expectations of the organizational culture, and the acknowledgement of possible hidden audiences—all of which the Cerner CEO failed to do in the above case. Instead, he used a shotgun approach, shooting in the general direction of the targets and hoping to hit a few.

Understand the Three Factors of Communication Context

This chapter looks in depth at Step 1 of the Straight Talk Writing Model: the processes involved in defining the context for a given message. This step in the strategy reminds you to learn everything you can about the context in which you are communicating. Specifically, this context includes the following:

- The situation or problem that causes you to produce your message. (Why are you planning to communicate? What is the need to write?)
- Your target readers: primary, hidden, and decision-makers. (To whom are you communicating? Who else may see the message?)
- Your desired objectives with those readers. (What do you hope to accomplish with your message? What do you want your readers to do or think?)

Understanding these three factors as you prepare to write a message will provide a foundation for a successful communication strategy. We'll start with the existing situation—the conditions that create the motivation to communicate. For example, a required sales report might be the situation that triggers a need for a written report showing sales results. A scheduled performance review, the need to gather some data, an assignment to write new policy guidelines or an opportunity to recommend an idea may be situations calling for workplace writing. The likelihood of success in all such situations will be improved by analyzing the context.

At the end of this chapter, you will find two Context Analysis Worksheets. One has been completed as an example; the other is blank for you to copy and use as you plan messages. Within each section of the chapter, we have also included the portions of the Context Analysis Worksheet that deal with the step of the Straight Talk Writing Model being discussed. As you read through the material, try to fill out the portions of the worksheet, using a recent example in which you read or wrote a message within an organization. If you cannot think of an applicable situation, try applying the worksheet to the opening story in this chapter.

Define the Situation

Three tasks comprise the process of defining the situation:

1   Limiting the problem.
2   Evaluating the problem within the external climate.
3   Evaluating the corporate (or organizational) culture that affects the problem.

Figure 2.1 shows the portion of the Context Analysis Worksheet that deals with this process. We look at each of these tasks in the following sections.

Limit the Problem

People can go on and on about almost any topic—there are an infinite number of things that can be said even about the most mundane topic. To illustrate this point, we know a professor who stands before his class, holds up a piece of chalk, and asks the class to respond to the question, "What

---

CONTEXT ANALYSIS WORKSHEET

[Defining the situation]

How should I limit the problem or topic of my message?

What factors in the workplace or industry environment may influence my readers' responses to my message?

What key elements in the corporate (organizational) culture should I take into account as I prepare my message?

FIGURE 2.1. Context Analysis: Situation

could you say about this piece of chalk?" Once the students begin to respond, they identify a wide range of topics associated with a simple piece of chalk. They suggest talking about uses for chalk, descriptions of its shape and size, the comparative advantages of chalk versus ink markers, its chemical composition, and even the history of the chalk industry. In short, any number of topics for messages could come from focusing on even a simple object. And, of course, most of what could be said is irrelevant to a communicator's purpose. Limiting the scope of your message is critical to good communication.

Limit your messages to the most pertinent ideas; avoid side issues.

Because overload is one of today's most pervasive barriers to understanding, your first challenge as a writer is to let your reader know what you will be covering and what aspects of the topic you will avoid. As easy as this may sound, isolating the specific issues that you want to address can be difficult unless you focus on the distinct reason for the message.

For example, if a labor union in your industry is threatening a strike, you might choose to limit your discussion to the current dispute and your opinions about how to resolve it. You should probably avoid discussing the history of labor relations, the pros and cons of having a unionized company or the personalities of individuals involved. Don't get sidetracked off-topic, even if the detour may be interesting to you. Limit your message to information that may best solve the problem or address the concerns of the situation—in this case, limit the topic to issues that may have an impact on the decision to strike.

Evaluate the Problem Within the External Climate

The best way to evaluate the external environment is to be current on what is happening in your specific industry, in related industries, and in the local and global markets that influence your organization. Watch business television, review websites that cover relevant news, read and clip articles from workplace publications. Simply commit to staying abreast of issues and events that could affect your organization.

The issue of internal memos being posted on the Internet described in our opening example is a current business concern. The writer should have been aware of the possible negative effects of mass distribution to hidden audiences. This and other employee misuse of the Internet is a real hot-button issue with businesspeople. While this broader topic may not be one to address with a particular message, it should be considered as background context.

Beware: "Internal" messages have a way of going public via the Internet.

Evaluate Aspects of the Corporate Culture That May Impact the Problem

The culture of an organization derives from its shared attitudes, beliefs, and meanings, which result in shared behaviors. Recent research summarized by Stephen P. Robbins shows seven primary characteristics that capture the essence of an organization's culture.[2]

- **Innovation and risk-taking.** The degree to which employees are encouraged to be creative, innovative, and to take risks.
- **Attention to detail.** The degree to which employees are expected to exhibit precision, careful analysis, and attention to detail.
- **Outcome orientation.** The degree to which management focuses on results or outcomes rather than on the techniques or processes used to achieve those outcomes.
- **People orientation.** The degree to which management decisions consider the effects of outcomes on people within the organization.
- **Team orientation.** The degree to which work activities are organized around teams rather than individuals.
- **Aggressiveness.** The degree to which people are aggressive and competitive rather than easygoing.
- **Stability.** The degree to which organizational activities emphasize maintaining the status quo in contrast to growth or change.

Self-Evaluation: How Could Culture Effect Communication?

Suppose you worked for each of the companies below. (You change jobs a lot. ☺) What would you expect to see in workplace writing in each of their cultures? What would you generally avoid in your writing? How might the tone differ?

1   An advertising firm that specializes in "edgy," highly innovative ad campaigns for companies targeting young consumers. WRITING MAY BE CHARACTERIZED BY SUCH THINGS AS:

_____

_____

_____

_____

2   A high-powered law firm that specializes in litigation (law suits) defending large corporations and government agencies. WRITING MAY BE CHARACTERIZED BY SUCH THINGS AS:

_____

_____

_____

_____

_____

3   A family-friendly sporting goods retailer that encourages customers to come in and play with products before buying. WRITING MAY BE CHARACTERIZED BY SUCH THINGS AS:

_____

_____

_____

_____

_____

4   An upscale, luxury auto dealership that sells to high-net-worth individuals and is well-known for pampering its wealthy clientele. WRITING MAY BE CHARACTERIZED BY SUCH THINGS AS:

_____

_____

_____

_____

Key Dimensions in Assessing Cultures[3]

Classic studies by organizational culture researcher Geert Hofstede evaluated work-related values of more than 100,000 employees in 40 countries. He found that managers and employees differ on five value dimensions of national culture. As you read these, think about how each might influence a person's communication behaviors.

- **Power distance.** Some cultures put strong emphasis on social classes or socioeconomic levels. People in higher positions would rarely be approached by those in lower circumstances. These class differences are quite rigid. Conversely, some cultures put little emphasis on such status and treat all people equally. The culture of the United States exhibits lower power distance.

- **Individualism versus collectivism.** Some cultures accept or encourage individualism. Others frown on it, instead stressing the value of collective behaviors. People who rate individualism highly tend to look after themselves and their families; people who rate collectivism highly tend to belong to groups and look after each other in exchange for loyalty.

- **Quantity of life versus quality of life.** Quantity of life is the degree to which the society values the accumulation of material things, skills, and attributes. Quality-of-life cultures focus on the value of relationships and showing concern for the welfare of others.

- **Uncertainty avoidance.** Some cultures value predictable and stable structure (individuals tend to become nervous and stressed when the routine is upset). Others encourage innovation and risk-taking, even when it may undermine traditional ways of doing things.

- **Long-term versus short-term orientation.** Some cultures are simply more patient than others, looking to the long run rather than pressing for more rapid changes.

Define Your Readership

The second step in defining the communication context includes identifying and learning about your target readers. The more specific information you have about your readers, the better you can tailor your message to their needs and achieve your specific purpose. The most common mistakes we make are generalizing and assuming things about our readers. The Straight Talk Writing Model provides questions to ask about your audiences that will take you beyond generalizing and assuming.

Identify All Potential Readers (Distinct or Overlapping)

Let's take a moment to review the three kinds of audiences—primary, hidden, and decision-makers.

- **Primary audience.** The primary audience is easy to identify because they are the individual(s) to whom you address your message. The primary audience is critical to the success of your communication. However, you should not limit your audience analysis to just these people. In almost every case, you need to think about other potential readers as well.

Most messages go beyond their primary readership. Others see them, too.

- **Hidden audience.** The hidden audience is composed of the indirect readers of your message. This audience may not be directly connected with your communication purpose or process but may have some power over you. An example is your supervisor, who may not directly read your message but who is likely to hear about it. Another example of a hidden audience may be a supervisor in another department who has had her eye on you for a possible promotion. A powerful hidden audience may be your target reader's spouse or significant other, who influences the reader's decisions—and is totally outside of your control. Your reading the opening story in this chapter makes you a hidden audience witnessing Mr. Patterson's email message to his employees. (Scary how many hidden audiences we may have, isn't it?)
- **Decision-maker.** The decision-maker is your most important reader(s), even in situations in which this audience gets information secondhand from your primary audience. In the workplace, this is likely to be your boss. Your work associates may be the primary audience, but the boss will be the one evaluating your job performance. Similarly, someone outside the primary readership may well make a final decision on your proposal. (Often organizations observe a chain of command, limiting formal communicating with only one's immediate boss. He or she then takes your ideas to his or her boss who holds the authority to decide. In such cases, the decision-maker may not even read your message firsthand.)

An example of these three types of audiences might be illustrated by a situation in which you write a sales letter to a customer. Your primary audience is the potential customer who reads your letter. Your hidden audience might be your manager, who tends to review the letters send out of the office and who has power over your career advancement. Another hidden audience might be colleagues of your customers who have had some experience with you or your company. Your decision-maker may be someone in the customer's organization who did not read your actually letter but who will make a decision based on the reports of the employees who did read it.

This may all seem complicated, but these are the realities of the business world. Communicators who simplify too much and think only of the obvious primary audience—the people addressed in the letter, memo, or report—often fail to accomplish their objectives. The Straight Talk Writing Model reminds us to think through some of these complexities.

Learn About Each Reader

Focus on the facts, attitudes, wants, and concerns of each potential reader. To the extent possible, learn as much as you can about each audience using the kinds of questions on the Context Analysis Worksheet. Make an effort to focus on the following four activities:

1   Gather personal and professional facts.
2   Consider audience attitudes.
3   Evaluate audience "wants" and your "needs."
4   Look for consistent concerns.

Gather Personal and Professional Facts

Some key information about your readers may include age, gender, education level, cultural background, religious preferences, personal values, job responsibilities, and status, as well as their knowledge of your topic. Although this data may not all be readily available, work to consider these and any other personal information that may be useful in better understanding your audiences. Let's look a bit more closely at examples of the potential value of some such data.

- **Age, gender, and education level.** Your message may be phrased much differently for an audience of young, ambitious, entry-level employees than for a group of senior managers. Younger, ambitious audiences may be more likely to be motivated by opportunities to make more personal income or develop their careers, whereas senior managers may find that much less relevant. Also, marketing research into various generations reveal wide differences about what works with each. For example, "Generation-Y" (people between 25–40 years of age, generally) responds far better to visual, symbolic images, and less well to text. Writing a long, wordy letter or report will probably be a waste of paper when dealing with Gen-Y audiences.

  Recognize, too, that gender (yours and the reader's) can influence communication effectiveness. Studies consistently show that men and women often communicate differently. And even when they communicate the same way, men and women are often perceived differently by their target audiences.

- **Cultural background, religious preferences, and personal values.** Someone's national culture as well as the cultures their families may have brought with them through the generations have an impact on their values and, thus, on what motivate them. Similarly, people who are involved in religious activities may base their thinking on how an idea fits with their view of ethics or appropriate behaviors. Personal values about such things as physical fitness, intellectual activities, social or political activism, family concerns, and use of financial resources can color the way people receive and process new information.

- **Job responsibilities and status.** People from different levels in an organization may look at issues in different ways. In traditional organizations, the higher the position a person holds, the better he or she is likely to be at dealing with complex problems and taking a larger view of recommended actions. Lower-level employees may see issues through the lens of their limited experience or their immediate department.

  As modern organizations become less hierarchical and more team oriented, this distinction between so-called levels becomes blurred. Many of today's organizations downplay status differences and work hard to be sure employees throughout the company are fully informed about all aspects of the business.

Modern organizations do more than ever to keep workers at all levels informed.

- **Knowledge of your topic.** How much people already know about your topic will impact how you should develop your message. If your readers have sufficient background experience, you can probably move more quickly through your material or ask for a greater commitment to your objectives. If your readers know little about your topic or may be confused, you will have to provide appropriate background before you can accomplish the "big idea" of your message.

Knowing about the demographics, values, attitudes, and predispositions of your audiences can give you hints as to how readers may react to what you say. For example, as we mentioned, older workers may be more loyal to the ways things have always been done and might be resistant to changes you are recommending. They tend to be less adaptive to technology, for example. Audience members who are active in religious organizations may respond well to your recommendation of a charitable activity or your discussion of ethical issues. People in lower levels of responsibility may resist additional overtime work whereas higher-level personnel may accept the need to work longer hours in order to maximize their bonuses.

Be careful, however, to remember that these generalizations are just that—generalizations. Communicators run the risk of stereotyping when they take an oversimplified view of groups of people. Ultimately, the best option is to come to understand people as individuals, not as categories.

Be aware that some generalizations may be inaccurate stereotypes.

Think carefully about past experiences you have had with the people to whom you will communicate. If you don't know them personally, consider your experience with similar people in similar situations. The longer you have worked with individuals, the more you are likely to know about them. Review all pertinent information and make notes. Then make your best guesses about how they are likely to respond to your ideas or proposals. You cannot predict with 100 percent accuracy how people will react, but the more information you have, the better your predictions will be.

Consider Audience Attitudes Toward You and Your Topic

Make some realistic inferences about your reader's attitudes about you, about your topic, and about having to actually read this message. Honesty may force you to acknowledge that your reader doesn't want to deal with you or your topic. They may prefer to never have to read what you wrote. They may be busy and disinterested and resent having to spend the time on this issue. They could be as turned off by your message as were the employees at Cerner Corporation in our opening story.

Realistic audience analysis prepares you for handling reluctant message receivers and likely reader objections. As disillusioning as it may be, you *will* face times when your reader would rather eat a bar of soap than read your report. Don't assume that just because it's part of their job to receive and respond to your message that they really care. Anticipate their specific needs and give them something to *motivate* them to care.

Believe it or not, not everyone is eager to read what you write!

Evaluate Audience Wants and Your Needs

After facing the potentially cruel realities of reader attitudes toward you, your next step is to determine exactly what your audience wants to know. Your job is to give them their "wants" before you ask them to do something that meets your "needs." In other words, you must satisfy their information hunger before you ask them to do or think something new. Until you tell people what they *want* to know, they will never hear what you *need* them to know to fulfill the purpose of your message.

For example, your task may be to write a document to explain changes in job responsibilities after a company reorganization. The employees, however, may not be willing to focus on the details of their job descriptions until you reassure them about the security of their jobs or the status of their benefit plans. Satisfy your audience's information needs first.

Look for Consistent Concerns
Most people regularly express continuing interest in some key issues or themes. In today's world, the threat of terrorism has become a consistent concern for business that had never seriously considered it a few years ago. Similarly, computer hackers or viruses, identity theft from unsecured data, exposure to legal suits based on non-discrimination legislation, possibility of reputation risk due to unpopular or unfortunate decisions—all these are consistent concerns that may have been unheard of a decade ago.

Remember to consider that each individual in your target audience might have his or her own consistent concerns. For most people, job security, personal safety, opportunity for satisfying work, and the need to balance work and personal lives are consistent personal concerns. If you write to college-age readers, they generally hold consistent concerns about career opportunities. Politicians have a consistent concern about being re-elected. Parents of young children have concerns about child safety issues. Various functions in a company have different consistent concerns. Marketing, accounting, human resources, and operations functions hold primary interest for the appropriate departments.

Figure 2.2 shows the portion of the Context Analysis Worksheet that deals with this step.

Define Your Objectives with Each Reader

The third element of defining communication context is to specify your objectives with each of your audiences. Most messages, no matter how apparently simple, encompass three objectives: an overall goal, a specific communication purpose, and a hidden agenda.

Define an Overall Goal

The overall goal is your long-range plan or major desired result. For example, a student's overall goal might be to graduate with a specific degree or prepare for graduate study. The overall goal for an employee seeking a job might be to get hired by a good company or to launch a new business. An overall goal for a career would probably be to move into higher levels of responsibility in

---

CONTEXT ANALYSIS WORKSHEET

[Defining the situation]

Who is My Primary Audience—The Actual Reader(s) of the Message?
- What do I know about them personally and professionally (age, gender, educational level, job responsibilities and status, civic and religious affiliation, knowledge of the subject, and cultural background)?
- What are their key attitudes about me?
  - About my subject?
  - About having to read my message?
- What do my primary readers *want* to know about my subject?
- What do I *need* my primary readers to know?
- What are the *consistent concerns* that I hear from my primary readers?
- What specific information addresses those concerns?

[Defining other possible audiences]

Who is My Hidden Audience?
- What do I know about him, her or them?
- What are the *consistent concerns* of my hidden audience?
- What specific information addresses those concerns?

Who is the Decision-Maker?
- What do I know about him, her or them?
- What is the *consistent concern* of the decision-maker?
- What specific information addresses those concerns?

FIGURE 2.2. Context Analysis: Readership

an organization or to build the company to a certain size. In corporate communication, the overall goal is often based on the mission statement of the organization. For example, the overall goal of a report about the budget for the next quarter might reflect the company's commitment to increase the value of its stock, or your United Fund memo to employees might focus on the company's initiative to "give something back" to the community.

While companies are not always faithful to their stated intentions, mission statements are intended to be a definition of an organization's vision and values—what it cares about and where it is going. Some companies do a good job of identifying—and talking about—their core values and how these impact the company. David Neeleman, the founding CEO of Jet Blue Airways (a remarkable success story in its early years and in a difficult industry), took frequent opportunities to recite the company's core values in speeches and interviews: "For our company's core values, we came up with five words: safety, caring, fun, integrity, and passion. We guide our company by them."[4] Such statements define constant concerns of the company's leaders. The overall goal of any communication within that company should involve being congruent with these core values.

Identify the Specific Purpose of the Communication

The specific purpose of a message depends on your needs and on your analysis of target audiences. Ask yourself, *"Exactly what do I want to occur* as a result of this message?"

We talked in Chapter 1 about the "big idea" of a message as "what you want the reader to do or think" after reading your document. Functional workplace communication often emphasizes the doing. Your goal will often be to get some behavioral response from the reader—to get them to do something based on your message.

Failing to articulate a specific purpose is an all-too-frequent pitfall for ineffective communicators. For example, in the job search process, the specific purpose of a cover letter may be to get an interview. The specific purpose of a first interview is to be invited back for a second interview. The specific purpose of the quarterly budget report might be to clearly explain each department's need to cut expenses and get them to take action that will do so. The specific purpose of a company's annual report would be to explain past performance, preview future actions, and keep people enthusiastic about their investment in the company.

Keep a focus on the big idea of the message—what you want the reader to do or think.

Be realistic about how much you can accomplish with a single communication attempt. Persuasion, especially, is a process that is seldom fully accomplished with one message. Most audiences consist of people with various levels of willingness to accept your ideas. Often, the best a writer can hope for is to move the reader a little closer to the overall goal—to move people through the "sales cycle"—the steps customers typically go through before actually buying. If, for example, you are in the market for a new computer, an effective salesperson would move you through the sales cycle by:

- Giving you information about the computer orally and offer a brochure.
- Inviting you to see the computer in the store or a demonstration room.
- Encouraging you to try the computer, using some of its features.
- Preparing the paperwork for the purchase.
- Delivering and possibly installing the computer.

Each of these actions is a step in the sales cycle. A typical buyer would go through all the steps. Each step in the process has a specific communication objective: to move the target audience to the next step in the cycle.

The Persuasion Continuum

Since your goal in functional communication is most often to persuade others, you need to be realistic about your chances. The process of your communicated message can be visualized as a continuum from 0 to 10, where 0 represents "I know (or care) nothing about this," and 10 represents "I'm ready to sign on the dotted line!" (Or, 0 is "Who is this Pat person mailing me a resume for the sales position?" and 10 is "Let's hire Pat for the job!")

Communicators hurt their effectiveness when they assume that their readers know or care more than they actually do, and ask those readers to move too quickly up the continuum. You must work to accurately assess where your reader is on the continuum, and then set a reasonable, specific objective. You generally can't get from 0 to 10 in one message. A more realistic goal would be to move them from complete ignorance to partial knowledge of an issue. For example, your specific purpose might be to take your audience from a "0" ("We don't need interns in our department") to a "3" ("An intern would be a low-cost solution for the extra help we need on our summer projects"). This is much the way a car salesperson moves a customer from browsing through the lot ("2"), to sitting inside a car ("4"), to taking a test drive ("6"), to going inside to discuss terms ("7"), to signing a contract ("10").

Realistically consider where your reader is on the persuasion continuum.

Acknowledge Your Hidden Agenda

Finally, as you specify your objectives, be honest about your hidden agenda—personal goals to which you are aspiring. Everybody has them. This is perfectly normal. Acknowledge that you have a hidden agenda and factor it into your planning.

For example, your business-related hidden agenda may be to be perceived by your co-workers as a leader, to earn a promotion, to move to another department, or to be considered for additional training. If you factor these goals into your planning, you can make a conscious effort to include information that would demonstrate your leadership potential or value to the company.

Figure 2.3 shows the portion of the Context Analysis Worksheet that deals with this step. We will look at each of these objectives in the following sections.

We all have hidden agenda when communicating!

CONTEXT ANALYSIS WORKSHEET

[Defining objectives with each audience]

What are my objectives with my primary readers?

What are my objectives with other possible audiences (hidden, decision-makers)?

FIGURE 2.3. Context Analysis: Objectives

Consider the Organizational Culture

Finally, our analysis of the context needs to consider the organizational culture. A culture emerges from a set of shared values or practices that become ingrained in the organization. How does the company normally function with regard to written communication? Is it commonplace for personnel to write memos or emails (as opposed to, for example, holding meetings, using the phone, or having face-to-face discussions)? Does the culture value having hard-copy documentation of messages? Is a "paper trail" seen as necessary or desirable?

We will talk further about media advantages and disadvantages in Chapter 3. But, for now, be cognizant of general expectations that seem to be consistent in the company.

Gather the Information You Need for Context Analysis

The process of defining your communication context requires gathering good information and using that information to tailor your message. This is where all the parts of your Context Analysis Worksheet come together. Getting this information is not always easy, but it is generally worth the effort. Writing your message without gathering sufficient information is a recipe for miscommunication and career damage.

The most common information-gathering approaches are listening, observing, and reading secondary sources. Below we talk a bit about each.

Use Listening as an Information-Gathering Technique

Ironically, of the four basic communication skills—reading, writing, speaking, and listening—only listening is rarely taught in formal classes. Yet, of all the communication skills, listening may actually be the most important. In any case, it deserves more attention than it typically gets.

Two forms of listening: support and retention.

Some people think that listening is passive—it's really just a matter of sitting back and letting the talker have his or her say. In reality, it is a highly active mental process that takes two forms: *support listening* and *retention listening*. Support listening consists of giving people enough feedback so that they thoroughly express their thoughts. Retention listening emphasizes techniques for capturing information from what is said. Let's look at each listening approach.

Use Support Listening
The intent of support listening is to learn what a person thinks and feels. When gathering information with support listening, avoid speaking except to encourage the other person to elaborate. (Yes, this can be *hard*!) Support listening seeks to draw out people's feelings and ideas by using non-evaluative responses such as the following:

- **"Go on" comments.** "Uh-huh" is the simplest kind of oral response and consists of saying "uh-huh" or "hmmm" as other people talk to encourage them to continue to clarify their thoughts. Open questions that cannot be answered with a simple yes or no statement are also useful.
- **Content reflection.** Repeat, mirror, or echo the statement made by another person in the form of a question. Be careful you don't use a tone of voice that implies a judgment. You simply repeat what was said in essentially the same words and wait for further elaboration or clarification.
- **Non-verbal encouragement.** Let the speaker know that you are focusing on him or her. Make eye contact. Nod your head (but recognize that the speaker could perceive an "I'm listening" nod to mean "yes"). Be aware of non-verbal behavior that could discourage the speaker.

Suppose you are gathering information from a colleague about an unpleasant experience they had. If you reflect their comments using support listening, it may sound something like this:

"I am very disappointed with the new cell phone the company got me. It sucks."
"You're disappointed. I'm sorry to hear that."
"I'm about ready to toss it and ask for a better one."
"Hmmm." (nodding)
"Yes, I thought the touch screen would be easier for text messaging."

"You want easier text messaging."

"Yeah, and this touch screen is too unresponsive for my big fingers, and I can't even read the screen in bright light."

"Uh-huh. I understand."

By using message reflection and support listening, you gained additional information about the reason for the person's dissatisfaction. Now you can offer ideas that may solve the problem. This supportive approach gets far better information than, for example, debating about the merits of the cell phone. If you had said, "I have one just like that and it's great," you would do little to create understanding.

Resist debating when using support listening. Simply restate and express understanding.

Use Retention Listening
Retention listening calls for techniques that help you remember and use information you hear. The following are some tips for improving your retention:

- **Minimize distractions.** Concentrate on the speaker. Force yourself to keep your mind on what the speaker is saying, and avoid multitasking. Trying to do other things while listening simply does not work.

- **Recognize opportunities.** Do your best to find areas of interest between yourself and the speaker. Ask yourself, "What's in it for me? What can I get out of what this person is saying?" Identify the speaker's purpose. Is this person trying to inform you, or persuade you, or is he or she perhaps just trying to entertain you?

- **Stay alert.** Avoid daydreaming. If the person you are listening to is a bit boring, force yourself to stay alert. If your thoughts run ahead of the speaker, use the extra time to evaluate, anticipate, and review.

- **Listen for central themes rather than for isolated facts.** Too often people get hopelessly lost as listeners because they focus on unimportant facts and details, and miss the speaker's main point.

- **Take notes efficiently.** The simple process of writing key ideas as you hear them helps you retain information. People are often flattered when you convey that their ideas are worth jotting down.

- **Plan to report the content of a message to someone within 24 hours.** (Even if you won't really do this, listen as if you will be required to do so.) This forces you to concentrate and to remember. It is a good practice technique.

Use Observation as an Information-Gathering Technique

Legendary baseball manager Yogi Berra once said, "You can observe a great deal by watching." Well put, Yogi. Much of the information needed to tailor your writing can be gathered by observation. This is particularly true when considering the corporate culture (many facets of which are readily observable) and the external climate. We learn about these things by systematically observing and carefully reading.

Systematic observation and careful reading pay off for better context analysis.

Of course, be aware that you may not get good information based on one or two haphazard observations. A better technique is to plan to systematically observe in certain ways over a period of time so that what you see is more likely to be common occurrences, not fluke behaviors. Multiple observations of the same or similar behaviors are better than just one look.

Avoid drawing conclusions based on haphazard observation.

If you suspect a problem or sense that an issue needs to be researched, make the effort to observe relevant behaviors systematically. For example, if a particular product in your store is not selling as well as it should, you may schedule systematic observations of customer behaviors. Select random times to observe how people look at or touch the product. Observe customer traffic patterns in your store. Do people seem to walk past the product without looking at it? Are customers hesitant to pick up the product or look more closely at it? Do they seem to react negatively when they see the price? Is the packaging hard to hold or so dull that people don't seem to notice it? These are the kinds of questions that can be answered in part by observation of customer behavior.

Gathering context information in an organization may involve observing how employees implement (or fail to implement) policy changes or new directives. For example, do workers seem frustrated or annoyed by the requirements of a new process?

Read Secondary Sources as an Information-Gathering Technique

A secondary source of information is an article, report, statistic, or other document already written about a topic. Researchers often look first at such sources to see what has already been discovered rather than starting from scratch and repeating someone's efforts. Reading such printed materials or studying information on the Internet are excellent ways to gather information about the context of your message. In the past, reviewing secondary sources required library research, but today your "library" exists in cyberspace. With the Internet you have a wealth of information available at the stroke of a few keys.

With a little effort, you can become very familiar with the kinds of issues facing any industry or company. Using an Internet search engine (Google, Bing, Yahoo, and Ask.com are popular), you can simply type in the name of a company and find a wealth of articles about it. Use this secondary information to enrich your knowledge of the company or industry and to better define the context of your message. If your research reveals that the industry is facing serious profit problems due to increased competition, for example, you need to consider that fact as you plan your messages.

> **An enormous amount of information about virtually any topic is accessible via search engines such as Google or similar tools.**

You can also gather a lot of information about individual audience readers. Using a search engine such as Google.com, simply type in the name of a target reader and see what comes up. People need not be famous to be listed. If your target reader has written articles, been listed on the company webpage, or engaged in various activities, there is a fairly good chance that he or she will show up on Google.

> **Googling individual readers before writing can provide excellent insight.**

Use the Context Analysis Worksheet

Figure 2.4 is a completed Context Analysis Worksheet for a business document. The writer's assignment is to prepare a persuasive document encouraging workers in the company to accept a proposed company reorganization. Let's see how this might look.

Figure 2.5 (see page 54) is a blank Context Analysis Worksheet that you may photocopy for your own use. This worksheet pulls together all the separate worksheet elements you have seen throughout the chapter. As you review it, be sure that you understand what information should be placed in each section. If you are unclear about any section, review the material in this chapter.

CONTEXT ANALYSIS WORKSHEET

TOPIC: Persuade employees to accept company reorganization

How should I limit the problem or topic of my message? Limit to three-phase reorganization plan. Do not introduce other possible variations. Present supporting data from consulting firm recommendations. Emphasize advantages to employees throughout.

What factors in the business environment may influence the audience's response to my message? Another similar company (ABC Corp) reorganized in similar way 2 years ago and went out of business within 10 months, resulting in loss of 300 jobs. Industry is going through rough time with big players taking over small to midsize firms like ours.

What key elements of corporate culture should be taken into account as I prepare my message? Stable, low risk-taking, traditional manufacturing environment. Management slow to change existing processes that have worked for many years. Have had no significant reorganization in 10+ years. Workers value stability.

[DEFINING THE PRIMARY AUDIENCE]

Who is my primary audience—the actual reader(s) of the message? Employees, most of whom are hourly workers with specialized skills. Many do repetitive jobs on assembly lines and tolerate boredom by enjoying strong friendships with co-workers. Do not want to disrupt those friendships.

What do I know about them personally and professionally (age, gender, educational level, job responsibilities and status, civic and religious affiliation, knowledge of the subject, and cultural background)? Tech school training without a lot of employment options outside industry. Average age is late 40s. Forty percent of workforce is over 55 yrs old. Very skilled in what they do but could not easily find comparable jobs elsewhere. Strong work ethic. Many have worked for company throughout adult lives. Have lived in community for generations. Multicultural mix but predominantly Hispanic

What are their key attitudes about me? I am seen as the "new guy"; they see me as the college hot-shot who some fear will be a "hatchet man." They suspect I do not share loyalty to company that they do. Overall, they seem to like me but are suspicious of me. Trust is questionable.

About my subject? They know little about organizational design and fear extensive change. They are concerned that reorganization = layoffs, less security, separation from their work friends.

About having to read my message? Some are eager to see the report to confirm or dispel rumors. They know some change is coming and will appreciate seeing it in "black and white" so they can study the details. They are generally willing to take time to read it, although reading skill levels are not exceptionally high. Nevertheless, the fact that it is written reassures them that it is a concrete plan, possibly reducing concerns.

What do my primary readers *want* to know about my subject? How this plan affects them personally and their work relationships.

What do I *need* my primary readers to know? Job security also a concern. Will they keep their jobs? Will the company be stronger?

What are the *consistent concerns* that I hear from my primary readers? Why must companies always seem to "rock the boat?" Things have been good for a long time and workers value this consistency.

What specific information addresses those concerns? Explain competitive pressures and absolute need to respond to these. Change is a fact of life in today's business world. If we do not engage in planned, constructive change the company will be in danger of losing market share and possibly the whole business.

[DEFINING OTHER POSSIBLE AUDIENCES]

Who is my hidden audience? My boss. She wants to see how well I can convince the employees of the need to buy in to the change. My spouse, who wonders why I took this job instead of the more "traditional" one offered by her father.

What do I know about him, her, or them? Boss is looking for the next generation of leadership for the company and considers this assignment very important.

What are the *consistent concerns* of my hidden audience? Cost pressures while maintaining a stable workforce. Wants to keep our reputation as a good employer to attract best available people.

What specific information addresses those concerns? Plan includes numerous opportunities for employee engagement in the process. Cost pressures will be reduced with better alignment of workforce and reduction in need to hire additional people now.

Who is the decision-maker? The union leaders must be won over to help convince the workers that the plan is a good deal.

What do I know about him, her, or them? Union guys have been tough but fair. They are smart enough to recognize competitive pressures and the need for some reorganization. They are worried about job changes and the impact on their ability to represent workers in a reasonably cordial atmosphere. No one wants an increase in grievances.

What is the *consistent concern* of the decision-maker? Protecting employees against unnecessary or unfair management actions. Also, need to keep economic stability of company and satisfaction of union members.

What specific information addresses those concerns? The recommendations in report are based on objective economic data. Competitive changes require us to change for the benefit of all company employees and management.

Other observations: This is my first significant leadership challenge since being promoted to current level. I need to pull it off and impress the boss while strengthening my relationships with union leaders and employees. I want to be seen as the good guy in all this.

FIGURE 2.4. Context Analysis Worksheet

CONTEXT ANALYSIS WORKSHEET

TOPIC:
How should I limit the problem or topic of my message?

What factors in the business environment may influence the audience's response to my message?

What key elements of corporate culture should be taken into account as I prepare my message?

[Defining the primary audience]

Who is my primary audience—the actual reader(s) of the message?
What do I know about them personally and professionally (age, gender, educational level, job responsibilities and status, civic and religious affiliation, knowledge of the subject, and cultural background)?
What are their key attitudes about me?
About my subject?
About having to read my message?
What do my primary readers want to know about my subject?
What do I *need* my primary readers to know?
What are the *consistent concerns* that I hear from my primary readers?
What specific information addresses those concerns?

[Defining other possible audiences]

Who is my hidden audience?
What do I know about him, her, or them?
What are the *consistent concerns* of my hidden audience?
What specific information addresses those concerns?

Who is the decision-maker?
What do I know about him, her, or them?
What is the *consistent concern* of the decision-maker?
What specific information addresses those concerns?

Other observations:

Figure 2.5. Blank Context Analysis Worksheet

Applying the Straight Talk Writing Model

Let's look back at our opening story to get what one radio commentator used to call "the *rest* of the story."

A few days after Patterson's critical memo found its way to the Internet, he sent an email discussing it and apologizing. "First and foremost, it is clear that my direct language offended some committed, hard-working Cerner associates," Patterson wrote.

"To this group, I sincerely apologize to you if I offended you. I have invested the majority of my adult life, along with many other long-term associates, trying to create an uncommon work environment in order for us (collectively) to achieve great things. The approach in my email last week did real damage to this culture."

Patterson said dozens of employees had sent him emails thanking him for the second memo.

Cathy Wickern, a product specialist for Cerner's ProFit, was among them. "Thanks for recognizing that you have many hard-working, loyal ASSOCIATES who believe in what we do and care very much what happens to Cerner," Wickern said. "I've spent the past week trying to talk some of our best folks into staying at Cerner. The only objection I couldn't overcome was the use of the word EMPLOYEES. Your email will soothe that wound."

There is no doubt Patterson's earlier March 13 memo sent a chill through the workforce. "It hit people hard," said Stanley M. Sword, chief people officer for Cerner. "The people who are working very hard took this personally. I took it personally when I first read it . . .

"Those that [*sic*] know Neal know he was overstating to make a point. And, by golly, it worked."

Patterson said he had been talking about the changing Cerner work ethic for about a year. He said he decided to take action after he had ridden an elevator with a longtime employee. "I asked her how bad it had gotten. She said, 'Neal, the work ethic has gotten bad.' "

Interestingly, the original memo was sent out the same day Cerner ran a full-page ad in the *Wall Street Journal* designed to raise the company's profile on Wall Street. Cerner has been on an upswing for more than a year, and was one of the best-performing stocks on the Nasdaq stock exchange over the past 15 months.

Although the company's stock suffered because of the memo, analysts dismissed the tempest as a short-term storm.

Investors have posted nearly 200 comments about the memo on a Yahoo bulletin board where investors talk about Cerner stock. Many were negative, with some comparing Cerner to a sweatshop.

"The CEO's prime objective is to increase shareholder value, and unfortunately Patterson let his emotions get in the way of sound judgment, and he needs to be held accountable," said one Web posting.

But not everyone disagreed with the tone of Patterson's memo.

Another Yahoo post read: "Yes, there are other ways to communicate this, but from the e-mail it looks like they did not work.... In the era of sensitivity training, I think it is refreshing to see someone trample on people for a change."

The memo drew a sharp response from Judy Ancel, director of the Institute for Labor Studies, a joint program of the University of Missouri-Kansas City and Longview Community College.

"People have fought long and hard in this country for the eight-hour day, so they could have a life," Ancel said. "Obviously, Mr. Patterson thinks his employees don't deserve to have a life."

Marilyn Taylor, a professor of management at UMKC's Bloch School of Business and Public Administration, said Cerner is "facing a number of challenges."

> Although Mr. Patterson's memo is not diplomatic by any means, he is clearly issuing a clarion call for higher contribution levels to the firm.... Some will have to examine whether Cerner is the place they want to work. Some may decide that Cerner is not for them.

Sword acknowledged that the commotion over Patterson's email may make it tougher for Cerner to recruit employees. The company plans to more than triple its workforce by 2010.

"But I think a lot of good will come out of it," Sword said, adding that the episode should lead to clearer expectations among Cerner workers. The email flap underscores a basic change in the workplace with the increasingly common use of email and the Internet.

"This is an example of the potential problems that arrive with the use of email. It's really not a very private medium," said David Sobel, general counsel of the Electronic Privacy Information Center in Washington, D.C. "It's a medium that lends itself to being candid, but there's a permanence there that people might not take into account."

Probes

1   In light of the ideas discussed in this chapter, how did Patterson's message go wrong?

2   If you were advising the Cerner CEO on how to deal with the situation, what would you tell him?

3   Which aspects of context analysis could have helped Patterson avoid this mess?

Performance Checklist

After completing this chapter, you should be better prepared to use key principles of written communication and avoid some common pitfalls. Specifically, you should now understand that:

- Message effectiveness is dramatically affected when you take the time and make the effort to carefully define the context for your writing.
- The communication context consists of the specific problem or issue, the audiences (readers), and your specific objectives with each audience.
- Limiting the problem, evaluating the external climate, and evaluating the corporate (or organizational) culture are important planning activities.
- Factors such as age, gender, and national cultures have an impact on people's work values.
- Key dimensions of different national cultures include power distance (status differences), individualism, quantity of life (materialism), uncertainty avoidance (versus risk-taking), and long-term versus short-term orientation.
- Three groups of target audiences should be considered as you define your context: primary, hidden, and decision-makers. These may be different people who have different informational needs and wants. These groups can also overlap.
- Context analysis information can be gathered by careful listening, systematic observation, and review of secondary sources.
- The Context Analysis Worksheet is a useful tool for planning any message.

What Do You Know?

Activity 2.1: Defining the Context

Complete a Context Analysis Worksheet for one of the following situations. Try to get into the role and use reasonable information based on your best experiences.

1   Your boss asked to draft a sales letter to sell a product or service students about to complete an MBA program would find useful. Select a product or service that costs less than $200 and that can be explained in a clear one or two page letter. (Hint: if you are drawing a blank, consider technology devices, professional development coaching, planning systems or software, or physical fitness facilities. But don't limit yourself to these. Be creative and have fun with this.)

2 You want to prepare a message advocating a zoning change that will permit a youth recreation center to be built in an area where several senior citizen apartment complexes are located. You anticipate some resistance to this but hope to win over community support. You will distribute this letter to the seniors.

3 You are preparing a position paper to advocate voting for or against a current law or rule change. (This may be for an apartment residents' association, a rule in some organization you are familiar with or a legislative issue.) Target your message at people who are undecided or may oppose your position.

Activity 2.2: Determining How Well Others Define Their Contexts

Do an Internet search of current business magazines to find companies that are experiencing unfavorable publicity. These may be companies whose products are defective, whose service practices are substandard or unethical, or whose sales results are declining sharply. Review the ways they are communicating with their various audiences in light of the material discussed in this chapter. Prepare a brief written report (three pages or less) on why these companies have been effective or ineffective, and how they have used or failed to use effective context analysis.

Activity 2.3: Gathering Information on Corporate Culture

Recent graduates from school are a valuable resource for information on the corporate culture in which they work. Plan to conduct an interview with a recent graduate to gather information about what he or she sees in an organization's corporate culture. Design questions you can use to discover the seven primary culture characteristics of the company:

- Innovation and risk-taking (example question: "Can you tell me about a time when an employee was rewarded for innovating thinking or risk-taking?").
- Attention to detail.
- Outcome orientation.
- People orientation.
- Team orientation.
- Aggressiveness.
- Stability.

Reinforce With These Review Questions

1 True/False Although many writers (and speakers) do some audience analysis, most are better off getting right into composing their message.

2 Context analysis reminds writers that they are likely to have three kinds of audiences or readers: (1) _____, (2) _____, and (3) _____.

3 True/False Defining the communication situation involves limiting the problem and evaluating it in association with the external and organizational cultures.

4 Name four of the seven aspects of corporate culture described in this chapter: (1) _____, (2) _____, (3) _____, and (4) _____.

5 True/False Many experts believe that Generation-Y-age people have a strong preference for less text in written messages.

6 Name three ways of gathering information about the communication context as described in this chapter: (1) _____, (2) _____, and (3) _____.

7 True/False Realistic audience analysis prepares you for handling reluctant message receivers and likely reader objections.

8 True/False Because overload is one of today's most pervasive barriers to understanding, your first challenge as a writer is to let your reader know what you will be covering and, often, what aspects of the topic you will avoid.

9 True/False The "big idea" of any functional message is defined by what you want your readers to do or think after they have read your document.

10 True/False The overall goal of a workplace message may relate to the organization's mission statement—its long-range plan or major desired results.

three

Consider Your Media, Source, and Timing Options

The fewer data needed, the better the information. And an overload of information, that is, anything much beyond what is truly needed, leads to information blackout. It does not enrich, but impoverishes.

(Peter F. Drucker, *Management: Tasks, Responsibilities, Practices*)

Analyzing Conditions that Impact Message Effectiveness

Before you reach for a pen or limber up your keyboarding fingers, take a step back and think: is this message one that will benefit from the media advantages of writing? Am I the one who should be writing this, or might it be more effective if written by (or at least signed by) someone else? Is this a good time to distribute this written message?

These questions may sound simplistic and their answers may be obvious, but many a written missive has missed its target or generated an unexpected reaction because its writer didn't take the time to think it through. This chapter gives you guidelines for systematically considering media, source, and timing issues using the second step in the Straight Talk Writing Model.

Performance Competencies

When you have completed this chapter, you should be able to:

- Recognize the advantages and disadvantages of using different communication media, timing, and source options.

- Describe how communication media trigger certain expectations in message receivers, present tradeoffs between efficiency and effectiveness, and have unique capabilities.
- Explain the distinction between communication efficiency and communication effectiveness.
- Apply appropriate media based on characteristics such as speed, feedback capacity, hard-copy availability, message intensity and complexity, formality, and relative costs.
- Describe some ways to mix media to improve effectiveness.

The Way It Is ... Wilbur Matheson's Outburst

The following message is fairly clear, but it fails miserably to accomplish its goal. See if you can determine why.

Wilbur Matheson, the department manager, was upset. He arrived late for work yesterday after a doctor's appointment where he talked with his physician about the chronic headaches he was having. Sure enough, just as he suspected, his employees were goofing off. It was 10:22 a.m. and coffee break was still going on. Wilbur was fried.

He marched straight to his office and wrote a memo and printed copies. Within 30 minutes, every employee had a paper copy on his or her desk. That will shake things up, thought Wilbur.

The memo was brief and to the point (Wilbur prided himself on being direct and clear), and read as follows:

> It has recently come to my attention that department employees are taking excessively long coffee breaks. These violate company policy. Employees caught taking more than fifteen minutes in the morning and afternoon will be terminated. If things don't improve, the coffee break room will be closed. I trust you will obey policy in the future regarding this matter.

What problems do you see with this memo? You could cite its tone and its abruptness, but a more basic problem arises from Wilbur's decision to write in the first place. A memo is an ineffective communication medium for this message. Wilbur chose the "easy way" to deal with a problem and, in so doing, probably created more problems than he solved.

Suppose that you work for Wilbur and that you have been very careful to limit your coffee breaks to less than 15 minutes. Further suppose that you often forego breaks to meet the demands of your job. How would you react to this memo? Suppose Wilbur's message was sent shortly after you had put in large amounts of volunteer overtime to meet heavy production demands. How would that make this reprimand even worse?

A critical step when initiating a message is to consider media and timing options. The term "media" refers to the channels or mechanisms for conveying a message. Each medium has certain characteristics, advantages, and disadvantages that make it more or less effective under various circumstances. The decisions you make at this phase of your planning can have a considerable impact on the overall effectiveness of your communication.

Be Aware of the Many Media, Source, and Timing Choices

Although this book focuses on workplace writing, we need to consider the broader question of media selection. Sometimes writing is not the best choice for getting a message across.

Never before have we had so many media options available. Traditional media such as letters, memos, presentations, interviews, meetings, and telephone calls are now supplemented with faxes, email, teleconferencing, Web pages, videos, and DVDs, to name a few. You can use any of these, or combine several to deliver your messages. Effective communicators evaluate the pros and cons of each option in relation to the message context, their audience, and their objectives. Less effective communicators too often make media choices out of habit or based on what's easiest, instead of considering the needs and preferences of their target audiences.

Avoid choosing a communication medium out of habit. Take a moment to think about its relative effectiveness.

Consider Your Media Options

Now we go back to media selection. Your choices from the many media options can dramatically impact your message's outcome. An otherwise effective message can fall flat (or even backfire) if you use an inappropriate medium.

Each communication medium:

- Triggers certain expectations in the message receivers.
- Presents a tradeoff between efficiency and effectiveness.
- Has unique capabilities.
- Plays within certain "ground rules."

The combined effect of all these media characteristics is that the medium you select for a particular message becomes a part of the message—it conveys information about the message.

Personal Tech: Communication Intimidation?[1]

Secretly don't know what Twitter is, but you're afraid to ask? Worry no more.

We know—it's hard to keep up. You just figure out how to set the clock on your coffee maker, and all of a sudden there are a dozen new technologies you've never heard of. For those of you too afraid to ask someone, here's a guide to get you up to speed on the basics of how people communicate these days. And, just to make you feel smarter, we threw in a couple of old favorite methods. Because, sometimes, there's just no excuse for a little face time.

Face-To-Face

In a nutshell. Since you're reading this, we're hoping we don't have to explain this one to you. But, just in case: You talk, someone listens.

Got its start. This is a tough question to answer. Linguists debate that language debuted anywhere from 100,000 to 30,000 years ago.

Hit the big time. Vocal communication really started to become a bigger deal when it was paired with writing, most likely Cuneiform around 3400 BC.

Best used for. Sometimes, there's no substitute for being there. Face-to-face communication allows you to hear words and see body language.

Pitfalls. You're close enough to smell and/or be slapped or punched by your conversation partner.

Getting started. Turn to your left. Now, your right. If you see another human (or very smart pet), begin speaking.

Telephone

In a nutshell. Allows for real-time voice communication between two people. Users dial a 7–10 digit number via keypad to contact another party.

Got its start. The actual inventor is disputed, but Alexander Graham Bell was the first to be awarded a patent for it, so we're going with him.

Hit the big time. Around the turn of the twentieth century, the "candlestick" phone made it easy for anyone to operate it simply.

Best used for. Personal communication between two people. Phones are great when you need an instant response, and want the nuance of talking.

Pitfalls. Although the federal Do Not Call list has helped, unwanted phone solicitations are still an inconvenience.

Getting started. We're guessing that, if you don't have a phone, it's not because you don't know how to get one. Can we move to the tough stuff?

Email

In a nutshell. Anyone with a computer and Internet access can send email, which is about as close to its physical-world counterpart as you can imagine.

Got its start. Email grew out of the federal 1960s ARPAnet project. Email today is largely unchanged since the 1980s, although the addition of photos and Web-styled formatting is more commonplace.

Hit the big time. In 1993, America Online shifted to a standard email format, opening access to a range of people. In 1998, the Tom Hanks movie *You've Got Mail* made the audience even broader.

Best used for. One-to-one communication with someone you know, or as a way of sharing things with a group of friends.

Pitfalls. Due to the fire-and-forget nature of email, it's easy to say something you wouldn't say to a face. Spam—unsolicited junk email—is also prevalent, averaging 94 percent of all sent mail.

Getting started. If you have Internet access, your provider has likely given you an email account. If not, sign up for a free service such as www.gmail.com or mail.yahoo.com.

Text Message

In a nutshell. Texting, or SMS messaging, is a popular way to send short messages from one cell phone to another. Most cell phones today have the ability to send text messages, but costs apply.

Got its start. Text messaging came about in the early 1990s when phone companies realized they could use the blank space in the "header" of a digital phone call as a way to squeeze in brief messages.

Hit the big time. In 2003, 35 percent of all cell phone users worldwide already were using their phone's text message capabilities.

Best used for. One-to-one messaging or sending a notice to a group of friends. Why not just call? Sometimes, a brief text message can be less obtrusive than taking up the recipient's time with a phone call.

Pitfalls. Too many messages—even if you're just receiving them—could harm your wallet. Make sure you have an unlimited text plan if you do a lot of texting. Also texting while driving (or walking) is a major distraction.

Getting started. Phones vary, but you can generally find a recipient the same way you call someone (by using your phone's contact list), and, instead of pushing the call button, send a message.

Instant Messenger

In a nutshell. Instant messaging is real-time communication between two people typing. There are several IM programs: AOL Instant Messenger, Microsoft Instant Messenger, and iChat are a few. These programs work on their own networks, meaning they're not always compatible.

Got its start. Like many of the things on this list, IM history is tied to the Internet itself. QuantumLink allowed Commodore users to send and receive messages instantly; the company later became America Online and popularized the service.

Hit the big time. AOL Instant Messenger moved from a proprietary service to public Internet in 1997, making it the first big company to offer IM service easily.

Best used for. Rapid communication while you're stuck at your computer. If you're a fast enough typer, an IM conversation can be a great way to share Internet links, photos, and thoughts while still working on other things.

Pitfalls. Because the communication is happening so fast, your brain can sometimes interpret it as a vocal conversation. But without the subtext of inflection, you might misinterpret a message or read too much into someone's sentence.

Getting started. If you have a Mac, iChat is installed by default. On Windows, MSN Live Messenger is already there. In order to use it, you must know someone else on the service. Find out his or her contact address (often an email address) to begin an IM session.

Facebook

In a nutshell. Facebook allows you to connect with family, friends, and co-workers. A user posts updates about his or her life on their "Facebook wall." Once someone has added you as a "friend," you can view their updates and see their photos.

Got its start. In 2004, then Harvard student Mark Zuckerberg created "The Facebook," which was a place for Harvard students to post their photos and bios. It was opened to the public in 2006.

Hit the big time. Its traffic surpassed that of rival MySpace. According to ComScore, Facebook became the world's most-used social networking site in April 2008. Since then, its traffic has continued to climb, while MySpace is seeing a slow decline.

Best used for. Connecting—or reconnecting—with family and friends. While Twitter seems best suited for connecting with people you don't know, Facebook is most often used for sharing life events with people you know in real life.

Pitfalls. One profile per person and real name usage can mean a potentially dangerous blurring of public and private lives. (People have been fired over unprofessional Facebook photos.)

Getting started. Visit www.facebook.com and sign up for an account. Once you're registered, you can begin posting updates and photos. Usually, your old acquaintances will come out of the wood-work of their own accord and find you.

Twitter

In a nutshell. Twitter combines the texting ability of phones with the reach of a blog. It allows you to send out 140-character "tweets" to anyone who cares to listen. If people like what you're saying, they "follow you." It's like twenty-first-century CB radio.

Got its start. In 2006, a podcasting company brainstormed a short-messaging service inspired by cell phone text messages. It launched as a full-scale public version later that year.

Hit the big time. CNN started featuring it on its news broad-casts. Twitter also enjoyed time in the limelight when it was used in Iran as one of the primary ways of getting information out to the public when mainstream media outlets were shut down.

Best used for. Connecting with strangers and groups of people who share common interests. Twitter is also a great tool to drive traffic to websites, blogs, and shared points of interest.

Pitfalls. The 140-character limit can sometimes lead to superficial communication. Also, Twitter lacks a business model, only making money through venture capitalists and fundraising efforts, leading some to believe Twitter is a fast-burning fad.

Getting started. Visit www.twitter.com and sign up for an account, then use the search tool to find others with common interests. You'll find it starts snowballing from there as others follow your tweets.

Media Choices Trigger Receivers' Expectations

People come to expect certain types of messages to be communicated via certain media. Some examples may be:

- Your workplace may put out an employee newsletter.
- Your company may make heavy use of email.

- Your family may send written party invitations.
- Your job may call for telephone follow-up with all new customers.
- Your boss may use a weekly staff meeting to share information, etc.
- Your company may use regular one-to-one performance reviews.

These and many other media options are used, often out of habit or tradition. This common use provides an opportunity—a savvy workplace communicator can try using a different medium or combination of media to give a message extra impact.

If, for example, a change in work schedule is normally posted on a bulletin board, a supervisor may get better audience attention by calling a meeting or talking with each worker individually about an unusual change. Similarly, a letter sent to a worker's home will have a different impact than will a general public address system announcement—or even the same letter distributed at work. Customers who expect little or no follow-up after a sale may be impressed by a personal, handwritten note. Apply creativity, some thought about media characteristics, and some educated guesses about likely effects of messages, and you can develop an interesting and effective media mix.

Creative media use—breaking from the expected—can give a message added impact.

We are all bombarded with an enormous number of messages every day. We awake in the morning to messages from our clock radio. We watch the morning TV news, drive to work and see billboards and hear more radio messages, etc. The average person is targeted with thousands of messages every day. We come to develop expectations about how we are likely to receive certain types of messages. "Violating" those expectations—that is, using a different medium than is normally used—can provide a way to break through communication overload. For example, suppose that you typically get your information about traffic conditions from the radio, but on a particular day while stuck in traffic, you are approached by a police officer who gives you information about an alternative route. This would be a case of violating expectations with an alternative medium (personal contact versus radio) to break through with a message.

Media Efficiency is Not the Same as Effectiveness

Consider the costs of communicating. In a broad sense, we can best calculate costs by distinguishing between communication *efficiency* and communication *effectiveness*.

Communication *efficiency* is a simple ratio between the resources expended to generate a message (including time, materials, and effort) and the number of people to whom the message is sent. To improve efficiency, we simply increase the number of people reached or reduce the message preparation costs. A large mass mailing, group presentation or broadcast TV ad can be *efficient*.

Communication *effectiveness*, however, is quite another matter. To remember the four-part definition of communication effectiveness, use the acronym RURU. Communication may be said to be *effective* when a specific message is:

- **R**eceived by its intended audience.
- **U**nderstood essentially the same way by the recipients as intended by the sender.
- **R**emembered over a reasonable period of time.
- **U**sed when appropriate occasions arise.

The dilemma for the message sender is that, in most cases, the communication methods that are most efficient are least effective, and vice versa. In almost every case, for example, face-to-face conversation with individuals is the least efficient, least convenient, and most costly method of communication. It is also often the most effective. And, for some types of messages, including Wilbur's problem with the coffee breaks, it is essential. Wilbur's *efficient* announcement results in a shotgun approach that is likely to hit the wrong people (violating effectiveness condition number one above) by striking the innocent as well as the guilty. This could cause huge resentment.

Media that are most efficient are often the least effective.

In some cases, of course, a message is very simple or not important enough to use expensive media such as individual, face-to-face interaction. In many cases, organizational size or complexity forbids it. You need to strike a balance between efficiency and effectiveness.

Avoid choosing a medium out of habit, without considering the merits or drawbacks of possible alternatives. Avoid selecting what is easiest for *you* to do—rather than thinking about the preferences of your audiences. For example, you may prefer to email extensively because you are at your computer all day. Or perhaps you prefer to use the phone extensively, drop in on people to talk in person, or call frequent meetings. These media choices may be fine as long as you choose purposefully, not just out of habit.

Each Medium Has Unique Capabilities

Each medium has specific advantages or disadvantages based on its capabilities and limitations. Let's look at some of the capabilities of workplace media that make one preferable to others in a given situation. Key capabilities include speed, feedback capacity, hard-copy availability, ability to handle message intensity and complexity, and formality.

Speed

The speed of a medium depends on several factors, including preparation time, delivery time, and assimilation time (the time it takes for the receiver to comprehend the message being delivered). A letter is generally slow getting from sender to receiver (although overnight services have reduced delivery time), but an oral presentation of the same information may take considerably more preparation time. The time-consuming work of producing a videotape or slide presentation may be offset when repeated showings can efficiently present the same information to many audiences. Normally, the spoken word is faster than a print medium, except when we are comparing a formal oral presentation with a handwritten note.

Feedback Capacity

The amount and promptness of feedback are important media considerations. Written media are asynchronous (source and receiver of the message take turns and cannot interrupt in real time). Messages elicit no feedback from your audience while you are writing the message. By the time you get a response, it is too late to adjust and clarify the original message. Telephone conversations provide immediate feedback in the form of questions, comments, tone of voice, pauses, hesitations, and so on. Face-to-face communication situations provide all this plus other, non-verbal feedback in facial expressions, body movements, and postures. Writing's feedback capacity is more restricted.

The asynchronous nature of writing restricts timely feedback.

Hard-Copy Availability

Whether a tangible, permanent record of the message is *normally* retained or not is another media characteristic. Ordinarily, interviews, informal conversation, and telephone messages leave no record. (Of course, these can be recorded, but that is not routine practice in most organizations.) Email messages can be easily printed or maintained in electronic files so a hard copy is easily accessible. Written communications such as letters, reports, and most memos are often maintained on file. An informal note, however, may be discarded and is therefore usually a non-record medium. Of course, a non-record medium can have advantages where candid, "off the record" expression is called for. Putting it in writing seems to make the message more formal or "official," a situation that may also call for less openness in expression.

Email and Hard Copies

Writers should treat email the same as a hard-copy document. Even if the message is never printed on paper, it still remains available and, as such, is a hard copy.

An attorney friend of ours calls email "evidence mail" and uses such electronic exchanges as documents of proof in legal actions. A client can win breach-of-contract-type lawsuits on the strength of email exchanges alone, without having traditional hard copies.

Ability to Handle Intensity and Complexity

Some media are more appropriate for conveying complex or highly intense messages. A high-intensity message may be one that conveys unpleasant information or in some way plays upon the receiver's emotions. Examples are messages that criticize the reader's behavior or seek to persuade a course of action. Most persuasion plays on emotions to some extent. Readers need to have their emotions engaged (hope, anger, frustration, desire for better situation) to bring about the big idea. Typically, a formal letter, a carefully planned oral presentation with handouts, or a written report would meet these requirements. Casual conversation or a brief memo would be less appropriate.

High-intensity messages involve reader and writer emotions.

Messages that require careful explanation of underlying reasoning are often best communicated by a medium that can carry complex data in a relatively structured format. Oral reports may do this, especially if supplemented with handouts, but written reports are also useful, especially if you can't get the audience together for a presentation. Similarly, a document requiring extensive data or an explanation of relationships between many factors will be best handled by written media. Such media allow the reader to review and process the information at his or her own pace.

Formality

Some media are more appropriate for formal occasions, and others fit well in informal settings. A letter of congratulations to an employee seems more formal and has a rather different effect than, say, a casual, unplanned remark conveying the same information. The letter makes it official. An informal handwritten note sent to the board of directors by a worker may be considered out of line. When you write a message intended for internal consumption only (within the organization), its format may be less formal than if it were to be publicly disseminated. For this reason, memos and email are used internally, while written correspondence sent outside the organization takes the form of letters—a slightly more formal format.

Legal documents or formal policy statements are always in written form. (This may be the written equivalent of a diplomat reading a speech word-for-word.) Any detriment to the flow of the message is compensated for by the precision of the language. And for legal or policy issues, language precision is important.

Legal documents, agreements, and policy statements use written media to certify their formality.

Table 3.1 summarizes key characteristics of some common communication media. The bolded items suggest characteristics that may be the most significant reason for choosing a particular medium.

Media Have Certain Ground Rules

Another way to determine the best media is to think about the "ground rules"—the underlying and often unspoken assumptions associated with each option. These ground rules for the use of a particular medium are usually assumed by participants rather than prescribed in advance. For example, the medium called "polite conversation" usually works under the following ground rules:

- Whoever is talking may continue to talk until he or she appears to be finished.
- No speaker should talk for "very long" at a time, which may vary from a few seconds to two or three minutes, depending on the circumstances.
- Nobody may interrupt the speaker unless he or she agrees to be interrupted.
- When a silence occurs, each participant has an equal opportunity to begin talking; that is, nobody is intentionally excluded.
- Anybody who is talking may change the subject without getting permission from other participants.

When such ground rules are violated, participants in the communication situation are thrown off. Imagine a polite conversation in which any of the rules listed are violated—let's say, for example, that interruptions abound—and you are likely to picture an ineffectual and decidedly impolite conversation.

Table 3.2 suggests additional examples of the kinds of ground rules (which are often unspoken) for several spoken and written/graphic media.

TABLE 3.1. Characteristics and Costs of Business Communication Media

Media	Speed	Feedback Capacity	Hard Copy Available	Formal/Informal	Can Handle Complex/ Intense Messages	Cost (High/ Low)
Informal conversation	**Fast**	High	No	Informal	No	Low
Telephone conversation	**Fast**	Medium	No	Informal	No	Low–medium
Voice mail	**Fast**	Low	No	Informal	No	Low
Formal oral presentation	Medium	Medium	Maybe	**Formal**	**Yes**	Medium–high
Informal note	Medium	**Low**	Yes	Informal	No	Low
Memo	Medium	Low	**Yes**	Either	Possible	Medium–high
Email	Fast	Low	**Yes**	Informal	Possible	Medium
Fax	**Fast**	Low	Yes	Either	Yes	Medium
Letter	Slow	Low	Yes	Formal	**Yes**	Medium–high
Formal report	Very Slow	Low	Yes	Very formal	**Yes**	High

TABLE 3.2. Examples of Ground Rules for Media

Some Possible Ground Rules	Spoken Media				Written/Graphic Media		
	Conversation (Telephone or Face-to-Face)	Interview	Meeting	Presentation	Letter/ Memo/ Email	Report	Visuals/ Display/ Charts
Receivers may interrupt and/or seek clarification	Yes	Yes	Yes	No	No	No	No
Participants may change subject	Yes	Sometimes	Yes	No	No	No	No
One may talk for extended periods	No	No	No	Yes	No	Yes	No
Participants have equal opportunity to initiate ideas	Yes	Sometimes	Yes	No	No	No	No
Messages presented in standard format	No	Sometimes	No	Yes	Usually	Yes	No
Supporting data, detail presented with conclusion	Sometimes	No	Sometimes	Yes	Sometimes	Yes	No
Artistic or aesthetic qualities shown	No	No	No	Sometimes	No	Sometimes	Yes

Written communication is asynchronous as opposed to the synchronous nature of most spoken media. Synchronous media are those that allow people to interact in real time (responding or interrupting as needed). Asynchronous media requires that each communicator takes his or her turn. Obviously, written media are asynchronous. I write something, you read it, and vice versa.

Written media are asynchronous in nature and allow no immediate, real-time responses.

Although we don't consciously consider each rule every time we communicate, these ground rules can provide a rational basis for deciding what medium to use for specific messages. If, for example, you need to convey some highly technical, intricate, and complex information, you would likely avoid the friendly conversation medium. Such messages may involve presenting a lot of information without receiver interruption. Recognizing the ground rules in operation may alert you to potential communication failures.

Differences Between Oral and Written Communication

Most of us intuitively understand that there are differences between oral and written language. All communication involves the transfer of information from one person to another. Writing is a fairly static form of transfer. Speaking is a dynamic transfer of information. Spoken language produces a higher level of immediacy and a lower level of retention.

Written language can be significantly more precise. Written words can be chosen with greater deliberation and thought, and a written argument can be detailed, intricate, and lengthy. These attributes of writing are possible because the pace of involvement is controlled by both the writer and the reader. The writer can write and re-write at great length. Similarly, the readers can read quickly or slowly, or even stop to think about what they have just read. More importantly, the reader always has the option of re-reading. The written word appeals more to a contemplative, deliberative style.

Consider Media Mixing: A Sound Alternative

Bear in mind that you are certainly not limited to the use of a single medium for a given message. Often a combination of several media does the job very nicely, since disadvantages of one medium can be offset by another. For example, the slow-feedback characteristic of written media can be offset by an accompanying oral medium. Table 3.3 suggests some ways to combine commonly used media to offset such disadvantages.

Experiments studying the effects of combining media have produced inconclusive results, primarily because of the difficulty of accounting for all possible variables—especially non-verbal ones. Nevertheless, some tentative findings have emerged. In one classic experiment, specific factual information was transmitted using each of the following media or combinations of media:

- Oral only.
- Written only.
- Posted on a bulletin board.
- The grapevine (no formal message sent).
- Both oral and written.

Several days after the messages were delivered, researchers tested the recipients to see how much content they could accurately remember. The results showed that the written-plus-oral message combination resulted in the greatest retention. Oral exchange alone was second in recall accuracy, followed by the written message used alone. The bulletin board was next, and the grapevine came in last.[2]

TABLE 3.3. Combining Media for Effectiveness

Medium	Major Limitations	Supplemental Media
Conversation (phone or live)	No record; little non-verbal feedback with phone use	Record notes; send additional written material; tape-record
Formal oral presentation	Preparation time; no record	Written handouts; outline of presentation; supplemental readings
Informal note	Low feedback; may look overly casual or unimportant	Telephone or conversation follow-up; insert with printed card
Memo	Low immediate feedback; medium often overused	Telephone follow-up to check for understanding
Email	Informal; may get lost among overload	Follow-up hard copy or supplemental information; telephone or conversation follow-up
Formal report	Preparation time; low feedback; cost of printing, etc.	Meeting or presentation to discuss, clarify, and provide/receive feedback

In a later study of communication within a company, researchers asked supervisors to rate the effectiveness of (1) written, (2) oral, (3) written and then oral, and (4) oral and then written communication for different types of situations. In general, the oral-followed-by-written technique came out best. Supervisors saw it as most effective for situations that required immediate action, passed along a company directive, communicated an important policy change, reviewed work progress, called for praising a noteworthy employee or promoted a safety campaign. The written-only technique was judged best for passing along information that required action in the future or was of a general nature. An oral-only message was suggested for reprimands or to settle a dispute among employees.[3]

Tools Used in Workplace Communication

People today are bombarded with enormous amounts of information. So how can the effective communicator be heard above the din of competing messages? Try creativity in media selection. Creativity and innovation start with a look at what's being done now. The following describes the kinds of communication media and tools used in organizations. This listing represents popular use, not necessarily the optimum use of communication tools. As you will see, there is considerable breadth of media options available to today's communicator.

Tools to Convey Job-Related Information

Organizations use the following tools to convey information such as work directives and policy clarification that people must have to be effective:

- Published job descriptions, procedures, practices, or policy manuals.
- Instructional interviews, performance reviews briefings, or training sessions.
- Newsletters and in-house magazines.
- Organizational Web pages.
- Benefits statements (individual accounting of the value of an employee's benefit package).
- Reprints or summaries of technical articles (distributed online or via paper copies).

Tools to Convey "For-Your-Information" Messages

Companies use "for-your-information" tools to convey messages that are likely to be of some interest but are not crucial to the job functions of employees. ("For your information" messages are often abbreviated as "FYI." Messages described as "FYI" generally don't require a reply.) Such FYI messages serve to keep organization members "in the loop."

- Announcement emails and memos (used to explain personnel changes, promotions, appointments, etc.).
- Information/reading racks (stocked with pamphlets, how-to booklets, and magazines or journals of varying topics).
- Bulletin boards.

Tools to Motivate Employees

Companies use the following tools to build and strengthen organizational identification and loyalty:

- Auto windshield decals, bumper stickers, or license plate frames.
- Open houses, family nights (programs including tours of the plant, exhibits, demonstrations, samples, and refreshments), and alumni or retiree activities.
- Letters and cards (sympathy, birthday, anniversary, etc.).
- Recreational and social activities (such as athletic leagues, picnics, and outings).
- Uniforms, coveralls, hard hats, and name badges marked with the company logo.
- Displays and exhibits (photos, artwork, videotape, or slide presentations on subjects such as company history, company products, or statistical data regarding employees, management, and stockholders).

Tools to Convey Upward Feedback

Companies use certain media to encourage upward feedback from subordinates or customers to management. Examples of these media include:

- Advisory councils, focus groups, or similar groups to identify employee or customer concerns.
- Grievance interviews where employees or customers can speak face-to-face with a company representative.
- Exit interviews (interviews with employees who are leaving the company, attempting to understand why they are leaving or what concerns they have about the company).
- Suggestion systems.

> ■ Online feedback systems (blogs) that allow employees and customers to communicate with organizations and receive responses to their complaints, complements, suggestions, or questions. (Two examples of such systems can be found at www.AllegianceTech.com, and www.SilentWhistle.com.)
>
> These listings represent only a sample of tools used in organizations to communicate and create understanding.

Consider Source and Timing Options for Message Success

You have looked in-depth at media options and are convinced that your written letter, memo, email, or report is the best choice. Okay. Now you also need to be aware of the potential impact of the *source* and *timing* of your message.

Source Options

Sometimes you are not the best person to send a particular message. This is not a knock on you—you may be well informed and knowledgeable—but your message may have greater impact if someone else delivers it. Functional business communication asks us to set aside our ego if the outcome can be better achieved by someone else. This situation is especially common in organizations where a person with more formal authority or higher perceived credibility is likely to be more effective delivering a particular message.

Again, this should not be seen as diminishing you in any way. Many professional people produce letters, memos, reports, presentations, and such that are delivered by others. Speech writers, communication directors, and ghost writers are common for executives and political leaders, for example. Using these people does not mean that the originator of the ideas (the writer) is not as bright—it simply means that the message is more likely to be effective if some other source delivers it.

Sometimes you are not the best person to send a particular message—it will be more effective over another person's signature.

Organizational authority is not the only reason you might want to have someone else deliver your messages. Sometimes other people or groups have greater credibility,[4] are better known to the audience or possess some characteristics that help them better establish a connection with the audience. If your intention is to communicate functionally—that is, to get your receivers to do something—the cold fact is that someone else's signature on your writing may have greater impact. Set aside your ego and enlist them into the effort.

Timing Options

The timing of your messages is another critical consideration. When should the message arrive for maximum impact? Improper timing of a message can diminish its effectiveness. For example, sending a thank-you note months after you receive a gift won't win you much goodwill, and writing a progress report before you have progress to report will have little positive effect. Similarly, explaining an advanced application for a software product will do little good if the audience doesn't understand the basic uses. You get the picture. Don't just communicate at your convenience. Be sensitive to whether your audience is mentally prepared, capable of understanding, and available to receive your message.

Good timing requires reader readiness to get your message.

Your decisions about timing can be further complicated when you communicate with multiple audiences or repeat the message. You need to think about the sequencing and spacing of your messages. Who should you write to first? How much time should you allow between messages? Companies normally expect messages to go through channels of authority. You would not, for example, write directly to a senior manager with a question that your immediate supervisor could answer. Conversely, the senior manager should not tell you about a decision before telling your supervisor.

Also, certain audiences should receive information before others. For example, an employee who is being promoted or reassigned should get this message before others do. The supervisor of that employee should announce changes to the people involved in advance of a public announcement. Violating these timing issues can lead to embarrassment and the feeling of being "out of the loop" in the organization.

Timing decisions should also consider organizational protocol. Who should receive the message and in what order?

Self-Evaluation: Timing Blunders

Think back on a situation where a message's timing was awkward or ineffective. What was the outcome in regard to communication effectiveness? Did the mistiming convey any unspoken messages? Was the message sender's success impacted? How? Why?

Here are a few examples to start your thinking:

- You received a routine thank-you note for a wedding gift given six months earlier.

- A magazine ad showed a Nissan SUV poised to race down a runway with the Concord supersonic aircraft. The ads appeared shortly after the fatal crash of a Concord.

- A newspaper chain was revealed as having pre-written obituaries for some elderly famous people in case these were needed on short notice.

- An organization announced the hiring of a high-profile executive before he had officially accepted the offer (or announced that he was leaving his current company).

- An ominous email summoning an employee to meet with the boss on Monday arrives at closing time Friday (causing the employee to fret about it all weekend).

Add your own examples.

What do these examples say about media and timing choices?

Avoid Mistiming Messages

Poor timing decisions can ruin even the most carefully crafted message. This can occur when we communicate at our own convenience rather than being sensitive to our audience. Timing of messages can also have a dramatic effect on their acceptance and understanding. The following sections offer some suggestions for making the most of media timing.

Be Aware of Competing Audience Concerns

Sometimes leaders deliver their messages at poor times. One manager sent an email message to a subordinate asking her to call his secretary to schedule a meeting to talk about "performance issues." The email arrived at 5 p.m. on a Friday, giving the receiver all weekend to wonder and worry about this vaguely threatening message. In another case of poor timing, a manager told a subordinate that his contract was not going to be renewed on a day that marked the three-year anniversary of a tragic auto crash that killed the man's wife and daughter.

You can best avoid such timing mistakes by knowing your audiences and being sensitive to their needs. Put yourself in their shoes and ask, "Is this a good time to receive such a message?" If competing concerns or emotions are likely to overshadow the message, its likelihood for achieving its function is diminished.

Anticipate possible factors that make timing unproductive to your message's function.

Shun Communicating When You Are Upset

Many of us have fired off a blistering memo, made an angry phone call, or spouted off in a meeting while upset. When our message is written or emailed, it can produce lingering embarrassment. It's especially difficult to later eat our words when they are there in black and white. If a situation prompts you to send an emotionally charged message, write or draft your thoughts, but hold on to them for a day or two. Letting the message ferment and then editing it carefully can help you avoid embarrassment and serious credibility damage.

Always think twice before sending an emotional message. Write a draft and hold on to it for review when you can be more dispassionate.

Be Aware of Message Sequencing

Additional timing considerations are *sequencing* and *spacing* of your messages, especially with multiple audiences. Sequencing means deciding who will get the message first, second, and so on. An effective communicator will decide which audience is to receive which message in what order. Organizational protocol and common courtesy usually provide good guidelines. Don't announce a decision before it has really been decided. Don't direct an action to subordinates if their supervisor has not been notified.

Also consider how much time to allow between messages. For example, if you are given the task of training people about a benefits change in all your company's locations, you need to decide whom you will present to first, second, and so on. If the message is about retirement program changes, you may well choose to talk first to older workers, who will be affected soonest by the change. Likewise, organizations generally want information to follow the chain of command. You may need to get approval from your supervisor or even that person's manager before distributing a message. Sending out unapproved messages is a serious social blunder that can hurt your career.

Information should normally follow the organizational chain of command.

The Straight Talk Writing Model Applied

The medium that communicators choose for their messages sends important signals to the receivers. In the case of Wilbur Matheson in our opening story, he chose a brief memo sent to the larger group without an opportunity for feedback. The effect was to convey some possible unspoken messages to its readers such as:

- This message isn't very important. If it were, I'd present it more formally and allow discussion.
- You are not important enough to receive this information from me personally.
- I am too busy to convey this information to you in a more personal way.
- I don't care about the appearance of my message; this "quick-and-dirty" approach is good enough.
- This matter is so urgent I had to sacrifice personalizing and professionalism to get the information out quickly.
- This is routine information that you will readily understand.

Unfortunately, Wilbur apparently gave little thought to the medium he chose. In failing to look at his options, he failed to consider the fact that the medium itself makes a comment about the contents of the message. When criticizing personal behavior, mass memos or emails are not likely to be functional. In short, they won't work. If he were really interested in changing his employees, Wilbur would have met with people individually in an interactive conversation. This would cost more (in time and effort), but if the message is truly important and demands behavior changes, conversations are a far superior medium.

Performance Checklist

After completing this chapter, you should be better able to apply some principles for selecting the best media and timing options for your message. Specifically, you should now understand that:

- The media, methods, or approaches we choose when communicating can enhance or detract from our communication success.
- Each communication medium triggers certain expectations in the message receivers, presents a tradeoff between efficiency and effectiveness, and has unique capabilities.

- What receivers might expect should be factored into media choice decisions. At times you will want to use the expected media; at times you may want to use unexpected media to direct special attention to your message.
- Efficiency and effectiveness are different and should be weighed in your media decision. Communication efficiency is a simple ratio between the total costs of a message and the number of people reached by that message. Communication effectiveness is determined by the degree to which a message is *received* by the intended audience, *understood* correctly, *remembered* for a reasonable period of time, and *used* when appropriate occasions arise. (The acronym "RURU" can help you remember this.)
- Capabilities inherent in a given medium should be considered when selecting that medium. Among the salient characteristics are speed, feedback capacity, hard-copy availability, message intensity, and complexity, and formality.
- A communication medium operates within a generally accepted set of ground rules. These ground rules play a large part in determining the medium's effectiveness in a given situation.
- Mixing several media can offset the disadvantages of one of them, resulting in more effective communication.
- Written media are asynchronous, meaning that participants in the communication take turns and may not interrupt each other.
- Consider timing options for your message by being aware of your audience's competing concerns, avoiding communicating when upset and being sensitive to message sequencing.
- A wide range of communication tools is available to you. Creativity and innovation will help your message stand out from the massive amount of information bombarding people today.

What Do You Know?

Activity 3.1: Experiencing Media Choice Problems

Recall an experience you have had in which you received a message through an inappropriate medium. Describe how that media choice damaged the effectiveness of the message. What medium would have been better? Why?

Activity 3.2: Recognizing Media Ground Rules

List eight communication media you use regularly. Then, articulate at least three ground rules for each medium. Finally, identify the most important characteristic that would cause you to choose each medium.

Media I Use	Ground Rules	Strongest Reason for Use
1	_____	_____
2	_____	_____
3	_____	_____
4	_____	_____
5	_____	_____
6	_____	_____
7	_____	_____
8	_____	_____

Activity 3.3: Recognizing Habits of Media Use

We all have media preferences and tend to use those media that we are most comfortable with. Analyze your media use over several days. Make a log of which media you use for various communication situations. Based on the material in this chapter, describe in a brief report your tendencies or habits of use. Are you using media optimally? Do you seem to have a disproportionate preference for written versus spoken media? Is that giving you optimal results? What might you change to boost your effectiveness?

Reinforce With These Review Questions

1 True/False Written media are synchronous, allowing significant interaction with the message receiver.

2 Communicators should be aware of options with regard to three things: (1) _____, (2) _____, and (3) _____ _____.

3 Using a source other than yourself can add _____ to your message.

4 True/False Timing, while important in oral communication, is far less relevant when dealing with written messages.

5 Communication effectiveness, as defined in this chapter, is defined by four characteristics (RURU): The message is (1) _____, (2) _____, (3) _____, and (4) _____.

6 True/False Communication media trigger different expectations in message receivers.

7 Communication media operate within generally accepted ground rules that play a large part in determining the medium's effectiveness in a given situation.

8 True/False Best communicators select only one medium for each message.

9 True/False At times you may want to use unexpected media to direct special attention to your message.

10 Communication efficiency can be described as a simple ratio between _____ of a message and _____.

four

Select and Organize Your Message Content

Turning out a first draft is far and away the most decisive part of the writing process. For this is when you begin to commit yourself to a specific course of action; to a detailed and precise architecture of the finished product.

(Herbert E. Meyer, *How to Write*)

Putting Ideas Together

Once you have analyzed the context and considered the media, source, and timing options available to you, it is time to pull ideas together and organize your message for maximum impact. This, incidentally, is the step in the Straight Talk Writing Model where many people begin: the sit down and start writing! But we now know better and understand the importance of assessing the foundation of the communication event as described in the model.

Getting started on the initial draft of a written message can be daunting for some. Writer's block is fairly common. That is why you need to focus on the word "draft." Rarely will what you write first be the final version of your message. Re-writing and editing is not only commonplace, but essential in all but the simplest messages.

This chapter shows you some concrete steps for selecting and organizing the meat of your message. These tips are especially applicable to workplace writing—functional business communication.

Performance Competencies

When you have completed this chapter, you should be able to:

- Choose an overall select-and-organize approach for your written messages.
- Identify the key ingredients in effective informative, persuasive, and bad-news messages.
- Understand the "big idea" and use of BIF and BILL patterns of arrangement.
- Justify different structures for messages with different purposes.
- Identify key factors that may damage goodwill in bad-news messages.
- Explain how the principles of organization covered in this chapter can be applied to long documents.
- Utilize proven principles for outlining a longer message and checking its consistency and flow.
- Apply the STEP test to determine document integrity.

We now get to the part of writing that some less effective communicators begin with! Too frequently, people start by writing the ideas they want to convey before (or instead of) thinking through the many elements of the communication context or the media, source, and timing options. By thinking about what we want to convey before thinking about possible reader reactions, we set ourselves up for failure.

Less successful writers erroneously begin to write before working through the foundation steps of the Straight Talk Writing Model.

Review Your Decisions about Context, Media, Source, and Timing

As you face the task of selecting and organizing ideas for your message, take the time to review the context of your message. Specifically, jot down relevant facts about the situation, your audiences, and your objectives with those audiences. Your Context Analysis Worksheet will remind you of all the questions you need to ask yourself. Failing to have a clear picture of this context makes it nearly impossible to succeed as a communicator. Remember, the most successful communicators focus their thinking on their readers' viewpoint.

The "default" position for any message is that it must have an effective introduction, body, and conclusion that are appropriate for the situation, readership, and objectives. To produce these elements, you must first be clear about your main objective, or what we have described earlier in functional communication as the *big idea*. To review, the big idea can be defined as what you want your reader to *do*, *think*, or *feel* as a result of getting your message.

If you don't have a clear, hoped-for outcome, or if you don't take the time to consider your audience, the big idea of your message will be unclear, and your message won't be functional. If you don't know what you are trying to accomplish, your reader won't either.

Choose an Overall BIF or BILL Approach

A good starting point for determining how to arrange a message is to focus on the big idea. What, exactly, do you hope to achieve with your writing? Put another way, what do you want your reader to do (or think) after reading your message? This is a critical question for functional, workplace writing.

Next determine if the *big idea* should come *first* (BIF) or if the *big idea* should come a *little later* (BILL). For most functional writing, BIF is appropriate. The big idea—what you want the reader to do—can be presented up front. This is particularly the case when you convey routine or positive messages the reader is not likely to resist. For example, if you are writing a letter or sending an email to order a product from a company, how is that reader likely to respond? They are probably going to be glad you ordered—that's good news. Telling them what you want them to do (the big idea—send me the product) is not likely to cause them to resist or get their feelings hurt.

Routine messages or those that will be seen as good news should use a big-idea-first (BIF) approach.

Some message situations, however, may hurt people's feelings or convey disappointing information the reader would rather not get. Refusing someone's request, for example, may lead to negative reactions. In such cases, the big idea (the refusal or bed news) should come a little later in the message via the big-idea-a-little-later (BILL) approach.

Another situation where BILL makes sense is when you are attempting to persuade someone to do something they would not be likely to do without your message. A sales letter, for example, may flop if it starts out with the big idea because the reader will resist it until you can provide reasons to do the big idea. If your letter's purpose is to get someone to buy from you, it rarely makes sense to tell them that too early. Starting a letter with "I want you to buy some insurance from me" (which is the big idea, of course) will be less effective than giving them some reasons before getting to the "close."

The common element in the decision to use BILL instead of BIF is when the reader's *emotions* will come into play. In bad-news messages, these emotions may be disappointment, frustration, hurt feelings, etc. In persuasive messages, the emotions are enthusiasm, desire for your product or idea, and the like. Almost every buying decision has an emotional component—we buy because we get excited about a product or service. As a writer of persuasive messages, we need to get people's emotions excited before they are likely to buy our product/idea.

Look Inside: Should This Be BIF or BILL?

Let's see if you understand the distinction. For each "big idea" listed below, determine if the BIF or BILL approach would make the most sense.

- You want your readers to agree to change their work schedules, although the new schedule may be less convenient.
- You want your subordinates to use a new form to report work data. The form is simple to use and will require less time to fill out than the current form.
- You are inviting people to an open house to celebrate some occasion.
- You want your reader to vote for a particular proposal or person.
- You want your colleagues to see last month's sales results.
- You want your readers to be aware of the time and location for next week's regular staff meeting.
- You need employees to voluntarily participate in some community action project.

If you are thinking that the BIF versus BILL distinction is not always absolutely clear, you are right. What a reader may see as bad news—say, a memo announcing an inconvenient work schedule change—may be presented directly as BIF so long as the reader knows that these things happen and everyone takes turns doing the crummy shifts. On the other hand, routine monthly sales results may be better received with a BILL approach if the reader is fearful about his or her performance, is still learning the job, and you don't want to be discouraging. Ultimately, your overall approach depends on the context.

Selecting Information to Include in the Message

Selecting information to put in a message is a natural outgrowth of defining the context. In other words, you will discover questions that need to be answered as you apply the Straight Talk Writing Model and gain a clear picture of the situation, audiences, and your objectives. These questions—resulting in answers about what your message receiver needs or wants to know—determine the information you need for your message to succeed. Try to assume the perspective of your various readers and anticipate the questions they would likely ask. A complete and effective message answers all the receivers' potential questions.

Content of the message stems from what readers may be asking as they receive the message. Anticipate and answer reader questions.

Introductions: Attention-grabber, Benefit, Agenda

Because people constantly battle the problem of communication overload, you need to make your document or email stand out. To do so, employ a strong introduction. Typically we think of introductions in oral communication. A speaker tells a funny story or makes a startling comment that grabs our attention to what he or she is saying. The same principle can apply in writing.

An effective introduction must grab reader attention—it must pry your readers away from competing messages or distractions. You can accomplish this verbally (with your words) or non-verbally (with illustrations, document design features, etc.). For example, your memo or report might grab attention by:

- Using some graphic device such as a distinctive typeface, picture, graph, or eye-catching diagram (non-verbal).
- Using clear wording that creates mental images in readers' minds.
- Stating something that sparks their interest by offering or implying an advantage they can receive from reading your document or email.

In addition to grabbing attention, an effective introduction can accomplish two other things: it may imply or tell readers about the benefits they will gain by paying attention to you, and it may describe the agenda for the rest of your message.

Effective introductions gain reader attention, suggest reader benefit, and describe an agenda for the rest of the message.

Gaining reader attention is foremost in any introduction. Based on your context analysis, develop appeals that suggest personal benefits to readers— "what's in it for me" or WIIFM. By reading your message, the audience may receive something beneficial or avoid a loss with regard to their desires for success, power or status enhancement, self-satisfaction, or curiosity. People pay attention to matters of self-interest.

Introductions should tell or imply WIIFM to the reader.

Table 4.1 shows you some positive and negative appeals that may gain reader attention.

TABLE 4.1. Positive and Negative Attention-Getting Appeals

	Success	Power and Status Enhancement	Self-Satisfaction, Happiness, Fulfillment	Curiosity
Positive appeals	Acting will lead to success in accomplishing goals.	Acting will improve power and status.	Acting will lead to a sense of satisfaction.	Acting will answer questions the audience would like answered.
	Examples: "You can break into the premier sales club …" or "This report shows you four tips for remodeling your home and saving thousands of dollars."	*Examples:* "Do you want to master the art of negotiation?" or "Let me show you how to dramatically improve your ability to [add a skill] with just a few tips."	*Examples:* "I can show you how to achieve your goals of becoming your own boss," or "I can show you seven ways of boosting your life satisfaction and happiness."	*Examples:* "How would you like to know your competitor's exact sales strategy?" or "I can show you some little-known key indicators that will guarantee …"
Negative appeals	**Not** acting will lead to the failure to accomplish goals.	**Not** acting will cost the loss of power or status.	**Not** acting will lead to dissatisfaction or a missed opportunity for the audience.	**Not** acting will leave important questions unanswered.
	Examples: "Can you be satisfied with another average sales year?" or "Let me show you how to avoid the mistakes many home repair people make …"	*Examples:* "Are you coming up short in negotiations?" or "Here is why continuing to do [X] as you have been doing it, will destroy your ability to lead."	*Examples:* "How much longer will you work to make someone else wealthy?" or "Do you feel trapped in a rut?"	*Examples:* "Is what you don't know about the competition killing you?" or "Have you ever wondered how hackers can get into your computer?"

In addition to grabbing an audience's attention, some introductions also lay out an agenda for the rest of the document. Letting people know what you plan to cover provides *content preview* (as discussed in Chapter 1) and helps readers prepare mentally to receive your message. Such previewing may also describe what you *will not* be discussing, as well.

For example, a writer may say something like:

■   This report will deal with only the three most popular product alternatives identified by our customers based on July's research survey.

Or:

■   This memo will bring you up to date on the Harris Street construction but I will not be discussing other new branches.

An agenda statement almost always makes a message clearer for readers. It helps them focus on what you want to cover. This can be stated directly. For example:

■   This report will look at last month's sales results, will offer some competitor comparisons and highlight key strategies for targeting most profitable markets.
■   In this letter I will show you four reasons for the reorganization and specific ways it will impact each department.

Conclusions: Summary and Action Step

Any document that covers more than one main point should include a summary and action step(s) to reinforce the big idea. Summaries simply and briefly restate your key points. Be certain to limit summaries to the major points and do not reiterate the whole document. Also, be careful to avoid introducing any new ideas at this point.

Action steps stated at the end of a document have a particularly strong emphasis position. These will be the last words your reader gets from you. Leave readers with something that resonates and clarifies a clear action you would like them to take. This action is the "big idea" of the writing—the essence of what you are trying to accomplish.

Conclusions should leave readers with a clear action step.

Now let's look at some typical patterns of arrangement for various types of messages.

Organize Information for Positive, Routine Request, and Informative Messages

Positive and routine written messages answer simple questions for the reader. Typical workplace examples are requests for basic information, brief progress reports, routine announcements, invitations, or product orders. They convey information, update people, and/or provide good news. As we mentioned earlier, receivers of such messages are likely to be happy—or at least not unhappy—to get them. Since there will be little or no emotional resistance to the big idea, put it up front—use BIF.

Criteria to Apply to Positive, Routine Request, and Informative Messages

Positive, routine-request, and informative messages should include appropriate information that is complete and direct in answering reader questions. The selected information should be organized to get directly to the main point (BIF) and then follow with clarifying details and, perhaps, a friendly close. Apply the following criteria to this type of message.

Be Complete

Make sure you provide enough information to accomplish what you want your listeners to do or think. If you are inviting people to an activity, for example, be sure to include its location, time, date, and what to bring or wear. If your message conveys a simple change in a procedure (one they are not likely to resist), be certain to tell the receivers exactly how to make the change. If your document or email reports information, be certain that you include all the relevant information. Before sending the final draft, anticipate any questions the receiver may have, and be certain you have answered those questions.

Be Direct

The intent of good-news or routine informational messages is to tell people something they are glad to hear or, at worst, are neutral toward, so you can put the big idea up front and not worry about getting a negative emotional reaction. These are usually pretty easy to write, but be certain to follow the big idea of the message with all needed relevant, subordinate information that clarifies details.

Be direct and provide all needed details in these BIF messages.

Patterns of Arrangement for Positive, Routine Request, and Informative Messages

If your informative message calls for elaboration—is more than a brief thank you or a simple, routine request—help your receiver digest the details of your message with a clear introduction (attention-grabber, agenda, purpose, and benefit for the reader) and then elaborate with one of these patterns:

- **Chronological order.** Organize supporting information items as they occurred in time. For example: "In 2007 we opened the Riverwoods Branch followed by the Stadium Branch in 2009."

- **Problem-solution.** Tell your audience what problems you faced and how you propose to resolve them. For example: "Immediately after the department reorganization, we were concerned about employee reactions to the changes. So, we polled all employees to determine if they were experiencing any significant problems. The polling revealed some areas of concern, such as ..."

- **Topical or spatial order.** Progress systematically from one topic or place to another. For example: "Sales results are shown below for each branch." Or, "Three sources of customer complaints seem to be value, systems and people. Examples of each are shown in this report."

- **Cause–effect.** Tell your audience what happened and what caused it to happen. For example: "Customer dissatisfaction with the new Frequent Flyer Program has had a direct impact on our profitability in major hubs in the following ways ..."

- **STAR(R).** Describe a progression of information describing a *situation* you or the company faced, what *task* the situation required, what specific *action* you took and the *result*—what happened. (If applicable, the second "R" stands for "recommendation.")

Here is an example of STARR:

- **Situation.** The department's sales results were dropping for three consecutive months.
- **Task.** My assignment was to find a new incentive program that would reenergize sales people.
- **Action.** I offered "instant cash" bonuses for selling selected products.
- **Result.** Sales increased X percent.
- **(Recommendation).** We should consider similar cash bonuses to boost high-profit products.

Following the use of any of these patterns of arrangement, close your document with a conclusion (summary and action step), if appropriate.

Look Inside: Applying Order to the Body

Assume that you need to write the following documents. Which pattern of arrangement is likely to be the best option for each? Why?

1   A progress report on the building of a new branch office.

2   A summary of customer service complaints from each company office.

3   An explanation of an accident that injured several workers.

4   A discussion of options for dealing with increased absenteeism at work.

5   A memo summarizing significant contributions you have made to the company since being employed there.

6   A report dealing with workplace accident prevention efforts.

7   An annual recap of company highlights for the year.

Select and Organize Information for Persuasive Messages

Persuasive business messages are *action*-oriented. They seek to get readers to *do* something they normally would not do without some prodding. The message's effectiveness can often be judged by the action that results. The effective sales message sells. The effective collection message collects. The persuasive presentation sways opinion or moves people to action. The communicator's job is to motivate readers to expend the effort to change in the desired direction. Thus, the more you know about the reader's needs, wants, and motives, the more likely you are to motivate appropriately.

Persuasion, by definition, seeks to get people to do (or think) something they otherwise would not do (or think).

Criteria to Apply to Persuasive Messages

Successful persuasive messages involve reader emotions to be successful. In sales training, you may hear the expression "sell the sizzle, not the steak." It's the emotion of savoring the steak that causes people to buy. Stories and vivid examples that stimulate the senses trigger emotions and motivation. Appeal to reader wants or needs and relate the features of your product, idea, or proposal to specific benefits. Boost persuasiveness by applying the following criteria to your messages:

Appeal to reader emotions for successful persuasion.

Use Information That Appeals to the Reader

One of the best ways to overcome resistance to your solution is to select information that addresses your readers' anticipated objections. For example, suppose you wanted to propose that your department converts to a whole new computer platform. Two obvious objections likely to come to mind are: (1) cost and (2) time needed to train personnel on the new system. Now that you have anticipated these objections (and as many other possible objections as you can discover from your context analysis), address them in your message. You might overcome these objections by showing how they will be offset by increased worker efficiency and better system capabilities, for example.

Show your readers what personal benefits will be gained by doing what you want them to do. The recommended computer system, for example, may lead to increased company success which will impact employee bonuses. Many persuasive requests fail when the communicator forgets to phrase ideas in terms of the audience.

Use Information That Links Features to Benefits

Appeals you use to persuade will work best when the benefits of what you are offering relate closely to reader needs. If you have carefully analyzed the context of your message, you should have a pretty good picture of the nature of your readers—and what benefits are attractive to them.

When describing a product, service, or recommendation to readers, distinguish between features and benefits. A *feature* is simply some aspect or characteristic of your product, service, or idea. A vehicle may have a powerful engine; a vacuum cleaner may come with clever attachments; a package delivery service may guarantee against breakage at no cost. These are features. A *benefit* is a "what-this-means-to-you (the customer or reader)" statement.

To maximize the persuasive impact, features should be phrased in terms of the benefit your readers will get from them. For example, the truck can take you up the steepest gravel road; the vacuum can get disease-carrying dirt out of hard-to-reach places; intact delivery of your products will eliminate customer complaints and help your company be more profitable. You sell ideas and products with reader benefit. Use the phrase "and what this means to you" in showing the linkage your audience needs to see. A few examples of tying features to benefits are:

Feature of Your Product, Idea	Benefit Associated With That Feature (What This Means To You ...)
The new phone system will direct customers to the appropriate department	You will not be interrupted by calls you cannot handle
The hybrid truck gets more than 50 miles per gallon	You save money on fuel and lets your customers know that you are ecologically sensitive
Outsourced shipping services simplify processes	You will no longer have to package and transport product; the new service picks it up, saving you time
Phone system upgrade keeps a record of all calls, their duration, and timing	This provides backup information if needed to verify a customer request

Patterns of Arrangement for Persuasive Messages

Because persuasion, by definition, seeks to get people to do something they otherwise would not do, we usually prefer an indirect (BILL) approach. The big-idea-a-little-later approach leads up to the requested action and thus reduces the likelihood of turning the reader off before you present the big idea. The opposite—a direct (BIF) approach—would be like starting out saying, "I want to sell you some widgits." The indirect approach establishes some need before getting to that point (the big idea of the message). However, the direct approach may be effective when your reader is already predisposed to agree with your proposal, when your proposal does not require strong persuasion (perhaps the decision isn't very significant), or when the reader prefers that you get to the point.

For example, an email announcing a minor change in work schedule or abolition of an outdated procedure could be direct without much downside risk.

Once again, the ideal document would include a complete introduction and conclusion. In your introduction, remember to include an attention-grabber that engages your readers, an agenda that describes what you are going to cover, and a very specific benefit statement that articulates exactly "what's in it for them" to read your message.

One caveat about the agenda, however, is to not give away too much. "I want to sell you some insurance" is likely to be off-putting, not enticing—unless the reader is hot to buy some insurance. Instead, your agenda might be more generic, such as, "I'm going to describe some common financial concerns for our families and businesses and then how to protect them."

The ANSA Pattern

In theory, successful persuasion is simple. All you have to do is help your reader get answers to their questions or problems. The key word is "answer." With a little New England accent, answer becomes ANSA, which stands for:

Attention
Need
Solution
Action

Admittedly this is a bit hokey, but hokey can be memorable (like those awful commercials that you can't get out of your head). We want you to remember not only the four parts to the approach but also the key to successful persuasion—providing *answers*.

The ANSA pattern can work in almost any persuasive message. We will discuss each part as isolated steps in a four-step sequence, but these parts often overlap. Sometimes, the middle two parts are presented in a different order, with the solution coming before the need development. Sometimes, when the need is obvious, more emphasis is placed on getting attention and convincing the reader your product or idea really is the answer. With this understanding in mind, let's look at each part of the ANSA approach separately.

The ANSA pattern provides a systematic method of persuasion.

---

1 Gain reader *attention*. Yes, this is just like the introduction of any document, as we have discussed. Some techniques for grabbing reader attention include the use of a statement of the topic or reference to the occasion, a startling statement or statistic, a rhetorical question, a quotation, a definition or narrative, or a short story. To work best, these techniques need to appeal to specific readership needs by implying or offering some benefit. Such benefits are *persuasive appeals*. Four categories of persuasive appeals are widely used in communication to get listener attention. These are appeals to the audience's needs for

- Success.
- Power and status enhancement.
- Self-satisfaction, happiness, fulfillment.
- Curiosity.

These attention-getting appeals may be phrased positively or negatively. Positive appeals focus on what the message receiver stands to gain; negative appeals accentuate what the audience might lose if they do not pay attention to your message. Examples of such appeals were presented back in Table 4.1.

2 Develop the *need*. Often the attention-grabber combines interest-creating information with a description of a problem. Television commercials often follow this pattern. They present an unpleasant situation in such a way that we can identify with the victim of, say, embarrassment, discomfort, disappointment, or failure. Our reaction may be to empathize and feel the discomfort of some similar emotions.

Why does need-agitation move the reader to action? Psychologists explain this in terms of balance theory. People prefer to be in a state of psychological balance or equilibrium; they want perceptions to fit together, to make sense, to seem rational, to be comfortable. You create feelings of tension and imbalance when you expose a problem your listener can identify with. If strongly felt, this is agitating. To reduce this agitation or tension, the audience will try to restore psychological balance. That balance comes about by doing what you, the persuader, suggest.

3 Offer a *solution* to the problem. Once you have your readers' attention and have helped them identify a personal need, your job is to explain how to satisfy that need. You can best do this by giving the reader a solution. To convince your audience that you really do have the solution, you'll need to select believable evidence—information that supports and clarifies your big idea. Such evidence can take the form of:

- Descriptions of benefits your product or idea provides.
- Statistics and related facts.
- Quotes or testimonials (perhaps from others who have tried your solution).
- Product samples.
- Answers to possible objections about your product or idea.

4 Close with a call for *action*. An action close makes the difference between a merely informative message and functional one that gets results.

The action close seeks to do two things:

1 Persuades your listeners to *do* something specific.
2 Summarizes the benefit they can expect from taking this action. This becomes the conclusion of the message.

The tone of the action step should be assumptive—it should imply that you assume they will do what you ask. You should be moving from the conditional phrasing, such as "If you do it," that you used at the beginning of your message, to the more definitive, "Here's how you do it." Assume that your readers have understood and agree with your reasoning. They now simply need to be nudged a bit to obtain the benefits you promise.

The following are examples of action closes:

- Go to our website today, while you're thinking about it—and I'll send you a free examination copy of the Executive Planner. You'll be surprised how much time this modern management tool will save you. The impact on your productivity will be substantial!
- Authorize two additional employees to work on the taskforce, and I will pay to send them to the software training classes out of my departmental budget. The classes start in two weeks, so I need your approval right away.
- Get a copy of our booklet describing the specific benefits of [product, service, or idea] by calling our toll-free number (or responding to this email).

Select and Organize Information for Bad-News Messages

Sometimes you need to convey information your audience does not want to hear. When this is the case, you need to make a cost decision: is softening the message and maintaining goodwill with your readers important enough to expend some *extra* effort and cost in communicating with them? The alternative is to simply write the bad news and, if their feathers get ruffled, so be it. Of course, there is often potential damage to relationships when communication is too blunt. A tactful, carefully arranged bad-news message may take a bit more effort, but is likely to mitigate negative impressions your readers have toward you or your organization. The payoff in maintaining goodwill may be worth the effort.

When To Be Direct

Classic leadership studies by Fred Fiedler[1] identify key situational factors that can determine leadership effectiveness. Fiedler contends that these factors are:

1   **Leader–member relations.** The degree of confidence, trust, and respect the followers have for the leader.
2   **Task structure.** The degree to which the task the leader is directing is structured (clear) or unstructured (ambiguous).
3   **Position power.** The degree of influence the leader has over power variables such as hiring, firing, discipline, promotions, and salary increases.

The "favorableness of the situation" is determined by how strong each of these factors is relative to the task the leader is trying to persuade people to do. A very favorable situation would be one where the leader is well-liked, the task he or she wants done is clear, and he or she is seen as having sufficient power or authority. The opposite situation may be where, for example, a less personable leader is assigned an ambiguous task (say, designing a new marketing approach) and has little real power to get people to do what he or she says.

What does this have to do with communication? An interesting conclusion of Fiedler's research is that when favorableness of the situation is either very high or very low, the appropriate leader approach (i.e., communication style) is to directly tell people what to do (use BIF). When the situation is moderately favorable, the better leadership approach is to seek cooperation, be relationship-conscious (use BILL). When you think about this, it makes sense. If people love you, get the picture of what needs to be done, and recognize your authority, they are likely to do what you ask, even if you are very direct in how you ask. If the workers hate your guts, the task is unclear and you really have little power, you have little to lose by being direct. If your favorableness of the situation is somewhere in the middle, persuading is more important than directing.

Criteria to Apply to Bad-News Messages

The bad-news letter or memo gives readers a message they probably would rather not get. These messages may refuse requests or convey disappointing, embarrassing, or even possibly hurtful information the receivers would rather not receive. While sending such messages is sometimes necessary, the way you communicate can make a difference in how your readers perceive the message and react to you. If you come across as overly blunt or insensitive, relationships can be damaged. If you are overly vague or sound tentative, you may be seen as indecisive or weak and you may damage your credibility. For workplace writing, the trick is to convey information in an assertive, but not offensive manner.

> **Bad-news messages are simply messages people would rather not receive.**

"Assertiveness" is sometimes mistaken for aggressiveness. The best, simple definition of assertiveness is "being pleasantly direct." You can convey even negative information in a pleasantly direct way and the BILL approach, whereby you preface the bad news with explanatory information, is one excellent way to do this.

Assertiveness means being pleasantly direct.

The ideal outcome of such a BILL-approach message is for your reader to conclude that, "I am disappointed (or upset, or even angry) about the message, but if I were in the sender's position, I would probably make the same decision." If you communicate effectively, receivers will understand why you needed to give the bad news and will respect you for doing so with compassion and class.

The best possible outcome for a bad-news message is for the receiver to understand why you did as you did, despite his or her disappointment.

Have Empathy

Before preparing bad-news messages, empathize with your reader—put yourself into the shoes of the person or people you are writing to. Based on your analysis of the context, you should have some sense of what kinds of information will work best. If, for example, you are writing to a business person and must refuse a request because it would damage your profitability, use an appeal to the value of maintaining a profitable company. The reader should understand that line of reasoning. On the other hand, if you are communicating with someone who may not understand basic business needs (e.g., to be profitable), you may refuse a request on the grounds that it would be unfair to others. Most people understand the value of fairness and will accept that as a reasonable rationale for a decision. Look for common values that your readers would relate to.

Empathize by appealing to common values in conveying bad news.

Be Clear

Although conveying bad news is seldom pleasant, you need to be clear. Some people try to be so sensitive to their reader's reactions that they never really get to the point—they never actually tell the bad news. Sometimes they try to sugarcoat the negative information so much that the reader doesn't "get it." For example, telling a job applicant that he did not get the job should leave no doubt about your decision. Saying "the position has been offered to another applicant" may seem clear to you, but could leave ill-founded hope in the mind of a reader who may not know if only one position was available or if the other applicant has officially *accepted* the job. If you fail to make the bad news clear, you run the risk of leading people on. When the finality of the bad news eventually hits them, they will be more disappointed than ever.

Be Clear in Conveying Bad News

An example of lack of clarity posed a problem in a small training company owned by Brian and Glenn. Because of the success of the company, a steady stream of people approached the business owners and expressed a desire to become trainers for the seminars and workshops the company offered.

When people applied for jobs as trainers, Brian was constantly optimistic, implying that the company would be delighted to hire the applicant. He avoided directness and inevitably lead them on with vague promises and stalling tactics. He did this because he wanted people to like him and avoided telling people possible bad news.

Glenn then found himself having to play the role of the "bad guy." He found himself facing unhappy would-be trainers when they got tired of waiting for a definitive answer from Brian. Glenn was more frank when people were not going to be hired. The outgrowth of this is that Glenn—the one who was candid with applicants—had far stronger credibility than Brian, who told people what they wanted to hear. The moral of the story: bending over backwards to "save" people from receiving bad news can damage your credibility. Be clear in all your communications—even the bad news.

Pattern of Arrangement for Bad-News Messages

When faced with the task of organizing a bad-news message, these are your options:

1   Give the bad news and then explain the reasons (direct approach).
2   Give the reasons first, leading up to the bad news (indirect approach).

Your decision about which approach to use should depend on your context analysis. Your hidden agenda may play an important role. If you want to maintain goodwill with the person getting the bad news, use the indirect approach—unless you know that your reader prefers to get negative news directly. Most people prefer to have bad news softened a bit. For such people, use of a bad-news pattern as described below is generally your best bet.

The following "bad-news model" pattern of organization includes six key elements:

1   Buffer.
2   Transition.
3   Reasoning.*
4   Refusal or bad news.*
5   Alternative.
6   Optimistic close.

* Note: steps 3 and 4 may be reversed depending on your guess about reader preferences.

Now, let's look at the parts of this approach pattern for presenting bad news. Each step in the approach is highlighted in the message shown below and is discussed in detail in the following sections. Assume this is the body of a letter or email.

Example of a Message to Refuse a Request

I appreciate your interest in the kinds of employee motivation programs we are developing here at Synectic Systems. I considered your request that I speak to your group in November very carefully and found it personally flattering. [Buffer]

Although I welcome opportunities to speak with young people in groups such as yours, [Transition] after checking my travel schedule for the remainder of the year, I find that I have a conflict with the November 19 date you mentioned. I will be attending a conference in New York and will not return until November 22. [Reasoning and refusal] May I suggest an alternative? [Alternative]

Dr. Elliott Anderson has recently joined our organization. He brings excellent academic background and seven years' industrial psychology experience with a major manufacturing organization on the West Coast. He is eager to know more people in the area and has indicated a willingness to talk with your group on November 19.

Elliott is an excellent speaker, and I'm sure you'll enjoy his presentation. [Optimistic close—makes the alternative easy to accept] You can reach him via email at EAnderson@XYZcorp.com. I have asked him to look for a message from you to confirm his availability and to get more information about the topic you want him to address.

Again, thanks for thinking of us to speak to your fine group.

Let's look a little closer at this message.

1 Use a neutral or mildly positive *buffer.* The buffer sentences present neutral or positive information the reader is not likely to disagree with. The speaker's comments about "appreciating [the reader's] interest" and finding the request "personally flattering" are examples of such comments. Often this buffer thanks people for their interest or makes other complementary statements with which anyone would be likely to agree. This buffer is designed to get the reader into the rest of the letter—to avoid a premature turnoff before you've had a chance to explain the reasoning behind the bad news.

One caution: the buffer should not sound so encouraging that the reader is led to expect a favorable message. Keep it vaguely positive or neutral.

Opening with a buffer reduces the likelihood that your reader will be immediately turned off.

---

2 Make the *transition.* Once you have offered a buffer, step 2 is to transition carefully into your reasoning. A transition may be as short as a few words or as long as a full sentence. (For example: "Although I enjoy the opportunity to speak with young people ..." or "Please let me explain the concerns I have.") Its purpose is to connect thoughts and prepare the receiver for what is to follow. Some experts recommend that you avoid using "but" or "however," especially if these may sound like an abrupt shift in tone. An abrupt-sounding "but" or "however" may undermine the positive effects of the buffer.

An alternative to "but" or "however" may be "at the same time," "that said" or "that notwithstanding." For example, a buffer that begins a job-refusal letter may say something about appreciating the applicant's interest in your company followed by "at the same time" leading into a discussion of specific job requirements the company needs from an applicant.

Work to avoid an abrupt "but" or "however" when transitioning into your reasoning.

---

3 Present your *reasoning.* Bad-news messages should be based on your best reasoning and, it is hoped, should make sense to your audience. The task of this type of message is to convey that reasoning in such a way that your reader, although disappointed, will either agree with the decision or at least understand *why* you decided as you did. Remember the ideal outcome: the receiver will think, "This is bad news, but I would probably make the same decision if I were in his or her shoes."

The information you select to present should be factual, logical, and clear. If your decision is based on prudent reasoning, you should have no need to sound apologetic. But do use objective, specific reasons. For example, don't say "We just didn't see you as a good fit for the job" when you can, instead, say something like, "Your experience exclusively in the transportation industry does not meet the requirements of this position." In our example, the writer had to refuse the speaking request. The reasoning is simple—he or she will be out of town. In other cases, you may need to convey more detailed reasoning. Express specific reasoning clearly and unapologetically.

4 Give the actual *refusal* or *bad news*. Be tactful but conclusive. The phrase expressing the refusal or other bad news should be carefully worded and clear so that there is no misunderstanding on the part of the reader.

Passive voice can soften the blow of bad news, but it risks sounding imprecise or even indecisive. An example of passive voice is "Your request must be denied" versus active voice "I must deny your request." Passive voice tends to separate the action from the doer of the action. Some writers see this as desirable; however, it can sound like the writer is unwilling to take responsibility for the decision. Whether or not you use passive voice should be based on how you think your reader is likely to react and how important it is for you to be associated with the decisions behind the message.

Note that the other option to using this pattern is to offer the reasons first, and then give the bad news. Make this choice based on your context analysis—how your reader would most appreciate hearing the news—not on what is most comfortable for you. The organizational culture should be considered, too. In a military environment, for example, softening the decision or distancing oneself from it (such as via passive voice) would normally not be expected.

Another subtle way to soften the blow of bad news is to position the actual refusal so that it naturally receives less emphasis. The positions of strongest emphasis (which should normally be avoided for bad news) are at the very beginning and the very end of each paragraph. The first words the receiver reads have higher emphasis; the last phrases they read tend to linger in the reader's mind and are thus emphasized. Your refusal or bad-news phrase would be best positioned toward the *middle* of the message for de-emphasis. Don't de-emphasize it to the point where it is ambiguous; just soften it slightly.

Emphasis positions in a message are at the beginning and end of a paragraph (or the whole message). Avoid putting the bad news there to de-emphasize.

---

5 Offer an *alternative*. Perhaps the best way to reduce the impact of bad news is to give the bad-news reader some alternative to his or her original request. Our example of the speaker with a scheduling conflict does this effectively and sends a powerful message about the writer's willingness to make the refusal less painful by offering another speaker. Any alternative should be explained in a positive tone conveying the assumption that it will be accepted.

Offering an alternative can reduce the negative impact of a bad-news message.

Also, when offering an alternative, make it easy for the listener to accept. In some cases, communicators simply toss the ball back to the person making the request. They may say something like, "If some other date would be acceptable or if another person from our company could be of help, please contact me again." That would fail to achieve closure—the problem remains unresolved. If you offer an alternative, follow through on the new idea. Don't just give the problem back to the requester and start the whole cycle over again. Offering a lesser alternative should not be used as a way to avoid saying no. It should only be used when you genuinely want to offer an option to the person you are giving bad news to.

Make it easy for the reader to accept an alternative.

Step 6 Use an *optimistic close*. Once the refusal or bad news has been clearly and tactfully conveyed, deliver an optimistic close. The intent of such closing remarks is to further repair any damage to goodwill that may have occurred. Use this as an opportunity to express confidence that a good business relationship will continue. Our speaker example expresses appreciation for being invited to speak.

Do not apologize. Since your decision has been based on sound reasoning, there is no need to apologize. In fact, the effusive apology may cause your audience to question the reasoning, wondering if you feel guilty for some misdeed. Instead, confidently express a desire to maintain a favorable relationship with the message receiver.

As you can see, the bad-news message requires more thought and effort than the routine informational message. Its payoff lies in projecting a favorable, caring image, and not being seen as an insensitive communicator.

Organize the Longer Document

The ideas for selecting and organizing information presented in this chapter will help you organize effective messages. You can readily apply these to virtually any communication, including emails, memos, letters, or presentations. But what about longer workplace communications such as major reports? The answer is that the same principles of selecting and organizing information apply to long, complex documents.

When dealing with long, complex documents, consider each segment of the report as a separate message. The Introduction, for example, has a specific purpose, as does each other part or chapter. Determine the purpose of that part and decide if it can best use a BIF or BILL approach. Then select an appropriate pattern of arrangement as discussed in this chapter. Tie the overall report together by including internal summaries, transitions, and content preview for each section.

Organize a long document by treating each section as a separate message and organizing it according to its purpose.

An example of a long, complex document is a graduate school dissertation. Even writing as complex as this, however, can benefit from a fairly simple arrangement. Typically, a dissertation begins Chapter 1 by introducing the topic and describing the research problem. This first chapter should say what the research will cover (content preview), describe the current project's goals, and end with a summary and transition into Chapter 2.

A workplace report can use similar organizing principles. Here is an example of segments from such a report:

(*Opening*) This report looks at our company's ongoing challenge of e-commerce competition. This analysis will describe the extent and impact of such competition and identify ways to deal with it in order to remain profitable. (*Reader benefit*)

(*At the end of the introduction or first "chapter"*) In this introduction I have overviewed the nature of the problems we face and identified some major competitors. In the next section of this report, I will describe the extent of competitor effectiveness in tapping the e-commerce market. (*Summarizes and transitions into next section by providing content preview*)

(*At the end the next section*) In this section I have described competitor effectiveness in e-commerce efforts. In the next section, I will develop a strategy we can apply to deal with this competitive threat. (*Summary and transition to next section*) The next section of this report identifies specific costs of implementing the strategy I have recommended.

The key to developing continuity in a longer message is to make liberal use of content preview, summaries, and transitions. Doing so helps readers follow the logical development of your message.

Tie together the long report with appropriate content preview, summaries, and transitions for each section.

Developing Structurally Sound Text for Long Reports

Facing the task of developing a systematically organized long report can be daunting. We often feel overloaded with information. We may have good arguments for one section but face gaping holes in our logic in others.

We can best identify key ideas with some form of outlining. Experts recommend using either a top-down or bottom-up approach. Top-down outlining starts with the major ideas (categories) and moves to the details. Bottom-up outlining first lists the details and then uses inductive logic to determine the major ideas (categories). If you know in advance the main segments of the message, use a top-down outlining method. If you don't know what the major segments of your message will be, use a bottom-up approach.

Use either a top-down or bottom-up approach to developing the outline for a report.

Professor William H. Baker elaborates on this process for outlining reports:[2]

Use Top-Down Outlining

Three effective methods for top-down outlining include traditional outlining, information sketching, and mind-mapping.

Traditional Outlining
To create a traditional outline, first list the main elements and then list supporting elements beneath them. Identify the main elements with Roman numerals and supporting elements as shown in the following example:

I First main element
    A First supporting element under I
    B Second supporting element under I
II Second main element
    A First supporting element under II
    B Second supporting element under II
      First supporting element under B
      Second supporting element under B

All major word-processing software packages have an automatic outlining feature that can help with this process, including the ability to cut and paste lines of text after the original outline draft has been created. An advantage of traditional outlining is its familiarity; most people become acquainted with it as they go through school. A disadvantage is that some people find it too rigid and confining.

Information-Tree Sketching
Information sketching consists of creating a tree-like information sketch. For the trunk of the tree, write the main idea, such as, "Why we need a new police officer." For the branches that extend from the trunk, write the main supporting ideas, such as (a) population has increased and (b) crime rate has increased. Add secondary branches to the main branches as needed for more detail.

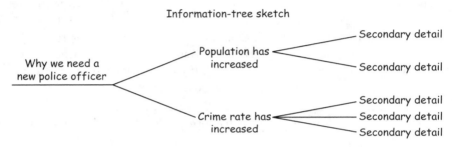

Information-tree sketch

FIGURE 4.1. An Information Tree

Mind-Mapping
Another top-down process is *mind-mapping*, consisting of the main topic identification inside a large circle or bubble in the middle of a page. The main circle is then connected by lines to subcategories, which may also be inside bubbles, with subcategory lines extending from them. Users of mind-mapping often like to add doodles and sketches as shown in the example opposite.[3]

Use Bottom-Up Outlining

Bottom-up outlining works opposite from top-down outlining. It begins with a list of details and then works upward from there. The detailed list can result from data gathering (e.g., conducting interviews, conducting a performance audit, or tracking quantitative trends) or from brainstorming (e.g., free-listing). Free-listing, which can be accomplished either on paper or on a computer, is described below.

Free-Listing
Free-listing is a good way to get spontaneous, unstructured information on paper for later organization and writing. Free-listing consists of:

1   Jotting down all the information bits you might want to include in your document.

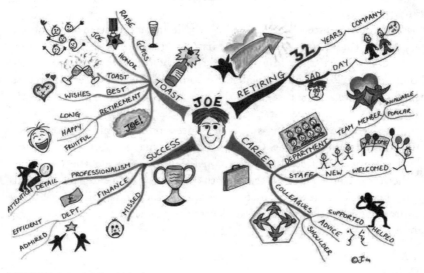

FIGURE 4.2. A Mind Map

2   Classifying the listed items into categories.
3   Sequencing the categories.

Create this list with your computer or handwrite the list on a blank sheet of paper. While creating the free-list, jog your mind by considering all aspects of your goals, the audience needs and expectations, and your strategy. Because this is just an informal working list, don't worry about capitals, spelling, or other writing mechanics while making the list. For example, here's a free-list for a document to be written about a problem in a printing operation.

Free-List

Small jobs used to tie up large expensive presses

Cost more than necessary

Delayed more critical large jobs

Small Job Shop established in 2007 to handle jobs too small for big presses

In small job shop, results have been bad

Lots of delays, customer complaints

Result has been good for large presses: improved costs and printing time

Problems = poor management, poor communication with customers (caused by bad job form), no accountability for press operators re. delayed jobs

Need to resolve 3 probs: Hire new mgr, revise job form, and track each job for better accountability

Savings = from replacing old supervisor with younger, designing new form, and improving thru put time

Classifying

After constructing a free-list, examine all the items and determine common-alities among the various items on the list. As you find two or more closely related items, choose a heading that describes the category of the items and use that heading as the category label. To complete the classification process, continue to create all the category titles and labels needed to include all the relevant items in your free-list.

You can accomplish the classification process on a computer or on paper, using a three-column format. On the computer, make a vertical list of the categories under the free-list as you consider each item on the list. Then drag the items from the free-list down to the appropriate categories, result-ing in the various headings listed vertically, each one followed by the appropriate free-list items, also listed vertically as shown in the following example.

Categorized List Created on a Computer

Background

Small jobs used to tie up large expensive presses
Cost more than necessary
Delayed more critical large jobs
Small Job Shop established in 1999 to handle jobs too small for big presses

Current Situation

In small job shop, results have been bad
Lots of delays, customer complaints
Result has been good for large presses: improved costs and printing time

Problems

Problems = poor management, poor communication with customers (caused by bad job form), no accountability for press operators re. delayed jobs

Proposal

Need to resolve 3 probs: Hire new mgr, revise job form, and track ea job for better accountability

Cost–Benefit Analysis

Savings = from replacing old supervisor with younger, designing new form, and improving thru put time

Three-Column List
If you're working with pen and paper, use a three-column approach to organize your free-list. On your notepad, draw two vertical lines to make three columns, as shown above. In the first column, create your free-list. In the second column, determine appropriate categories. In column three, create the final sequenced list. By adding appropriate opening and closing sections, you can use the final column as an outline for writing the document.

Sequencing
After classifying, arrange the information into an appropriate sequence. When deciding on the sequence, think of information as being either *non-chronological* or *chronological* in nature.

Non-chronological information is stationary, unmoving, and somewhat like a photograph. For instance, you might describe three different automobiles you are considering for purchase. Describing static information involves telling about different parts or different attributes of the whole at a certain point in time, not over a period of time. A description of three different

Proposal to implement Fitness Center HR

First data	Categories	Final data
-- HR at City Center overworked		-- City Center HR overworked
-- HR not serving fitness centre well	Workload problem	-- Not serving FC well
-- Need HR person for Fitness Center (FC)		-- 28 new employees in last year
-- Lots of turnover at FC	FC proposal	-- Establish HR position at FC
-- HR at FC would give more responsive service		-- Report to CC HR office
	Time line	-- Better service for FC
		-- Reduce workload at CC HR
		-- Better FC service to public
	Benefits	-- Announce July 1
		-- Fill by August 1
	Cost	-- Grade 8 salary
		-- Office equipment
		-- Benefits

FIGURE 4.3. Three-Column List

automobiles, for example, would probably include their price, reliability, efficiency, and so forth.

To arrange non-chronological information, arrange the information in a category order, quantitative order, or spatial order, depending on the information and the needs and expectations of the audience.

- **Category order.** City X is divided into six sections: NE, N, NW, SW, S, and SE.
- **Quantitative order.** City X has eight golf courses, City Y has five golf courses, and City Z has only one.
- **Spatial order.** Six banks are located from north to south along Highway 213.
- **Compare and contrast.** Company A and Company B both offer project-management software, but the software from Company A is more well integrated into their financial-management package.

Chronological information consists of a series of happenings, somewhat like a videotape. It involves different events that happen over a period of time, such as a few minutes, a few days, or even a few years. It is narrative: one thing happening after another. For example, you might describe the increase of traffic through an intersection over a five-year period, during which a neighborhood grows from just a few houses to a few hundred houses.

- **Time–series order.** Intersection X's traffic five years ago was 238 cars per day; now the volume is 307.
- **Problem–solution order.** Crime is up by 15 percent; *therefore*, we need more officers.
- **Cause–effect order.** If we adopt this plan, we'll be able to reduce crime by 25 percent.
- **Narrative.** The problem started when the delivery was late. Then when the customer discovered a partial delivery, he returned the package and canceled the order. Unfortunately, billing wasn't notified of the cancellation and sent an invoice, which further angered the customer.

No structure or sequence of information is absolutely correct. Therefore, consider the context of each situation and choose the sequence that seems to be most appropriate.

Evaluating Outlines with STEP

After you have created your outline, you might want to evaluate its structure, especially if it is an important and complex document. To perform the evaluation, use a procedure known as STEP (Structured-Text Evaluation

Procedure). STEP consists of evaluating each outline module, or cluster, starting at the first-level categories and then progressing module by module to the most detailed level of the hierarchy. (A module is one group of parallel categories, such as I, II, III, or A, B, C, D. Each occurrence of a I, A, 1, a, (1) or (a) in an outline signifies the first item in a module.)

Using STEP, conduct five tests on each module as follows:

1 **Inclusion (or presence) test.** Given the title or heading of a module, are all appropriate items included? If not, add the missing items or restrict the scope of the title or heading to fit the items that are present. Make sure every module contains at least two items (e.g., A *and* B, 1 *and* 2).

2 **Exclusion (or absence) test.** Given the title or heading of a module, are all inappropriate items excluded? If not, delete the inappropriate items, or expand the title or heading to fit all the items in the module.

3 **Hierarchy (or horizontal) test.** Are the items in the module hierarchically parallel? If not, shift the non-parallel items to the appropriate level (e.g., from the A, B, C level to the 1, 2, 3 level), and make other adjustments necessary to ensure hierarchical parallelism. In most cases you'll find no specific right or wrong hierarchy, because most subject matter can be organized in a variety of ways. Just decide which organization seems most logical in each circumstance.

4 **Sequence (or vertical) test.** Are the items in the appropriate sequence? Determine whether the module is of a noun or verb type, and then decide which sequence seems to be most appropriate for each module. Make this decision from the perspective of the audience.

5 **Language (or wording) test.** Are the items in the module grammatically parallel? If not, change the wording to achieve parallelism. Test 5 is important only if the items are used as headings in the final text. If they are not, you may skip this test.

Remember these tests by thinking of *presence* and *absence, horizontal* and *vertical*, and *wording*. Notice the two sets of opposites in Tests 1 and 2 and Tests 3 and 4.

The following example shows the STEP tests being performed on the first module (first-level categories) of the *Results of Management Audit of Administrative Services Division* outline.

STEP Test 1 *(Inclusion/Presence Test)*

Title: Results of Management Audit of Administrative Services Division

I   Introduction
II   Information Services
III Human Resources Department

IV   Accounting
V   Accounts Payable
VI   Accounts Receivable
VII   Marketing
VIII   Conclusions and Recommendations

Are all units in the Administrative Services Division present? No, the Purchasing Department is missing and needs to be included.

STEP Test 2 (Exclusion/Absence Test)

Title: Results of Management Audit of Administrative Services Division

I   Introduction
II   Information Services
III   Human Resources Department
IV   Accounting
V   Accounts Payable
VI   Accounts Receivable
VII   Marketing
VIII   Purchasing
IX   Conclusions and Recommendations

Are any units included that are not part of the Administrative Services Division? Yes, Marketing is not part of the Administrative Services Division and should be excluded.

STEP Test 3 (Hierarchy/Horizontal Test)

Title: Results of Management Audit of Administrative Services Division

I   Introduction
II   Information Services
III   Human Resources Department
IV   Accounting
V   Accounts Payable
VI   Accounts Receivable
VII   Purchasing
VIII   Conclusions and Recommendations

Are all the items in the module hierarchically parallel (on the proper level)? No, Accounts Payable and Accounts Receivable are divisions of Accounting. Therefore, they should be shifted to the second level as subdivisions A and B under Accounting and later be tested as a separate module.

STEP Test 4 (Sequence/Vertical Test)

Title: Results of Management Audit of Administrative Services Division

I   Introduction
II   Information Services
III Human Resources Department
IV   Accounting
    A   Accounts Payable
    B   Accounts Receivable
V   Purchasing
VI   Conclusions and Recommendations

Are the items in the most appropriate sequence? This module is a *noun-*type module; therefore, it will not be arranged in a time sequence. Items I and VI are arranged in the order in which we want the reader to encounter them in the report. Items II–V could be arranged by order of size (e.g., largest to smallest) or by order of management problems identified in the audit (e.g., most to least). However, an alphabetic arrangement seems to be more appropriate.

STEP Test 5 (Language/Wording Test)

Title: Results of Management Audit of Administrative Services Division

I   Introduction
II   Accounting
    A   Accounts Payable
    B   Accounts Receivable
III Human Resources Department
IV   Information Services
V   Purchasing
VI   Conclusions and Recommendations

Are the items parallel in language? No, items II, III, IV, and V are departments, but only item III includes the word "Department." Therefore, "Department" should be added to items II, IV, and V.

With all the necessary changes made, module I–VI now passes all five tests:

Title: Results of Management Audit of Administrative Services Division

I   Introduction
II   Accounting Department
    A   Accounts Payable
    B   Accounts Receivable

III Human Resources Department
   A   Employment
   B   Benefits
   C   Training and Development
IV Information Services Department
   A   Computer Systems
   B   Records Management
V Purchasing Department
VI Conclusions and Recommendations

After the tests are completed on the first module, they should be repeated on all remaining modules. For this example, you would next complete the STEP tests on the three remaining modules in the following order: (a) II, A–B; (b) III, A–C; and (c) IV, A–B.

If there were additional levels of sub-modules, they would be identified and tested in the same manner. For example, if Employment had two subdivisions, it would be identified as module III, A, 1–2 and would be tested after module III, A–C.

The STEP procedure is a comprehensive, yet relatively simple, writing tool. The five STEP tests encompass every type of change you can make in an outline:

1	Addition.	2	Deletion.
3	Horizontal movement.	4	Vertical movement.
5	Change of wording.		

Tests 1 and 2 help ensure that the proper *content* is included in each module; Tests 3 and 4 make sure the items are properly *located* (horizontally and vertically); and Test 5 guarantees proper *language* parallelism.

Four important benefits come from using the STEP tests. First, the tests help ensure the structural soundness of text. Second, they help produce clearer thinking. These tests methodically challenge your thought processes, helping assure that no content or organizational considerations are overlooked. Third, the STEP process helps you compose text more efficiently: writing becomes a straight-forward process of expanding the outline, rather than a perplexing process of not knowing what to write next. Fourth, the final text will be easier to read and understand. And that is something readers greatly appreciate.

Performance Checklist

After completing this chapter, you should be better able to apply some principles for selecting and organizing information for your message. Specifically, you should now understand that:

- You need to be clear about your big idea: what do you want your reader to *do*, *think*, or *feel* as a result of getting this message?

- Before choosing a specific pattern of organization, you should decide upon your overall *approach*. A direct approach puts the Big Idea First (BIF), while an indirect approach places the Big Idea a Little Later (BILL) in the message. Directness is appropriate for most workplace communication. It is efficient and generally clear. Indirect approaches may be helpful when the receiver's emotions may come into play, such as in persuasion or bad-news messages.
- Persuasive writing seeks to get readers to *do* something they normally would not do without some prodding. They awaken people's emotions.
- The ANSA pattern of arrangement is an often helpful persuasive tool. ANSA stands for "attention," "need," "solution," and "action."
- The bad-news message often uses an indirect pattern of arrangement, which includes these steps: buffer, transition, reasoning, refusal, or bad news, alternative, and optimistic close.
- For long messages, break the overall message into smaller units, apply an appropriate organizational pattern to each section and tie each section together with transitions, internal summaries, and content preview.
- Use top-down or bottom-up outlining and check a report's structure with the STEP test.

What Do You Know?

Activity 4.1: In-Basket of Writing Assignments

The object of this assignment is to respond quickly to a series of writing requirements. The items below make up an in-basket exercise. The following describes the role you are to play and gives some tips for successfully completing the exercise.

The Scenario

You are an executive with a mildly upscale chain, WunderBar Restaurants. You have been away for several days, and have come into your office a little after 7:00 a.m. to catch up and get ready for the day. Promptly at 8:00 a.m. you must leave to attend all-day meetings. Therefore, you have less than 60 minutes to handle the items in your in-basket. You pride yourself in your ability to work fast and keep on top of anything that comes your way.

Tips for Completing This Exercise Successfully

You will need to prepare several messages in a limited amount of time. Work efficiently. To do so, we suggest the following:

- Quickly read through all items and determine how you will budget your time. Determine a course of action. As appropriate, draft each message on your laptop.

- Apply the concepts of BIF versus BILL, content preview and accessing techniques.
- Apply the Straight Talk Writing Model as we have discussed it in this chapter.
- *Do not edit or re-work your writing after the allotted time.* The idea is to work within a tight deadline. Simply print your work exactly as written at the end of the time allotted.

ITEM 1

[This note is attached to the letter written by a personnel director, John Slager. The note is from your boss, Pete Zabriskie.]

Can you believe this guy? That bozo, Slager has all the sensitivity of a dump truck.

I intercepted this letter before it was mailed. This may be the last straw—Slager is on his way out.

Meanwhile, we need to let George Archer know we can't use him in franchise sales. But let's do it with some sensitivity. George has been with the company for a long time but we really can't transfer him as requested. I can't see him pitching potential franchisees. He has no discernable personality—he's an accounting clerk, for crying out loud—has no background for sales, other than a sincere desire.

Rework this letter for my signature, okay? I want to get this out ASAP.—Pete

[Slager's original letter]

Mr. George Archer
1334 Maison Rd.
Cincinnati, OH 32001

Dear Mr. Archer:

I received your recent letter requesting a transfer to franchise sales. Unfortunately, we cannot make that transfer at this time. Your work records show no selling skill whatsoever and we can't imagine why you'd think you are qualified for an important sales position in corporate.

Selling is a very demanding position, one that requires initiative, stamina, independent thinking, perseverance, good judgment, etc. We've found that guys as old as you (51) can't make the adjustment from working inside to outside sales.

Your interest in moving up is appreciated, but this isn't the job for you. If I can be of any further service, please do not hesitate to call upon me.

Sincerely,

John T. Slager

John T. Slager
Personnel Administrator
WunderBar Restaurants Corp.

ITEM 2

[Note attached to a newspaper clipping: What the @*&#*!@!* is this?? Fix it—quick! –PZ]

This newspaper article is talking about one of your *corporate* restaurants. As such it is supposed to be a model for possible franchisee owners. The manager is the sister of a Corporate VP.

Think through the Straight Talk Writing Model. Explain, in detail, what you will communicate. If you choose to use a written document, prepare that memo or letter. If you elect to use an oral medium, outline specifically what you will say. If you have another creative idea, go for it. But explain clearly what you are going to do.

What Our Attitudes Communicate to Customers

by Dr. Walter Lampson

Because my wife and I wanted to celebrate a special professional achievement, we asked the hotel concierge, "What restaurant do you recommend that's classy, but not overpriced?" She recommended the WunderBar Restaurant located a short cab ride away.

"You'll like the food and the scenery. It's one of the newest places around here. I know the manager, and you'll get very personal service."

Heeding her advice, we went there for dinner. The layout of the place was attractive, with an unobstructed view of the ocean. Our seafood was delicious, and prices were moderate. However, we decided—very quickly—that we won't return there when we're in that city again.

Why? Because the attitudes we encountered ruined our evening.

The kid at valet parking was not at all friendly. He seemed to think he was doing us a big favor by parking our car. We chatted up the waiter while he took our order, asking how he liked working there. He commented: "I've only worked here for a few months. At first, business was fine. Then, after the newness wore off, reservations declined drastically. Now, to be honest, it kinda sucks. Not many customers and, of course, not much in tips." Shrugging his shoulders and displaying a dejected look, he told us, "Guess I should look elsewhere for a job."

When our food arrived, so did the manager. Her greeting was cordial, and we asked how the restaurant got started. "Well," she answered, "we have other restaurants in Miami and across Florida that are doing quite well, so we thought the same concept would work here."

"So you came here from Florida?" we inquired.

"That's right," she said. "But I don't know how long we'll be here. This restaurant may not make it in a city like this—not very classy, you know. And the economy here is pretty lousy." After grousing a bit more about the lack of classy customers, she walked away.

We looked around. We saw only two other tables occupied, and just three people seated at the bar. The only noticeable noise came from a band and a vocalist, whose voice bounced around the nearly empty room. They band members looked bored.

"This small turnout doesn't surprise me," my wife noted. "Who wants to return here to listen to their bad news? Jeeze, *I'm* getting depressed!"

I agreed. "Yeah, they've sort of killed our celebration spirit. They misunderstand their purpose. Dining out means forgetting your problems—and not taking on anyone else's."

I'm confident that restaurant won't survive. Customers like to invest their time and money with winners, not with whiners.

ITEM 3

[Handwritten note from Zabriskie]:

> *Do me a favor. Send a sympathy note to Mrs. Perry Palliver. Old Perry died yesterday at the age of 83. Heart attack, I think. He was sort of a mentor to me way back when we worked together at Nabisco. Nice old guy as I recall—I haven't seen him in a couple of years. Tell her how sorry I am, and how much I liked Perry and all that stuff. Be warm and sincere—like me (!) (I like the "personal" letters much better than just a card, don't you?) Sign my name.*

[For the purpose of this in-basket assignment, type your note.]

Activity 4.2: Apply the STEP test

Select a recent report you or someone else in your company has written. To be most effective, this needs to be several pages in length.

Apply the STEP tests to determine if the organization and content are sufficient. Note any weaknesses you find.

Reinforce With These Review Questions

1 Define what we mean by the "big idea" of a message: _____
_____.

2 True/False Most workplace writing typically uses a BIF approach.

3 The key element that determines if you should use a BILL approach is the necessity to engage the reader's _____.

4 Name the four steps in the ANSA pattern of arrangement:
(1) _____, (2) _____, (3) _____,
and (4) _____.

5 True/False The bad news (BILL) pattern of arrangement is the only way to convey information your reader won't like.

6 True/False Long documents can readily apply the same patterns of arrangement as shorter ones, especially if the sections are linked with transitions.

7 True/False Sometimes, when conveying bad news, it is preferable to be vague and let the reader draw his or her own conclusions.

8 True/False The action close in a persuasive letter should tell your readers exactly what to do, should make it easy for them to comply, and should be assumptive—implying that you assume they will do what you recommend.

9 Describe the five steps of the STARR pattern of arrangement:
(1) _____, (2) _____, (3) _____,
(4) _____, and (5) _____.

10 The STEP test for checking an outline has four "tests." Name them:
(1) _____, (2) _____, (3) _____,
and (4) _____.

five

Enhance Your Writing With Graphic Elements

Graphic design and document layout can make you appear more confident, more professional, and more of an expert. It can also make the reader's task much easier.

Use Graphics and Visuals for Stronger Written Messages

The "stickiness" of a communicated message—how well the reader remembers—depends on how interesting, memorable, and effective the document is. While some people just seem to have a knack for getting and holding the attention of their readers, anyone can learn the techniques for doing this, using verbal and graphic elements. We can develop our own tool kit of tactics that greatly improve our likelihood for getting across to our readers.

Performance Competencies

When you have completed this chapter, you should be able to:

- Understand the importance of enhancing your message verbally with stories and examples.
- Recognize multiple options for enhancing your message with graphic and visual elements.
- Identify four basic graphic design elements that can improve readability.
- Describe the most commonly used visual formats and understand the use of each.

- Avoid over-complicating your graphic and visuals elements that may overwhelm your message.
- Evaluate feedback on your visuals in order to continually improve your design and delivery.

The Way It Is … Jerry's Underappreciated Report

Jerry finished his strategy recommendation report at 7 p.m. He had been working on it for days and, in all humility, felt he had produced a masterpiece. This document was going to re-energize the company's marketing strategy. "Good work, Jerry," he told himself, as he hit the print button. "I'll get these distributed to the executive committee first thing in the morning."

By early afternoon the next day he had heard no comments about his strategy recommendations. Jerry started to worry. "I thought for sure I'd hear something from someone. That is a great strategy—it's innovative, daring, and I explained it well. I wonder why nobody is in here congratulating me."

By 3 p.m. Jerry could keep quiet no longer. He went to his immediate boss and mentor, Harold, and asked if he'd seen the document Jerry had worked so hard to write. Harold's response was less than encouraging.

"Oh, yeah, I got it this morning," Harold told him, "but I haven't read it all yet. Look, to be honest Jerry, I found it a bit hard to digest. I'll take another shot at it when I am fresh and can concentrate better. It's pretty tough slugging. Seems like some good ideas, but I'm having trouble chewing through it. Let's get together in the morning and I'll give you some feedback before we meet with the exec committee."

"Tough slugging?" "Hard to digest?" "Chewing through it?" Those were not the responses Jerry had expected. And apparently it wasn't just Harold's reaction. Later that afternoon, one of his less diplomatic colleagues told Jerry he would have loved to read the whole document but was afraid his heart would stop from boredom. Zinger!

The axiom "A picture is worth a thousand words" might have been helpful to Jerry. His strategy report may well have died from lack of graphic design and visuals that would have helped his readers avoid heart-stopping boredom and, perhaps more importantly, gotten Jerry's message across persuasively and with enthusiasm.

Carefully prepared graphics can add an invaluable dimension to a business report and can project a positive image, reflecting favorably on the writer. As communication tools, graphics and visuals adds clarity to a report by presenting complex information in a visual, attractive, easy-to-understand,

and easily remembered format. Graphics and visuals serve a distinct purpose: to highlight, summarize, show patterns and trends in, and facilitate the understanding of, a complex process or situation.

Good graphics reflect favorably on the writer.

Although the bulk of this chapter focuses on graphic and design elements that help readers get your messages, we want to reiterate the importance of verbal elements for getting and holding reader interest as well. An increasingly important part of message delivery is the use of stories/examples and visuals or graphic aids. Almost any communication can be enhanced with the use of some form of support. Today's generation is the most visual in history. We have all been subject to far more visual stimulation than people who lived before the ubiquitous presence of television, movies, videogames, and computer graphics. In short, people expect to *see* something in addition to receiving just verbal messages.

Similarly, today's audiences expect some elements of entertainment in messages they receive. Think about people you regard as effective communicators and we are willing to bet they use stories.

First: Use Stories and Examples

We have all heard stories since we were little children. We bet you can still remember stories your parents or siblings told you when you were a tiny tyke. What is it about stories that make them stick in our memory?

Chip and Dan Heath's excellent book *Made to Stick*[1] explores the question of why some ideas succeed while others fail, and concludes that much of success has to do with how well the ideas are communicated. Stories, they argue, are one of the most powerful instruments for achieving message "stickiness."

Stories enhance message "stickiness" and reduce boredom.

While being a reader of a story may seem like a passive role, this passivity may be like the proverbial floating duck who, below the surface, is paddling like crazy. In other words, our minds are actively engaged. "When we read books, we have the sensation of being drawn into the author's world. When friends tell us stories, we instinctively empathize. When we watch movies, we identify with the protagonists."[2]

Example is a first cousin to the story. Typically examples amplify on a point but are less robust than a story. A message making a point about how certain sales behaviors (say, getting customers to test-drive the product) results in a better close ratio may enhance this point by describing several sales people who apply the behaviors and have had demonstrable improvement in their ability to close sales. For example: "Tara increased by 30 percent the number of hands-on demos her customers participated in. Her close ratio rose from 12 percent to 27 percent."

Stating a key idea with no further support is rarely effective. It is human nature for people to ask "why?" or "how?" to almost any assertion. Few are willing to take a directive without questioning it to some extent.

Stories in Today's Writing

Recent years have seen a particular genre of business books become mega-best-sellers. If you are familiar with books such as *The Tipping Point*, *Blink* and *Outliers* (by Malcolm Gladwell), *Freakonomics* and *Superfreakonomics* (by Steven D. Levitt and Stephan J. Dubner), *Influencer* and *Crucial Conversations* (by Kerry Patterson *et al.*), *Sway* (by Ori and Rom Brafman), and dozens of similar books, you will recognize the power of good stories. These books reflect the kind of writing that grabs and holds reader interest through the power of stories. Typically they present a memorable anecdote and then refer back to it as they develop the teaching points of their books.

Want to write best-selling documents? Use the same principles by telling stories. Flesh out enough detail that readers can visualize and empathize with the situations. Then tie the story into your theme. Business documents need not be dry recitations of facts. Enhance them with lively, interesting narrative.

Use Visuals and Graphic Design to Enhance Message Comprehension

Why use visuals in your writing? People are not accustomed to processing words alone—they want to see something presented graphically.

Visuals and Graphic Elements Help Both the Writer and the Reader

Visuals and graphics are vital to you as a communicator because they help fulfill at least five important functions.

Visuals help *writers* to:

- Develop the content of their message.
- Organize ideas and create continuity of thought.
- Strengthen the impact of their message.
- Clarify important concepts or associations.
- Provide attention-holding variety.

Visuals help *readers* to:

- Clarify and digest abstract ideas and relationships.
- Retain information.
- Avoid boredom, confusion, and apathy.

To make the most of these functions, you, as a communicator, should look at graphics as an integral part of your presentations, not as after-thoughts. Plan your visuals elements as you draft your message.

Consider graphics as integral parts of your document, not as afterthoughts.

Use an Appropriate Type and Overall Design Concept

Use graphic elements that are appropriate in terms of type and overall design concept. To select the appropriate type of visual displays, pay attention to the expectations about design elements in your industry, organization, or company. Carefully observe what other, successful people are doing, then meet or exceed these expectations. Of course, you can often find bad examples, but look at what the best writers are doing and emulate—or exceed—that behavior.

Become an observer of the effects of graphic elements and visuals.

Knowing the "appropriate" design concept involves reviewing the first step of the Straight Talk Writing Model—defining your context. You should do so by analyzing the situation, your readership, and your purpose. Use the details you gathered to make your basic choices for templates, colors, fonts, clip art styles or pictures, charts, and, especially, words. We will discuss each of these elements later in this chapter.

Graphic Design for Non-Designers

More matter is being printed and published today than ever before ... and *readers want what is important to be clearly laid out*. They will not read anything that is troublesome to read, but are pleased with what looks clear and well arranged, for *it will make their task of understanding easier*.

Ironically, Jan Tschichold made this statement in 1935! Even then, writers were concerned about the explosion of print materials—and that was way before Xerox machines and electronic media.

The point is, people do not want to read text-heavy "blobs of words." Consider your own experiences. Have you ever opened a book or document that had heavy paragraphs, no visual accessing, and no graphic elements? How did you feel about digging in? We're guessing this was not all that appealing.

People do not want to read "blobs of words."

Graphic design helps us reduce such reluctance to read our messages. Let's look at some simple, yet powerful, principles for improving the readability and functionality of your written documents. After this discussion, you will never look at documents, slideshows, signs, or graphics in quite the same way.

Four Basic Design Principles

As we develop graphic elements in our documents, we need to be aware of four key principles:

- Contrast.
- Repetition.
- Alignment.
- Proximity.

Contrast

Contrast has to do with the variances in such things as typefaces (fonts) and other graphic elements. The simple rule for effective contrast is that it must be significantly distinctive. If, for example, you wear a navy blue blazer with dark grey slacks, you are not showing much contrast. In fact, people may have to look closely to see if they are really different colors. The same navy blazer with khaki slacks exhibits dramatic contrast. In other words, contrast needs to be significant. Little contrast provides no advantages. Look, for example at the two business cards below. Which grabs your attention better?

Contrast needs to be significant, not subtle.

FIGURE 5.1. Examples of Contrast in Design

On a simple list, contrast in fonts can help categorize ideas for better reader comprehension. The list below illustrates this.

List without contrast:

CD ROMs
—Children's CDs
—Educational CDs
—Entertainment CDs
Educational
—Early learning
—Language arts
—Science
—Math
Teacher Tools
—Books
—Teacher guides
—Videos

Same list using simple contrast to categorize:

- ## CD ROMs
  Children's CDs
  Educational CDs
  Entertainment CDs

- ## Educational
  Early learning
  Language arts
  Science
  Math

- ## Teacher Tools
  Books
  Teacher guides
  Videos

Although this principle is simple, it can be a powerful way to enhance reader comprehension. To recap, apply these principles to create graphic contrast:

- Avoid elements on the page that are merely *similar.*
- If the elements (type, color, size, line thickness, shape, space, etc.) are not the *same*, make them *very* different.
- Contrast is often the most important visual attraction on a page.

Repetition

The second basic design principle is repetition. This element involves consistency of design. Check documents to be sure they:

- Repeat the same *visual elements* of the design throughout the piece.
- Repeat color, shape, texture, spatial relationships, line thicknesses, sizes, etc.
- Use repetition to develop the *organization*, strengthen the *unity*, and add *visual interest*.

Inconsistent design and layout distracts readers and damages your professionalism. Always re-check visual elements and ask for feedback from others. Specifically, ask a trusted associate (preferably one with an eye for detail) to review your document checking for consistency.

Alignment
Be conscious of where you place elements on the printed page. Find something to align with. If you have a graphic or illustration, consider how text should be associated with it. You may choose to "wrap" around an illustration or use a standard point of "justification" (the margin line your text follows). Word-processing software provides four choices in justification: left, center, right, or "full" (which aligns both left and right by adding spaces as needed to fill out the line).

Avoid using more than one text alignment on the page (don't center some text and right-align other text). Also, use center justification sparingly. It can be effective but often comes across as unimaginative, harder to read. The ad for construction workers shown below uses center justification (among other design flaws) and appears busy and confusing.

FIGURE 5.2. An Example of Bad Alignment

See how this same ad could be cleaned up using better justification and eliminating unnecessary graphic elements:

FIGURE 5.3. An Example of Good Alignment

The other rules for alignment can be summarized as follows:

- Nothing should be placed on the page arbitrarily. Think about ease of reading, consistency, and appropriate contrast.
- Alignment creates a clean, sophisticated, fresh look.
- Every element should have some visual connection with another element on the page.

This last point leads to the final basic design element, proximity.

Proximity
Readers often need to be shown how points in your document relate to each other. Proximity involves grouping related items close together. These grouped items then become one visual unit rather than several separate units. This helps organize information and reduces clutter.

To illustrate the principle of proximity, look at the two advertisements below. The first does little to group elements, making it difficult for the reader to dig out the meat of the message. The second uses the principle of proximity to associate related information.

NEVER BEFORE IN GALARIA HISTORY

HAS ONE BEEN ABLE TO TASTE 50 GALARIA RESTAURANTS AND 50 INTERNATIONALLY-ACCLAIMED WINERIES AT ONE LOCATION ON ONE DAY. DON'T MISS OUT! JOIN US FOR THE BIG EVENT OF THE 3RD ANNUAL GALARIA WINE & CHILE FIESTA THIS SATURDAY FROM 12 NOON UNTIL 4:30 P.M. AT THE EL DORADO HOTEL. $35 ADMISSION INCLUDES UNLIMITED TASTINGS, SOUVENIR GLASS & ENTERTAINMENT. PLUS, A PORTION OF THE PROCEEDS TO BENEFIT THE GALARIA FOOD BRIGADE HELPING US FEED OUR HUNGRY NEIGHBORS. ADVANCE TICKETS STILL AVAILABLE AT GALARIA NEWS AND AT OUR PLAZA AMERICADO BOX OFFICE. LIMITED TICKETS WILL ALSO BE AVAILABLE AT THE DOOR.

Never before in Galaria history...

has one been able to taste 50 Galaria restaurants and 50 internationally-acclaimed wineries at one location on one day. Don't miss out!

$35 admission includes unlimited tastings, souvenir glass, and entertainment.

A portion of the proceeds will benefit the Galaria Food Brigade, helping us feed our hungry neighbors.

Advance tickets are still available at Galaria News and at our Plaza Americado Box Office. Limited tickets will also be available at the door.

3rd Annual Galaria Wine & Chile Fiesta

This Saturday from 12 noon until 4:30 P.M. at the El Dorado Hotel.

FIGURE 5.4. Examples of Good (bottom) and Bad (top) Proximity

The design ideas we have shared in this section are, of course, very basic. If you produce documents requiring more sophisticated design, we encourage you to involve professional artists. That said, these ideas can improve even your routine documents. Keep in mind the four principles of contrast, repetition, alignment, and proximity (you can make that into an acronym if you like!), and you will enhance the impact and professionalism of your written documents.

Apply Common Visual Formats

Several tried-and-true formats help present information in written documents. Among these are word charts, pie charts, line charts, and bar charts. Additionally, reports often require discussion of processes or organizational hierarchy, which suggests the use of tables, flow charts, and organizational charts. (*USA Today* and other publications do a great job with the visual display of information. Look carefully at these to get creative ideas for your own graphics.)

Word Charts

A word chart states key ideas concisely and directly. It is probably your simplest visual and can highlight key ideas. In preparing word charts, economy of language is crucial. Here is an example from a document showing employees how to promote themselves for career advancement within the company:

Do Your Homework

- Find an interesting job description
- List the specific duties and requirements
- Determine needed education/experience
- Evaluate how you fit
- Plan a positive strategy

FIGURE 5.5. A Word Chart to Promote Career Advancement

This word chart reinforces recommendations for enhancing customer service:

Offer ancillary services, products

- Product line extensions
- Employee convenience
  - Chair massages
  - Recreational facilities
  - Refreshments
  - Concierge services

FIGURE 5.6. A Word Chart Offering Ancillary Services

The most common mistake in the use of word charts is too many words. Since this graphic is to reinforce ideas you should not post every word you have already presented in the text of your message. Don't even use complete sentences. As you draft your word charts, be a ruthless editor: cut out any words you can delete while maintaining the meaning you want to convey.

Word Charts With Graphics

Often word charts are made more interesting with the addition of clip art or graphics. The word chart below shows the relationship between three elements. This also shows the addition of art (in this case an illustration, but it could be clip art, cartoons, etc.) to add reader interest to a word chart slide.

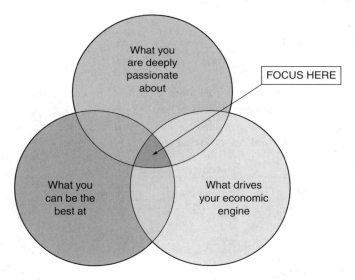

FIGURE 5.7. An Example of a Word Chart With Graphics

Pie Charts

A pie chart is a simple, circular illustration that is divided into segments to show part-to-whole comparison. It can effectively show only a few broad divisions (since a pie can only be sliced into a limited number of pieces). When creating pie charts, cut segments of the "pie" accurately, beginning at the top and moving clockwise for each new segment. Label each "slice," showing what it illustrates and the percentage it represents. Use large, clear lettering for the chart.

Graphics software packages like Excel™ or PowerPoint™ will automatically slice the pie correctly for you. You can also select a three-dimensional design, as shown below.

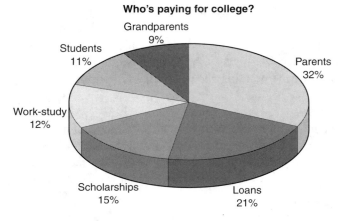

FIGURE 5.8. An Example of a Pie Chart

Line Charts

A line chart is a "trendy" way to show a continuous picture of trends or changes over time. It can also show simple comparisons of trends by color-coding different lines. An example of a multiple line chart is shown below. Be sure to use dramatically different line types and colors so that distinctions are clear.

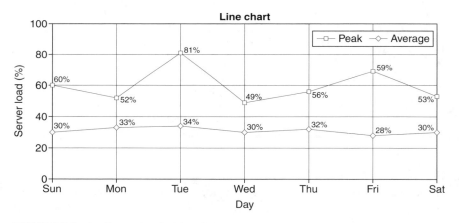

FIGURE 5.9. An Example of a Line Chart

Bar Charts

A bar chart compares one item with others. The most common types of bar charts are:

- Vertical bar charts, which are especially effective if you want to illustrate "height" and compare accomplishments, such as nearness to a goal or dollars of profit.
- Horizontal bar charts, which illustrate and compare distances over time.

- Segmented bar charts, which clearly visualize how different parts contribute to a whole over time.
- Grouped bar charts, which dramatically compare groups in specific times or areas, as shown below.

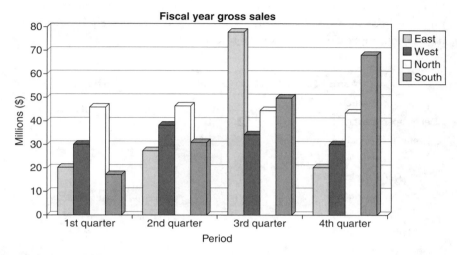

FIGURE 5.10. An Example of a Bar Chart

Area Charts

Area charts show comparative data in a slightly different way. The sample below shows relative sales in three different stores over a course of time.

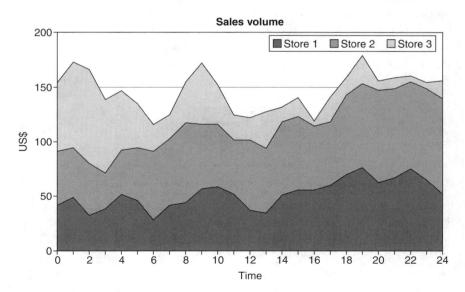

FIGURE 5.11. An Example of an Area Chart

Gantt Charts and Organizational Charts

Gantt charts (so named for their inventor, an early management theorist) and organizational charts usually require significant detail, so we recommend them for oral presentation visuals only when they can be made very simple. Flow charts show step-by-step progression of processes or procedures to simplify the receiver's understanding. They are particularly helpful in giving instructions or explaining the solution to a problem.

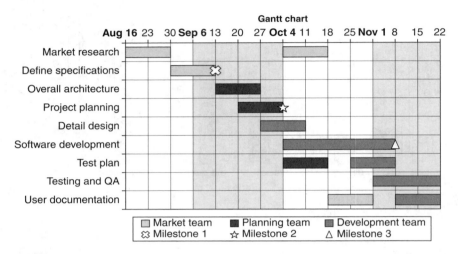

FIGURE 5.12. An Example of a Gantt Chart

Organizational charts illustrate the structure of a company, such as who works for whom and how many departments are in each division. Since many companies are very complex, organizational charts are useful to both internal and external audiences, since they show lines of authority (chain of command) and job responsibilities. Software packages often have templates for building organizational charts.

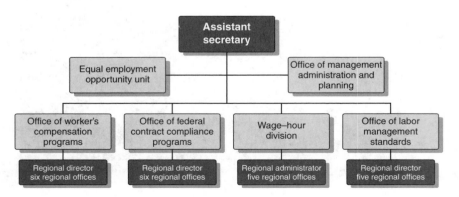

FIGURE 5.13. An Example of an Organization Chart

The Use of Photos

Photographs can add interest to documents. Communicators should, however, be aware of possible legal ramifications.[3] When messages are directed to internal audiences in an organization or to small groups, you are unlikely to risk legal action (with a few exceptions we'll describe below). Bear in mind, however, that when photos are used for public dissemination, advertising or widely distributed mailing, people in the pictures and the photographer may be entitled to credit and/or compensation for their work.

If you do not want to solicit permission or pay for a photo, you have several options. First, check online for materials that are copyright-free—photos that are "in the public domain." A second option is to take your own photos. Finally, you may want to purchase individual photos (or sets of similar photos) from the producer. Any limits to their use will be spelled out in a purchase agreement, but generally if you pay for a CD with related pictures, you are granted almost unlimited use of them. If you elect to use pictures captured off the Web, keep in mind some guidelines described below.

The most common problem you will run into is a photo with people in it. If you are using their images for editorial purposes (somewhere in a limited-exposure presentation), it's usually okay to use them without permission. If you are using photos with people in them for advertising, you need their permission. People have a right to profit, and to exclude someone else from profiting from their photograph or likeness.

In using images of people, be careful not to:[4]

- Defame the person in the image through captions or narration.
- Portray them in a false light.
- Libel them or slander them with falsehoods.
- Injure their reputation.
- Subject them to hatred or contempt.
- Hold them up to ridicule.
- Distort their image by cropping or altering.

In all of these cases, an individual can sue for monetary losses and mental anguish. If you have even the slightest concern about damaging a person, courtesy dictates that you show them the picture you plan to use to be sure they are comfortable with it. If the photo will be widely shown or distributed, ask the person to sign a release form okaying its use.

Check Graphics and Visuals for Design Consistency

This is important: your graphics and visuals should be consistent in terms of background, font, structure, capitalization, spacing, and illustrations. In the next few sections, we will look at each of these areas of consistency.

Maintain design consistency in visuals or you will distract your audience.

Background (Templates)

A *template* is a consistent design background for your document. This may be as simple as page borders or the use of other formats found in your word-processing software, or it may be more artistic. In selecting a template, choose only one and then stick with it for the entire document. Do not mix different templates, since this will cause your message to look inconsistent and unprofessional. Keep in mind also that the more illustrations you plan to use, the simpler your template should be. Otherwise, things get too busy.

When deciding upon a template, choose a style that symbolizes your message and shows respect for your target audience. For example, avoid overly "cute" templates (say, one with balloons or children's drawings) if you are writing a serious business document. If the context of your message is somber, select a conservative style. If your purpose is motivational, upbeat, or entertaining, consider a template with a border of stars, flags, cartoon characters, or other icons associated with the topic of the message. Be creative, but be certain that your overall design is suitable for the occasion, your readers, and your purpose.

Fonts

Your fonts (also called typefaces) should be consistent in terms of size and type throughout your presentation's visuals. All titles should be the same size and the same font from slide to slide, as should all body copy. (If the font is larger on one visual and smaller on the next, your audience will feel like the screen is moving toward and away from them, which is disconcerting.) However, the fonts for title and body copy may be different from each other.

Two basic types of fonts are serif fonts (in which the letters sit on small "platforms") and sans serif fonts (with no "platforms"). Serif fonts are traditional, and some experts consider them easier to read. Sans serif fonts look contemporary and may be more dramatic. Examples of some common serif and sans serif fonts are shown below.

Serif and Sans Serif Fonts

Examples of Serif Fonts	Examples of Sans Serif Fonts
Bookman Old Style, **Bold** and *Italic*	Arial, **Bold** and *Italic*
Garamond, **Bold** and *Italic*	Univers, **Bold** and *Italic*
Times New Roman, **Bold** and *Italic*	Comic sans, **Bold** and *Italic*

Fonts for titles or headings may be bolded, italicized, or significantly larger. Avoid using underlining because it will look like a hyperlink. Remember, too, the principle of contrast. Make the differences significant enough. Small contrast is no contrast at all.

> **What Are "Points?"**
>
> The term "points" refers to a sizing method for measuring type-faces. The term comes from the traditional printing industry, where 1 point equals 1/72 of an inch. This was a measure of how much "lead" to place in the molds used in old-fashioned printing presses. This form of measuring type sizes has carried over, although most printing presses no longer use lead type.

Font Sizes

Title (24pt)   Heading (18pt)
■ **Bullet points (14 pt)**

Title (24pt)   Heading (18pt)
■ Bullet points (14 pt)

Avoid the temptation to use many different fonts or many different sizes. You may mix a sans serif font for your titles with a serif font for body copy (or vice versa), but be certain they look sufficiently different from each other. Don't select similar fonts for titles and word chart copy; make them either exactly alike or very different to create sufficient contrast. You might add an additional display font occasionally for a special effect, but be careful. (Display fonts are such things as Maximus, **Century**, Bauhaus93, Auriol, and dozens of other artsy designs. Use those rarely.)

Generally avoid unusual or ornate display fonts.

Too much variety in fonts creates a "busy" look that can be distracting. Stick with the common, traditional fonts. Most people find serif fonts easier to read in text; sans serif can be okay for headings. Remember that the fonts you choose will make an impression on your readers. These can impact your credibility and professionalism.

Structure

Bullet points or enumeration enhance accessing (as discussed in Chapter 1). Look for opportunities to break up the text and to provide information that is easy to digest. Avoid big blobs of words!

Bullet points refer to listed items that are preceded by a bullet (■) or small symbol. *Enumeration* refers to such a list when each item is numbered (or lettered). Use enumeration when a list is sequential (e.g., step 1, step 2, etc., or (a), (b), etc.), or when you may need to refer back to the list of items.

When using bullets or enumeration, the points should be "parallel"—the grammar should be the same. If your first point begins with a verb, each succeeding one should also begin with a verb. Similarly, if you start with a noun, adjective, gerund (a word ending in "-ing") or adverb, start every point with the same word form. For example, notice the parallel construction in the following sets of points:

- Analyze the environment, Consider the options, Select information. (*Each clause begins with a verb*)
- Cost of doing business, Return on investment, Comparison with competition. (*Each phrase begins with a noun*)
- Overall goal, Specific purpose, Hidden agenda. (*Each phrase begins with an adjective*)
- Deciding on our mission, Communicating the goals, Encouraging participation. (*Each phrase begins with a gerund*)

Parallelism means starting each bullet point with a similar word form (noun, verb, gerund, etc.)

Capitalization

Use capital letters sparingly in headings. You may print your titles in all capital letters, but for the most part, a mixture of uppercase and lowercase letters is more natural and easy to read. All-caps feels like yelling to some listeners. (This has become a pet peeve in email use for exactly that reason.) Capitalize only proper nouns (names) and the first letter of the first word in each bullet point of body copy. Don't capitalize the first letter of each word because then everything will look like a title.

Spacing

Your titles or headings should begin on the same spot each time they are used (such as centered, flush left, or flush right). Also, start your body copy on the same line on each section. The space between your bullets should be consistent, as well. Avoid the urge to spread bullets out if you only have two or three. Use that extra space for a picture or other graphic instead. If you don't have an appropriate illustration, "white space" (the portion of the visual with nothing on it) is perfectly fine and is preferable to spacing that varies. Imagine reading a book that is single-spaced on one page and triple-spaced on the next!

Use consistent white space on all pages.

The space between bullets should be about one-and-a-half times the size of the bullet font. If your bullet is 36 point (about a half inch), the space between items should be about three-quarters of an inch. This is not an exact rule, of course. But be consistent with your spacing, even when you have only a few bullet points.

Illustrations

"Clip art" is an assortment of pictures, cartoons, illustrations, and icons (symbols) available in computer graphic programs. The term comes from the old days when graphic designers would physically cut and paste pieces of art onto documents or layouts. Clip art helps to illustrate your points and break up your documents. It can also project a personality and can help your reader focus on the words on your visual if you choose illustrations that "point." However, be careful with clip art because it can become too "cute" very quickly.

Here are some examples of clip art available in your PPT program.

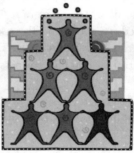

FIGURE 5.14. Examples of Clip Art

Graphics should be similar in size and type throughout your document. Since their purpose is to enhance your message, not distract from it, be sure the illustrations match the message. For example, don't mix cartoon-character clip art with realistic-looking photo art. Clip art available online through Microsoft is organized by family resemblance, making it easy for you to keep the pictures consistent. If you choose photographs, try to use them throughout your presentation. Mixing art types, like mixing too many fonts and sizes, looks haphazard. Consistency looks more professional.

Avoid mixing too many graphic element types.

Where, exactly, can we get art for our documents? This is easier than ever, thanks to technology. You may first check Microsoft for its download-able clip art. (In Microsoft Word, you can get into this by clicking "Insert," "Picture," and then "Clip art." Then type in what picture you want and follow the prompts. Other word-processing software may vary.) Another approach is to use a search engine such as Google.com and search for "images." Type in descriptions of what you want pictures of and you will get clip art, photos, etc. Then simply right-click your mouse on the images you want and save them to your computer. Be aware that the resolution (color and clarity) of the pictures may vary considerably, so check them before pasting into your document.

Get Feedback on Your Graphics and Visuals

Just as in other forms of communication, your learning process for using visuals does not stop with the actual delivery of your message. Step 5 of the Straight Talk Writing Model reminds us of the importance of evaluating feedback for ongoing improvement. In visuals or graphics, as in any other form of communication, the reactions of your readers can be valuable.

While you are designing your graphics, solicit feedback from trusted col-leagues. Often, another person will see gaps, missing data, confusing layout, or other problems that you miss. Ask them to react to the template or the colors (if used). Use open-ended questions and listen carefully to their responses. Be sure to have someone proofread your visuals. Typos, misspellings, or missing words can quickly undermine their effectiveness—and your credibility.

Get feedback on your visuals. Readers will inevitable note something you missed such as typos or other distractions.

Be willing to give others your feedback about their graphics as well. If the graphics are good and helpful, let them know; if not, suggest why they were not helpful. Share the guidelines in this chapter with your associates and you will all produce better visuals for better communication.

Performance Checklist

After completing this chapter, you should be better able to apply some prin-ciples for selecting and organizing information for your message. Specifi-cally, you should now understand that:

- Message content will be enhanced verbally with the use of appropriate stories and examples. These help engage readers and can lead to better retention.

- Graphics and visuals used in documents will help writers develop, clarify, and enhance their messages, and will help readers understand and remember.

- Your analysis of the situation, audiences, and objectives with your readers must be considered as you plan the appropriate graphics and visuals for your document.

- Common visual formats include word charts, pie charts, line charts, bar charts, tables, flow charts, organizational charts, and photos, or clip art.

- Consistency elements for your graphics include background (template), fonts (typefaces), structure, capitalization, spacing, and illustrations.

- Over-complicating is the most common mistake with visuals.

- Get feedback about your graphics and visuals from your peers and from the responses of your readers. Your visuals should clarify and enhance your message.

What Do You Know?

Activity 5.1: Preparing a Bar Chart

Using the hypothetical information given below, prepare a bar chart showing the top ten occupations in ascending order by percentage of growth. Use a presentation software package such as PowerPoint™ and select the style of bar chart that best expresses your message.

According to one survey by the US Department of Labor, the ten most rapidly growing occupations are as follows. The number following each reflects the percent of growth in employment between 2000 and 2010.

Employment interviewers	66.6
Computer programmers	73.6
Paralegal personnel	132.4
Tax preparers	64.5
Office machine and cash register servicers	80.8
Computer systems analysts	107.8
Food preparation and service workers, fast food restaurants	68.8
Data processing machine mechanics	147.6
Computer operators	87.9
Aero-astronautic engineers	70.4

Activity 5.2: What's Wrong With These Graphics?

Go back to pages 131–132 and look carefully at the graphic for the construction network. Using the four basic design elements discussed in this
chapter, describe how that ad violates these principles.

Do the same for the ad for the wine and chili fiesta on page 133. Be specific in your critical analysis. Remember to assess contrast, repetition, alignment, and proximity.

Activity 5.3: Review Some Documents

Gather a sample of three documents (reports, flyers, advertisements, bro-
chures) from your company or other sources and analyze their effectiveness.
Make a detailed list of ways the graphic and visual elements could be
improved. Also note what they did right and why.

Reinforce With These Review Questions

1 True/False Stories and examples tend to engage audiences better than
straight factual statements.

2 Name four common visual formats that help present information in
written documents: (1) _____, (2) _____,
(3) _____, and (4) _____.

3 Name the four basic design elements we should evaluate for documents:
(1) _____, (2) _____, (3) _____,
and (4) _____.

4 True/False Pie charts should only be used when presenting to someone
in the food industry.

5 True/False Headings should always use initial caps.

6 Three types of fonts are:
(1) _____, (2) _____, and (3) _____.

7 True/False The most common mistake with word charts is using too
many words.

8 True/False Clip art used should be from the same "family" if possible for
consistency.

9 The design element that says similar elements should be grouped
together is called _____.

10 True/False Turn toward the visual when talking about it. This will
direct your audience's attention to the right place.

Mini-Case Study: Jerry Gets Some "Advice"

Go back to the opening story of Jerry and his strategy report. Assume that you are Jerry's mentor. You know this about him:

- He is one of the brightest young minds the company has hired.
- He graduated from an excellent business school with a program that heavily emphasizes quantitative skills.
- He comes up with creative ideas and likes to participate vigorously in meetings and discussions.
- He isn't too crazy about writing. His skills in that area are adequate but his tone tends toward the rather pedantic reporting of dry facts.
- He is very logical, systematic, and linear in his thinking.

Assume further that Jerry's strategy report was, in fact, incredibly dry. He used no stories or illustrations, virtually no graphics (not even many headings), and the pages were heavy with verbiage. In short, his report suffered from the "blob-of-words" problem we mentioned in this chapter. Nonetheless, the content of his message was excellent.

What would you do to get Jerry to employ the ideas in this chapter? How could he enhance his writing with graphics and visuals? Be specific about recommending processes he could use.

six

Delivering Effective Workplace Writing

Every writer is a frustrated actor who recites his lines in the hidden auditorium of his skull.

(Rod Serling)

Writing with Personality

Delivery of your message in written form poses challenges for most people. When communicating with written media, we have fewer tools for conveying sincerity or enthusiasm than we would have when speaking. We cannot rely on facial expression, voice, or gestures. We can, however, project professionalism through the words we choose and our attention to reader needs.

So, what can we do to deliver written messages effectively? This chapter targets a few key tools that can affect the personality of your messages as well as their functionality.

Performance Competencies

When you have completed this chapter, you should be able to:

- Describe the importance of accuracy and tone in effective business writing for different types of business correspondence and reports.

- Explain how tone problems can create psychological stress and friction between writers and their readers.

- Describe various ways writers can use principles of good human relationships.

- Explain how you can resonate with reader self-interest by using reader-viewpoint wording.

- Contrast and provide examples of blanket tone versus personal tone and positive wording versus negative wording.

- Explain how to avoid tone problems such as abrasiveness, preaching, false sincerity, and sexist language.

- Apply the Fog Index to assess the readability of your documents.

- Break through writer's block.

The Bank Needs a Folksy Image

Tara is a communication consultant hired by Community Bank. Her client, Georgia Wilson, asked her to look at the letters the bank sends to its customers. "We need to be careful about how we communicate with our customers. We are supposed to be the friendly alternative to the big banks, so let's make sure we are projecting that folksy, local image." Georgia held up a letter. "I don't like the way this one sounds. If I were the customer, I would not feel warm toward Community Bank after reading it. Do you think you can fix this? Or better yet, can you develop guidelines we could use to write better?"

She then handed Tara the following letter written by Albert Hart and explained its background. The customer, Mr. Hocking, wanted to make no payment on his account this month but pay extra next month. His company had laid him off from his job and he needed a brief extension on the payment date. Mr. Hocking's credit history had not been outstanding in the past. He had been out of work several times and was, therefore, late in paying twice in the past seven months. However, he always caught up any past-due payments and his work situation looked like it would be more stable in the future.

Dear Mr. Hacking,

It's impossible for us to extend you another month before your next payment on your auto loan. Already you have been late twice this year. Such behavior shall have serious detrimental effects on your credit rating.

I sympathize with your problem. We all have problems. I find myself short of cash every now and then, too. But I always—always—pay my debts first, before spending money on luxuries. Your auto loan is a special obligation, one that should not be taken lightly. If we let you off the hook this month, we'd have to do the same for all our other thousands of customers. I am sure you can see that would be out of the question, since we are in the business of making a profit. My suggestion to you (the same suggestion I've made to other young men who seem to have such problems) is to forgo some other spending urges and, instead, make your car payment on time, as agreed when you borrowed the money.

Thank you for doing business with Community Bank and have a nice day.

Yours sincerely,
Albert Hart
COMMUNITY BANK
YOUR FRIENDLY BANKING PARTNER

Tara shook her head slowly as she read the letter. "What was Albert Hart thinking?" she asked herself.

The words we choose have impact on the tone, understanding, and relationship qualities of written messages. Careless phrasing projects a lack of professionalism in delivering written messages. This can have devastating effects on a business. Poorly written letters and memos can send all the wrong signals to customers, employees, and others involved in the organization's activities.

This chapter provides some useful guidelines on writing professional and effective business correspondence. Armed with the Straight Talk Writing Model, you have already defined the context of your message and considered your media, source, and timing options. You have also decided that your message requires a hard copy or a degree of formality, that the cost of writing is justified, and that a written document is the approach most likely to succeed. You have selected and organized the information you want to convey to your readers. You have considered graphic enhancements and now it's time to focus on delivering your message. Delivery, in written communication, is all about the words chosen and their impact on readers.

This chapter focuses on Step 4 of the Straight Talk Writing Model: Deliver your message using written media.

Written workplace communication typically takes the form of correspondence and reports. Some of these documents are form letters, memos, and routine reports. Hopefully these formulaic messages have been carefully designed. But business people also write more personalized, individual documents—the ones that address individual needs, situations, or problems in a systematic manner specific to the issue.

Email is, of course, a form of written correspondence, although we do not automatically produce a hard copy. What we say about letters and memos generally applies to email messages as well, although email carries an expectation of conciseness that may not be necessary in other documents.

Correspondence typically has one of three primary purposes (although we may incorporate several elements in any given message):

- To convey positive, routine information, or build goodwill.
- To persuade or sell.
- To deliver bad news or refusal.

Written business reports are documents we prepare to meet three general purposes:

- To inform readers by supplying necessary data and information.
- To interpret information by analyzing or integrating data.
- To recommend action based on analytical decision-making.

Regardless of the type of message, its delivery will be impacted by two elements: accuracy and tone. Accuracy determines how clearly the writing explains the ideas it intends to convey. Tone reveals the writer's attitudes toward his or her subject and readers. Attention to these two elements allows you to project true professionalism and produce successful documents. In the next few sections, we will discuss ways in which you can create messages that are both accurate and that convey an appropriate tone.

Accuracy and tone are critical elements of the delivery of a message.

Failure to be accurate can lead to all kinds of unwanted consequences, ranging from a loss of credibility to downright embarrassment. Many communicators have put messages in writing that they would love to be able to retract. Consider how the writers of the following simple messages must have felt:

> Buy one hot dog for the price of two and receive a second hot dog absolutely free!
>
> (Restaurant coupon)

> Our February 9 issue reported our earnings per share as $1.88 billion. The addition of "billion" was a typesetter's error, and we apologize for any ecstasy the error may have caused.
>
> (AT&T employee magazine)

There was a typo in lawyer Ed Morrison's ad. His logo is: "Your case is no stronger than your attorney," not "stranger."

(Tulsa, Oklahoma, *Gusher*)

Obviously, these messages have not accurately conveyed what they meant to convey. The following sections present some guidelines in forming accurate messages.

The Wording Was So Close

Deborah, a young, enthusiastic instructor, emailed an article to her department chair with this note: "I found this article in the *Journal* and thought it might be perfect for our undergraduate students." The department chair forwarded the article to faculty and students and wrote back to Deborah saying, "I resent this."

Deborah was crushed. Why would she resent my sending her an article?

The Chair, of course, meant "re-sent." Oops. Attention to detail; just one little hyphen would have eliminated the misunderstanding.

Choose Words That Communicate Accurately

Accuracy is largely a matter of careful word choices and attention to details. Attention to detail is a matter of polishing a document to be certain no glaring errors slip through.

Virtually no one produces flawless writing on the first take. Always consider the first draft as just that: a draft. Take the time to edit and polish your writing. Set aside your "pride in authorship" (just because you wrote it does not mean it is perfect) and ask difficult questions about the document. Some key questions might be:

- Will this message make sense to someone who knows less about the subject than I do?
- What unanswered questions are my readers likely to have?
- Am I presenting all the necessary information without over-killing with unneeded detail?
- Have I worded the information as clearly as possible?

Put yourself in the shoes of your audience and write so that you can answer each of the questions. Then proofread for "detail" errors such as typos, misspellings (like "resent" versus "re-sent"), grammar mistakes, and awkward wording which can cloud your meaning and damage your credibility. Do not rely solely on your software's spell- or grammar-checking functions. Such software can be helpful to catch "detail" errors, but it cannot identify all problems and may offer incorrect solutions.

In short, say what needs to be said with accuracy and professionalism. Write with your readers in mind and anticipate their questions, concerns, and possible confusion. Your goal is to be so clear that you deny the reader the opportunity to misunderstand.

Clarify the message so that you deny the reader the opportunity to misunderstand.

Some Conventional Elements of Written Messages

The business world holds certain conventions about how business correspondence should look, and may regard letters or memos that violate these conventions as inappropriate, thus damaging the writer's credibility. For example, letters are generally expected to have a salutation ("Dear Mrs. Shannon") and complementary close ("Sincerely"), etc.[1] That said, we also have opportunities for creativity so long as that creative effort advances the big idea of the message. You have, for example, more flexibility than ever to use graphics, illustrations, charts, and tables, thanks to the capabilities of word-processing and presentation software. Invest some time in learning these features, and use them appropriately. Consider the ideas for graphics in Chapter 5 as you design documents, but be careful not to get too cute at the cost of your professionalism.

Consider presenting information in creative ways, not always as straight text, so long as this does not endanger your professional credibility.

Conventional Elements of Email Messages

Email documents should have most of the same elements found in written correspondence, although they tend to be less formal. Use the following guidelines to be certain that your email will meet conventional expectations for effectiveness.

1   Provide your reader with adequate *context* by:
    - Using informative subject lines[2] to preview the upcoming message.
    - Write content preview in the opening remarks. (For example: "This message summarizes my ideas on the new ad campaign as you requested.")

- Quoting the email to which you are responding (you can cut and paste excerpts from the incoming email and respond to each point).

2 Be aware of page layout and *accessing* issues. Stick with:
- Short paragraphs with adequate white space.
- Lines under 75 characters long.
- Messages under 25 lines long.
- Plain text and simply graphics, charts, etc. as appropriate.

3 Find replacements for gestures and intonation (but don't overuse these):
- Smiley faces ☺ or simple avatars. A wide variety of such symbols or illustrations are available online. See, for example, www.unoriginal. co.uk/coolstuff.html or Google "email avatars" for more.
- All-capital letters (use sparingly—they come across to the reader as shouting).
- Occasional use of different typefaces (but understand that the receiver's computer may not be able to reproduce these).
- Font size variations (but, again, not extreme).

4 Be aware of what cues people will use to form impressions of you. These cues may include:
- Name, title, or domain name (do not get too cute with funny names or use suggestive or obscene domain names, for example: HotDude@msm.com).
- Grammar, punctuation, and spelling (it is still important, even in the relative informality of email).
- Presence or absence of goodwill statements. For example, a simple opening ("I hope all is well with you") and closing ("Have a great vacation" or "Please say hello to Kathy for me") can convey your personality.

5 Perhaps most important: be sure your message has something worthwhile to say.

Although workplace communication should be functional—that is, it tries to get something done—we must recognize that it is also *human* communication. A workplace document is a message from a person—a writer—to another person—a reader. To be effective, writers need to apply the same human relationship skills they would use in a face-to-face encounter. The ability to get along with others, even on paper, is essential in successful business communication. The letter Tara reviewed in our opening story could certainly use some improvement in this area.

In the following sections, we will consider some specific principles of psychology and human relationships that apply in written communication. These principles are rooted in the need to write with an appropriate tone, to consider reader emotions, to satisfy self-interest, to be treated as individuals, to receive positive information, and to avoid being offended.

Remember the advice of legendary grammarian William Strunk when he tells us to be concise and delete any unnecessary words "for the same reason that a drawing should have no unnecessary lines and a machine no unnecessary parts."

Respond to Writer Requests

If your message is responding to another person's message, but sure you answer the questions they asked. One of the great frustrations of email is the feeling that your message has dropped into an electronic black hole. Rule 1: give people the courtesy of a response, even if that response is brief.

We have all experienced the annoyance of an ignored request or an abrupt, incomplete response. Some email users prefer to be very brief and economical in their messages. This is fine, but runs the risk of sounding curt or even rude. It takes only a few seconds to add a "Thank you" or "Have a pleasant holiday" or some such expression of human caring. Even in cyberspace, human courtesy is important.

Any personalized, written message (electronic or hard copy) deserves a response—unless you absolutely don't care what the reader thinks of you and your company. Don't underestimate the ways blowing off a writer can hurt your future relationship. If at all feasible, take a few moments to respond to all written messages that warrant a response.

The Impact of Being Blown Off

Wayne is a member of the Board of Directors for his Credit Union. Several national organizations offer training seminars for credit union employees and volunteers. After attending one such seminar, Wayne wrote to the sponsoring organization to tell them that he does regular training in customer loyalty and that he would like to explore the possibility of working for them on an occasional basis as a speaker. He sent the organization a letter, his resume, and a free copy of a book he had published in the topic.

The training organization ignored his letter. What they overlooked by ignoring him is that Wayne not only regularly attends training seminars but that he often recommends such training to his fellow board members. He has become quite outspoken about why people should *not* attend the training sponsored by this company and they have lost many thousands of dollars because of Wayne's recommendations.

Wayne isn't upset because they wouldn't hire him to speak at their training—he was upset about being blown off, ignored after taking the effort to contact the training company with a proposal. Nothing discounts a person so much as their being ignored.

Write with Appropriate Tone

As damaging that poor wording or violated writing protocols may be, even greater problems can arise from inappropriate tone. Business writing should be courteous and polite. An otherwise accurate message can lose its effectiveness if the tone is offensive. For example, suppose you are chairperson of a committee in your organization and you write to invite members to attend the next meeting. Which of these sentences conveys the best tone?

1   The next planning meeting will be held on May 13.
2   We look forward to working with you at our next planning meeting on May 13.
3   You are expected to attend our next planning meeting on May 13.

Each of these sentences conveys the same essential information, but each projects a different tone. The tone conveys subtle messages about the reader's relationship to the writer. The first statement is strictly informational—it conveys neutral feelings and implies no differences in status between the writer and reader. The second statement seems more positive—it conveys a pleasant, collegial tone and an implication that working together in the past has been a pleasant experience. The third statement sounds almost dictatorial and demanding. It seems to indicate a boss–subordinate relationship, which is probably inappropriate, especially in a volunteer organization.

Albert Hart's tone when trying to collect past dues for Community Bank leaves much to be desired. Look back at his letter at the beginning of this chapter and you will see a preachy, condescending tone.

Develop sensitivity to your message's tone.

Consider Reader Emotions

Tone problems can create psychological stress and friction between communicators and their audiences. Below is an excerpt from a memo to the manager of a training and development department. The company president, Butch Rocco, is not too happy about a recent training program and is quite clear about his feelings. How do you like the tone of his message? How would you feel if you were Chris Gardner, the recipient of this memo? Would the writer be likely to speak face-to-face with the reader using the same tone?

Memo Example With Inappropriate Tone

To: Training and Development
         c/o Chris Gardner, Manager

From: Butch Rocco, President

Date: February 16, 2005

MY REACTION TO YOUR DEPARTMENT PRESENTATION ON TEAM BUILDING

Chris, as department leader, I want you to convey my message to the other members of your group. Whenever I say "you" in this memo, I am talking to all department members unless otherwise noted. Tell them that.

Overall, I was disappointed in the latest training sessions. They were lousy.

You gave a lot of information but few specifics on how to build and utilize team efforts. Training sessions like these need to focus more on specific behaviors. It is not important that the little people understand concepts so much. You got into your touchy-feely mode of teaching abstract ideas rather than actions because this is what you people learned in college. Corporate training should follow a different model.

You should have done a better job of identifying what you want us to do before charging forth with the presentation. What is it our guys can DO now that they couldn't do before your little show? I'd be hard pressed to answer that question.

What do you think of the accuracy and tone of that message? Accuracy may be fine. Perhaps everything Butch Rocco says is true. He does say what he wants to say, and he goes on to support his ideas with specific examples. (This support was not included in the excerpt we show here.) But the most significant problem with Butch Rocco's memo is that his tone is likely to be offensive to the reader. If his goal is to improve future training, he may have so intimidated the reader that such improvement will be difficult.

Let's look at a way he could have conveyed his message with a more diplomatic tone, as shown below.

Memo Example With Better Tone

To: Training and Development
        c/o Chris Gardner, Manager

From: Butch Rocco, President

Date: February 16, 2011

MY REACTION TO YOUR DEPARTMENT PRESENTATION ON TEAM BUILDING

Chris, because you are department leader, I would appreciate it if you would convey my message to the other members of the group. Please advise them that whenever I say "you" in this memo, I am referring to all department members unless otherwise noted.

Overall, I was disappointed with the latest training sessions. I do not feel they were very successful in moving our company toward its goals.

I felt that you presented a lot of information but offered few specifics on how to build and utilize team efforts. I believe that training sessions like the ones you did need to focus on behaviors that are more specific. To me, it is less important that the employees understand concepts so long as they can apply the kinds of behaviors that will improve performance. The training seemed to focus more on teaching abstract ideas rather than specific actions. Perhaps this model is appropriate for college classes, but in corporate training, I think we need to follow a different approach.

Corporate training requires that we identify specifically what we want employees to be able to do. An evaluation of the training should answer the question, "What is it our people can DO now that they couldn't do before the training session?"

I welcome your comments.

Appeal to the Reader's Self-Interest

People are egocentric; that is, they are strongly interested in themselves. The unspoken question for any message is "What's in it for me?" (WIIFM). It is human nature to be concerned with and motivated by one's own personal needs, wants, and interests. This self-centeredness is normal and not particularly harmful unless carried to extremes where there is no caring about others.

Always address the "WIIFM" for your reader.

When people speak or write, they reflect this egocentricity in their language. Studies have shown that as much as every fifth word written or spoken is "I" (or one of its derivations—me, mine, my, we, ours, us). Even though we are all self-centered to some degree, most of us learn to temper the tendency to focus on and talk about ourselves exclusively. Indeed, we avoid the extremely egocentric person like someone with a contagious disease. The point here is that business writers can turn this egocentricity into an advantage if they recognize the reader's needs. Effective communicators learn to express concern and appreciation for the views of others in letters, memos, reports, and other documents. This, of course, assumes that they have done their homework and carefully defined the context of their message.

An important way to reflect consideration for your reader is by phrasing your message in terms of reader viewpoint. Expressing appropriate reader viewpoint involves much more than just selecting certain key words. Genuine reader viewpoint causes a document's tone to reflect a sincere interest in the reader. Self-centered writers think of themselves first. Reader-oriented writers think of and convey their messages in terms of what the reader wants or needs to know.

Phrase messages in terms of reader viewpoint; don't overuse the first-person pronoun.

One "red flag" that the writer should look for is over-use of first-person pronouns "I," "me," "my" and the plurals "we," "our," "us" and so forth. These quickly produce a writer-centered tone. Second-person phrasing (using "you") often conveys more interest in the reader. Third-person phrasing (using "the data show" or "the results indicate …") can convey greater objectivity.

However, do not conclude that you should try to eliminate the use of "I" and its variations from your business writing. To do so may be impossible in many cases, and trying to do so may result in rather tortured syntax and excessive wordiness. Besides, the use of "I," "we" or "me" does not always indicate a lack of reader viewpoint. For example, the person who says, "I hope you will be happy with this purchase," is not really violating a reader viewpoint, even though the sentence begins with the word "I."

The overall tone and sense of caring for the reader are far more important than simply avoiding the use of first-person pronouns. In addition, if a supervisor says, "I appreciated your report," the meaning is different from, "You did a good job with your report." Most people would prefer the first message.

Look at the following sample sentences and see the difference in the tone of the I-centered versions compared to the reader-oriented ones.

I-Centered Examples

- *I* am applying for this job because it would give *me* some great business experience.
- *We* require that you sign the sales slip before *we* charge this purchase to your account.
- *I* have been teaching *my* social studies students for 22 years.
- *I* think you'll be interested in *my* young investor's program.
- *We* are happy to announce that *we* now offer a 24-hour drive-through service.

Reader-Viewpoint Examples

- I am applying for this job because I feel that my qualifications could benefit *your* company.
- For *your* protection, *your* account will only be charged after you have signed the sales slip.
- *Your* training department can benefit from my 22 years of experience in teaching social studies.
- As a businessperson, *you* will readily see some important benefits in this investor's program.
- Now *you* can shop with us conveniently with a 24-hour drive-through service.

Write to People as Individuals

Your written documents have a more appealing tone when you phrase information as though you are talking to individuals rather than to groups. A personally addressed letter or memo singles out a reader for individual attention. Such a message conveys a more sincere regard for the specific person than one addressed to "Dear Customer" or "Fellow Employees."

Address readers as individuals, not groups.

Word processing can easily insert names or other information while most of the letter remains the same for all readers. Explore these possibilities when you consider a mailing. If using email, consider techniques that will make each message look individual as opposed to a long list of addresses in the "To:" box.

Avoid Blanket Tone

When a document makes the reader feel lost in the crowd, the "blanket tone" may be responsible. Blanket tone uses the same message for all readers and, thus, lacks any personalization, any sense of individual communication. Contrast the blanket tone versus personal tone in the excerpts from the following letters.

Blanket Tone Examples

- When we receive thousands of requests from prospective customers, we feel pleased. These requests show that our product is being well-received.

- We appreciate the cooperation of our charge customers in paying their account. By paying on time, they allow us to give better service.

- All of our customers agree that prompt service is important, however, we have limited resources that force us to prioritize requests.

Personal Tone Examples

- We are sending a copy of the booklet you requested today. Thank you for your interest in this material.

- We certainly appreciate your paying the account. Your prompt payment allows us to give you better service.

- We sincerely appreciate your many years as a loyal customer and hope that we can continue to meet your family's needs for the best in personal healthcare products.

Address Your Reader Directly

Appeal to an individual reader's benefits by using direct address. Direct address uses "this means you"-type statements. Each day we see examples of this approach in television and radio commercials. The announcer "personally" addresses each of the several million people who may be listening and attempts to make them feel that they are being spoken to as individuals.

Direct address conveys personalization; blanket tone does not.

Direct address shows your readers how your message applies to them and how it can meet their individual needs. One way to show this application is to clarify features and benefits. Tell readers how your ideas or the product's features can be of benefit to them with "what-this-means-to-you" statements. Avoid letting the feature stand alone without tying it to a specific benefit. Some examples:

Feature	Benefit
We offer free home delivery	You will save time and travel expenses
Fully cooked meals ready to go	You can serve them in the comfort of home
Most powerful engine in its class	Gives the power to carry the heaviest loads
Private dance lessons available	You avoid potential discomfort of a larger class

Communicate with Positive Wording

People appreciate messages with positive wording because they sound more upbeat and because they actually convey more information than do messages with negative wording. Rather than telling a person what is not the case or what you cannot do, focus on the positive—what is or what you can do. For example, if you say, "I do not live on 14th Street," it conveys very little information—it only rules out one possibility. On the other hand, the positive statement, "I live on 20th Street," conveys more, specific information. Positive language also has a more pleasant ring to the ear. Work to reduce the use of common negative phrases that so often appear in business writing.

Positive wording conveys more information that negative wording.

To illustrate the difference in tone between positive and negative word choices, here are two responses to a civic group's request to use a company meeting room. The first response uses many negative words (which are underlined) and has an unnecessarily negative tone.

> We <u>regret</u> to inform you that we <u>cannot</u> permit you to use our large meeting room for your function because the Little Town Book Club asked for it first. We can, however, let you use our conference room, but it seats <u>only</u> 25.

The use of negative wording in this response undermines the actual good news of the message, which is that the reader can use the conference room. "We regret to inform you" is an unmistakable sign of bad news, and "cannot permit" contains an unnecessarily harsh meaning. Furthermore, you handicap the one good-news part of the message by the limiting word "only." A more positive response to the request might be written like this:

> Although the Little Town Book Club has reserved our large meeting room for Saturday, we can offer you the use of our comfortable conference room, which seats 25.

This version avoids the use of negative words. Both approaches yield the letter's primary objective of denying the request and offering an alternative, but the positive wording in the second response does a better job of building and holding goodwill for the company.

Let us look at a few more examples of sentences with negative and positive wording. Listen to the tone of each. (The negative words are in italics.)

Negative Wording Examples
- You *failed* to give us the part number of the muffler you ordered.
- You were *wrong* in your conclusion because paragraph three of our agreement clearly states . . .
- We *regret* to inform you that we must *deny* your request for credit.
- We *cannot* deliver your order until Wednesday.

Positive Wording Examples
- So that we *may* get you the muffler you want, will you please check your part number on the enclosed card?
- You will *agree* after reading paragraph three of our agreement that . . .
- For the time being, we *can* serve you only on a cash basis.
- We *can* deliver your order on Wednesday.

Be Sensitive to Potentially Offensive Wording

Message tone can be offensive when the writer sounds abrasive, preachy, insincere, or exclusionary. The following sections discuss various ways in which you can avoid offensive wording.

Beware of Abrasive Tone
Abrasiveness refers to an irritating manner or tone, the kind of writing that sounds demanding or critical. When people have a somewhat abrasive personality, this will come across in their writing and can hurt the tone of their messages. To determine if you tend to have an abrasive personality, you might ask yourself questions such as these:

- Are you often critical of others? When you supervise others, do you speak of "straightening them out" or "whipping them into shape?"
- Do you have a strong need to be in control? Do you strongly favor having almost everything cleared with you?
- Are you quick to rise to the attack or to challenge?
- Do you have a strong need to debate with others? Do your discussions often become arguments?
- Do you regard yourself as more competent than your peers? Does your behavior let others know that?

Answering "yes" to any of these does not necessarily mean you are generally abrasive, but you may come across that way at times. The abrasive personality will tend to communicate in a manner that can be irritating to others. Try to recognize in yourself the degree to which you have a strong need to control or dominate other people. If you suspect that you do have this need, make an extra effort to soften the tone of your written communications.

Abrasive wording creates damaging conflict and disagreement.

Replace Abrasiveness with Assertiveness

Assertiveness can project a productive tone whereas abrasiveness is generally damaging. The best definition of assertiveness we have heard is "being pleasantly direct." Assertiveness simply means that you express your feelings and observations in a manner that is clear and direct but non-threatening to other people. For example, instead of saying to someone, "You don't make any sense," the assertive person would say, "I am having a difficult time understanding what you are saying." Or rather than saying, "Deadbeats like you burn me up," the assertive person might say, "People who consistently make late payments cause us extra work and lost revenue." Few people are offended by assertiveness.

Assertiveness means being pleasantly direct, but not abrasive.

Avoid a Condescending or Preaching Tone

People tend to be independent creatures and like to be treated as equals, not talked down to. Thus, writing that suggests that the writer and reader are not equal is apt to make the reader unhappy. Preaching, in the context of this discussion, refers to a tone that talks down to the reader or otherwise emphasizes status differences. Again, we encourage you to review Albert Hart's letter in our opening story. Usually, writers do not intend to be preachy in documents; it occurs when the writer is trying to convince the reader of something, as in this example:

> You must take advantage of savings like this if you are to be successful. The pennies you save pile up. In time, you will have dollars.

In this case, the point may be valid, but saying something so elementary, as if the reader did not know it, is insulting. Likewise, messages that "remind" the reader of obligations may irritate. Here are some examples of condescending "reminders":

- When you agreed to serve on this committee, you knew that you had a responsibility to meet each week.
- The extension of credit is a privilege we give to those who have shown trustworthiness. Along with this privilege goes the obligation to make prompt, regular payments on your account.

Better phrasing might be:

- Committee membership requires weekly meetings so that we can get the needed work accomplished.
- The continued extension of credit requires that you make regular, prompt payments.

Avoid False Sincerity

An overall impression of sincerity—an expression of caring—is a composite of much of what we have discussed in this chapter. Do not overdo the good-will techniques (such as referring repeatedly to your reader by name), but do have a sincere desire to convey the best possible image of your company. Avoid terms that suggest an exaggerated sense of sincerity. One example of such exaggeration showed up in a form letter a company president sent out to each person who signed up for a new charge account. It sounds artificial and lacks believability:

- I was delighted to see your application for a Belko's charge account.

Or, consider this one, taken from an adjustment letter of a large department store, which also overstates the "sincerity":

- We are extremely pleased to be able to be of service to you and want you to know that your satisfaction means more than anything in the world to us.

Avoid the use of superlatives and overly enthusiastic phrases such as "delighted" and "extremely pleased" unless you really mean it.

Be careful when using superlatives. They can sound overstated and insincere.

Avoid Sexist or Exclusionary Language

Language can offend or even perpetuate discriminatory behavior by emphasizing the differences between people, by implying that one group is superior to another, or by excluding some people. The most common business mistakes regarding biased language are:

- Choosing the word "he" as a generic pronoun.
- Including unnecessary qualifiers.
- Selecting gender-specific titles.

AVOID "HE" AS A GENERIC PRONOUN

In general, avoid "he"/"she" and "s/he" entirely. Use "he" or "she" and "her" or "him" only when necessary. Try one of these replacements in a sentence such as "Each worker must wear his or her hard hat":

- **Convert to plural.** *"All* workers must wear *their* hard hats."
- **Use second-person.** "Wear *your* hard hat."
- **Replace the pronoun ("his" or "her") with an article ("a," "an" or "the").** "Each worker must wear *a* hard hat."

AVOID UNNECESSARY QUALIFIERS

Omit words that call inappropriate attention or offer irrelevant identification, such as *Hispanic* lawyer, *female* construction supervisor, *elderly* stockroom worker, *handicapped* receptionist, or *male* nurse.

In addition, avoid descriptions for one gender and not the other. Since you would not describe the suit the male keynote speaker was wearing, do not describe the woman's clothing either. Too often we read examples like, "Molly Hill, an attractive 35-year-old lawyer, and her husband, Jon Hill, a noted scholar." Instead, write equitably; for example: "Molly Hill, a lawyer, and her husband, Jon Hill, a scholar." Similarly, avoid "male secretary" or "minority candidate."

AVOID GENDER-SPECIFIC TITLES

Replacing the generic "man" is not always easy. For example, changing "manhole cover" to "personhole cover" is ridiculous. However, follow these tips whenever you can:

- Avoid words that exclude women, such as "chairman" and "policeman." Instead, use words such as "leader" and "police officer."
- Avoid words that exclude men, such as "stewardess" and "actress." Instead, use words such as "flight attendant" and "actor."
- Replace words that collectively include men and women but imply only men, such as "manpower" and "forefathers." Instead, use words such as "staff" or "human resources" and "ancestors."

We acknowledge that some of this smacks of "political correctness" and becomes tiresome, but it is a reality of the workplace. Writers can trip on their insensitivity to current verbal conventions. Stay alert.

Make titles, names of positions or occupations, and common references gender-inclusive. The following are some additional examples of gender-inclusive positions, occupations, and common references:

Avoid	Prefer
businessman	worker, manager, executive, retailer
chairman	chair, chairperson
coed	student
Congressman	member of Congress, representative, legislator
delivery man	delivery driver
draftsman	drafter
fireman	firefighter
foreman	supervisor
housewife	homemaker
husband, wife	spouse
mailman	mail carrier, letter carrier
man-hours	staff-hours
mankind	human beings, humanity, people
man-made	manufactured, artificial, synthetic
newsman	reporter
repairman	service technician
saleslady, salesman	sales associate, clerk, salesperson, sales representative
spokesman	representative, advocate, spokesperson
waiter, waitress	server
watchman	guard, security officer
workman	laborer, worker

You run the risk of demeaning at least half your readers by using sexist language. Whether such language offends you or not is irrelevant. Someone you write to could be more sensitive. Even if unintentional, your language can offend or even perpetuate discriminatory behavior by emphasizing differences between people or by implying that one group should be excluded.

Avoid sexist language that implies gender exclusion.

Applying good principles of human relationships and avoiding the common pitfalls described in this chapter can do much to create appropriate tone in your messages. Workplace communication is functional in nature, but it need not lack human qualities. Sensitivity to tone helps a writer sound like a concerned, thoughtful, caring person. The positive overall impression created in the minds of your readers will be worth the slight extra effort expended.

Much of what we have discussed in this chapter clearly applies to memos, letters, email, and correspondence. If you are working on longer documents such as business reports, the writing principles are basically the same. A long report is just a series of shorter sections, each of which can be treated using the principles we've discussed in this chapter. In the next few sections we will outline the elements of a workplace report and discuss how you can break through writer's block, which is a common problem experienced by writers of longer reports.

Those who write clearly have readers; those who write obscurely have commentators. (Albert Camus)

Understand the Key Elements in Workplace Reports

A report can be defined as an orderly and objective communication of factual information that serves some business or organizational purpose. A report should describe findings and analysis, not express undocumented opinions. It should use facts, data, and documentation. When you present opinions, guesses, hunches, or predictions, clearly label them as such so the reader will not mistakenly assume they are facts. In addition, of course, the report should be functional, offering specific recommendations. Three key elements of the typical report include:

- Defining the report's problem or topic (Why are your writing this?).
- Stating the goal of the report (What do you hope to accomplish?).
- Detailing the research procedures (How will you get there?).

Define the Report's Problem or Topic

Clearly, defining the report's problem or topic is crucial to its ultimate success. Remember that your reader may view the nature of any given problem differently than you do. By stating the nature of the problem—even when it seems obvious—you can validate that the reader is working from the same information and definitions as you are. Or, if not, you can address any differing perspectives to get on the same wavelength.

An objective, unemotional statement of the problem should be your goal. Avoid emotional language that may be overly judgmental or convey biases. The following examples illustrate this:

(*Emotional/judgmental*): Supervisors are incapable of writing good per-formance reviews.

(*More objective*): Most first-line supervisors are writing performance reviews that do not meet company standards.

Also, avoid stating the problem in terms that are too broad or vague. When the problem is too grandiose or unusually wide in scope, the report loses focus. The following examples illustrate this:

(*Too broad*): This report will study the effects of foreign competition on our business.

(*More objective*): This report will study the marketing strategy of the three foreign competitors that are having the most impact on our share of the market in cable television: Sony, Panasonic, and Mitsubishi.

(*Too vague or ill-defined*): This report will examine safety problems in our manufacturing operations.

(*More specific*): This report reviews lost-time accidents reported in the past 12 months in our manufacturing plant and corrective actions taken to prevent recurrence.

State the Goal of the Report

State the goal or objective of the report in concrete, specific language so that readers will understand exactly what they will be reading. Avoid being overly vague in this statement. The following examples illustrate this:

(*Too vague*): This report suggests some ideas for changes to cope with rising labor costs.

(*More specific*): This report recommends a three-step approach to cutting labor costs in the assembly plant.

Detail the Research Procedures

Relate the specific methods used for gathering and processing information. For example, "This report reflects results of interviews with 200 recently hired employees in four major divisions along with an extensive Internet search of comparable organizations" or "The findings are based on a review of data gathered from 17 organizations facing similar problems in the past two years."

Make Writing Readable!

This heading sounds like a statement of the obvious. Of course we want the reader to be able to digest what we are saying, yet some communicators get it wrong. The most common problem is that they are more concerned with impressing readers than expressing ideas. (We discussed this back in Chapter 1.)

Robert Gunning, an American executive interested in linguistics, created a simple algorithm for calculating the "readability" of a written document. This "Gunning Fog Index" is still a good rough measure of how difficult or easy a piece of writing is for readers.

The "Fog Index" provides a simple measure of readability.

The number calculated by the Gunning Fog Index indicates the number of years of education your reader supposedly needs to comfortably read the paragraph or text. The formula implies that short sentences written in plain language achieve a better score than long sentences written in complicated language. Here is the formula:

$$0.4 \left(\left(\frac{\text{words}}{\text{sentence}} \right) + 100 \left(\frac{\text{complex words}}{\text{words}} \right) \right)$$

If you are like your authors, your eyes just glazed over. (We just put that in there to impress you, clearly violating our advice to express rather than impress.) Here is a less foggy explanation of how to calculate the Index:

1 Take a full passage that is around 100 words (do not omit any sentences).
2 Find the average sentence length (divide the number of words by the number of sentences).
3 Count words with three or more syllables (complex words), not including proper nouns (for example, "Csikszentmihalyi," "Bienvenu," "Carolina"), familiar jargon or compound words (for example, "bookkeeper," "woodcutter"), or words that become three syllables by adding common suffixes such as -es, -ed, or -ing (for example, "focusing," "divided").
4 Add the average sentence length and the percentage of complex words (for example, +13.37%, not simply + 0.1337).
5 Multiply the result by 0.4.

Fortunately, the miracle of technology comes to our rescue! You can check the readability score (Fog Index) for a sample of writing by simply pasting it into a box found at this helpful Web address: http://simbon.madpage.com/Fog/

What does this all mean? The short answer is that some writing is unreadable. One of your authors (Timm) co-authored an article years ago called, "If You Can't Read the Budget Manual, How Can You Cut the Budget?"[3] In that article, we calculated Fog Index scores for a variety of publications:

The children's story, *Cat in the Hat*	4.25
A then-popular novel, *Love Story*	7.64
An article from *Playboy* (we didn't look at the pictures)	11.46
A government EEOC guideline	25.53[4]
Eligibility requirements for Food Stamp Act	26.41
Twenty city budget manuals	11.3–18.2

Today, the *New York Times* maintains an average Fog Index of 11–12, *Time* magazine is about 11. Typically, technical documentation has a Fog Index of between 10 and 15, and professional prose almost never exceeds 18.

Firms with Hard-To-Read Annual Reports Have Lower Earnings

ANN ARBOR, Mich.— There's a reason why some annual reports are difficult to read—they're hiding something, says a University of Michigan business professor. A study by Feng Li, assistant professor of accounting at the U-M's Ross School of Business, shows that annual reports of firms with lower earnings are harder to read.

"Consistent with the motivation behind the plain English disclosure regulation of the Securities and Exchange Commission, managers may be opportunistically choosing the readability of annual reports to hide adverse information from investors," Li said. "Firms with lower earnings not only tend to file annual reports that are more difficult to read, but a decrease in earnings from the previous year also results in annual reports that are harder to read, compared with the previous year's reports."

Using a sample of more than 55,000 firm-years since 1994, Li measured annual report readability by examining syllables per word and words per sentence in companies' 10-K filings. He used the Fog Index, which indicates the number of years of formal education a reader of average intelligence would need to read and understand the text. According to the study, profits of firms with annual reports that are more difficult to read are less consistent in the next one-to-four years. In fact, companies use more complex language in their annual reports even when presenting good news—if it is only fleeting.

On the other hand, Li found no significant evidence that firms make their annual reports harder to read to hide more persistent bad news.

Li's research also found that larger companies and growth firms (those with higher market-to-book ratios) tend to have annual reports that are more difficult to read. In addition, annual reports with more negative special items are harder to read.

Industries with annual reports most difficult to read include insurance, health services, and electric, gas, and sanitary services. Those that are easier to read belong to the airlines and the stone, clay, glass, and concrete products industry.

Although the study found a correlation between earnings and annual report readability, Li says none exists between readability and future stock returns. "Contrary to the SEC's concerns, small investors may not be affected by the lack of readability, since the stock market seems to impound the implication of annual report readability into prices," he said.

Overall, annual reports of public companies, in general, are difficult to read, Li says. The average Fog Index for all annual reports is 19.4 (a score of 12–14 is ideal and higher than 18 is unreadable).

"Interestingly, there is an obvious drop in the indices in the years immediately after 1999, suggesting that the SEC's plain English disclosure regulation of 1998 did make companies take efforts to make their annual reports more readable," Li said. "However, this trend reversed dramatically after 2002 and the annual reports filed by public firms seem to have become even more difficult to read, compared with the pre-1998 years."

Reprinted with permission of the University of Michigan News Service, June 6, 2006, www. ns.umich.edu/htdocs/releases/ story.php?id=283

Break Through Writer's Block

A long report can look like a huge mountain to climb. A common response to this is writer's block—the inability to get started on a writing project. Every writer has his or her own techniques for breaking through writer's block. One approach is using raw writing. Raw writing is a simple, three-step process for managing the task of writing long documents. The steps are:

Use "raw writing" to break through writer's block.

1 Set a deadline. Determine a realistic amount of time you will need to convey your message. After collecting the raw data, you may decide to set aside two or three hours to write the finished report. Set your alarm clock for one-half of that time.

2 Use half your time for outlining and fast writing. Use the first half of your allotted time to sketch out an outline of the key ideas and to get something down on paper (or on the computer). Write fast. Capture any ideas you think may be relevant in light of the context (your audience and objectives). Do not be overly concerned about exactly the right wording, spelling, grammar, or any other details of presentation. Just capture your ideas and arrange them under a rough outline covering your main points. If you cannot think of the right word, just leave a blank.

If you cannot write in the way you want to, don't worry. At this point in the process, dumping relevant data into your draft document is the most important activity.

When the allotted time is up, stop writing and look at where you are. Even if you feel frustrated at not having written enough or you have not figured out exactly where each idea goes, stop.

3 Use the second half of your time for fixing and polishing. Apply the second half of your allotted time to ensuring that ideas are in the right places, revising, moving text around, editing, and polishing the draft you made in the first half. Shift your mental gears from composing to being a ruthless, skeptical, rigorously logical editor. Polish the document by reading and asking others to review the draft document.

The key to breaking through writer's block is to separate the writing from the editing processes.

Other Techniques for Breaking Writer's Block

1 Stop in mid-sentence when you are finished writing for the day or are taking a break. Leave the document up on your computer screen. Then, when you return to work, the first thing you will see is the unfinished sentence on the screen, which you can then finish. With your fingers (and mind) moving, you will be more likely to continue writing.

2 Try doodling on a sheet of paper. The act of literally getting your pencil or pen moving—even if just drawing circles or sketches— can get the ideas flowing for some people.

3 Take breaks. Talk with someone about what you are writing and gather his or her ideas or reactions. This can trigger additional ideas useful to your report or document.

Why Your Writing Delivery Style is Important

Written messages reflect upon the writer and the organization he or she represents. If messages are inappropriate, poorly worded, or excessively difficult to read, they speak volumes about the company's courtesy, refinement, and concern for others. Take a few moments to look back at our opening story.

Community Bank is trying to project an image as the friendly alternative to its big-bank competitors. To do so, it needs to communicate in a personal and sensitive manner. The tone of the letter written by Albert Hart does not support the objectives of friendliness and caring. His blunt, direct communication is conversational but not friendly or courteous. Saying "Thank you" and "Have a nice day" do not make up for his abrasive and condescending tone.

Albert would be wise to apply the ideas in this chapter as he delivers his messages, being direct yet much more sensitive to his audience when making recommendations for guidelines for company writing. Tara should encourage her colleagues to strive for accuracy in their messages and to apply human relationship skills to their writing. This includes writing with an appropriate tone, considering the reader's emotions and needs, and being sensitive to offensive wording. Making such changes will allow Community Bank to project the warm and friendly image it values.

Performance Checklist

- Remember that delivery of effective writing calls for message appropriateness (use of the right medium), accuracy (of content correctly presented), tone (application of psychology to meet reader needs), and readability.

- Create appropriate tone in a message by recognizing that workplace communication is human communication. Good delivery requires that you consider reader feelings. You achieve effective tone by appealing to reader interests, addressing readers as individuals (avoiding blanket tone, using direct address), and using positive rather than negative wording whenever possible.

- Use assertiveness (being pleasantly direct) to project clarity. Avoid abrasiveness, which can annoy your reader.

- Eliminate sexist or exclusionary language that can demean some people and seriously affect the tone of a message. Avoid using "he" as a generic pronoun, adding unnecessary qualifiers and selecting gender-specific titles.

- Calculate readability using an algorithm called the Fog Index. Scores indicate the educational level needed for a reader to digest the message comfortably.

- Break through writer's block by using raw writing—forcing yourself to limit the time you use to produce rough drafts and the additional time you use for editing and polishing.

What Do You Know?

Activity 6.1: Fixing Butch Rocco's Tone

Take another look at Butch Rocco's original memo to his training manager (page 157). Consider the tone of his message. What possible problems are likely to arise from this document?

Identify examples of:

1 I-centered phrases.
2 Blanket tone.
3 Negative wording.
4 Abrasiveness.
5 Preachiness.
6 Sexist language.

Activity 6.2: Avoiding Sexist or Exclusionary Language

Replace the following terms with ones that are not sexist, exclusionary, or otherwise potentially offensive:

mailman	stewardess	fireman
coed	male nurse	chairwoman
salesman	the black actor	the gay manager
receptionist	migrant worker	junior executive

Activity 6.3: Calculate Readability Scores for a Company Document

Select one or more samples of writing from your organization. These may be internal documents or public ones. Calculate the Fog Index for each. Write a memo commenting on the appropriateness of the readability of each document in light of its intended readership.

Activity 6.4: Deal With Writer's Block

Try using one of the techniques described for breaking through writer's block. Write a memo describing how it worked for you. Use the ANSA pattern of arrangement.

Reinforce With These Review Questions

1 True/False Tone reveals the writer's attitudes toward his or her readers.

2 True/False Writers need to apply the same human relationship skills they would use in a face-to-face encounter.

3 When a document makes the reader feel lost in the crowd, the _____ tone may be responsible.

4 Direct address shows your readers how your message applies to them and how it can meet their individual needs. One way to show this application is to clarify _____ and _____, or "what-this-means-to-you" statements.

5 A simple definition of assertiveness is "being _____ _____."

6 True/False Negative wording generally conveys more information than positive wording.

7 Describe three ways to avoid the potentially sexist use of the masculine pronoun (he): (1) _____, (2) _____, and (3) _____.

8 Three key elements of the typical report include: (1) _____, (2) _____, and (3) _____.

9 True/False One technique for dealing with writer's block is to stop in mid-sentence when you are finished writing for the day or are taking a break and to leave the document open on your computer screen.

10 True/False The way we deliver written messages reflects upon us as individuals and upon the organization(s) we represent.

seven

Evaluate Feedback for Continued Success

The trouble with most of us is that we would rather be ruined by praise than saved by criticism.

(Dr. Norman Vincent Peale)

It takes a lot of courage to show your dreams to someone else.

(Erma Bombeck)

Feedback as a Form of Coaching

At its most basic level, feedback is crucial to any kind of improvement, and writing is no exception. While positive feedback is nice—we all love a compliment—it is usually the *negative* feedback that helps us the most. Despite people saying, "I always welcome your feedback," most of us need to work to overcome the "feedback hurts" mentality. Of course, it isn't always pleasant to hear negative comments about what we are doing. Sometimes these comments hurt our feelings or wound our ego. Sometimes the feedback strikes us as, well, stupid. That said, let's consider a shift in our perspective.

Try this: think about feedback as a form of *coaching*. When we work with a coach, he or she is constantly giving us negative feedback—and we appreciate it. A golf coach, for example, will correct the way you hold or swing the club, and you are delighted to get the negative feedback. Career coaches point out behaviors that are detrimental to our success and we appreciate it. In fact, you pay for all these "criticisms."

There is no positive change without negative feedback. We all need feedback (which often takes the form of criticism) to improve our performance. It makes us better at what we are learning to do—and writing is all about constant learning. Those who provide honest feedback are our coaches. The final step in the Straight Talk Writing Model shows us how to give, solicit, and receive external (from others) and internal (self-assessment) feedback.

Professional Competencies

When you have completed this chapter, you should be able to:

- Recognize that writing is an ever-evolving process that only improves when we get useful feedback.
- Appreciate the importance of feedback in the process of improving writing skills.
- Enhance your skills at soliciting, receiving, and evaluating feedback from others.
- Improve your ability to give helpful feedback to others.
- Use the principle of internal feedback to evaluate yourself with a credibility checklist.

The Way It Is: Our Love–Hate Relationship with Feedback

Rob had spent countless hours developing his report detailing the reasons his company should seriously consider franchising its business. He researched similar companies that did so—successfully or unsuccessfully—and compiled a small mountain of relevant data. The final document met all the requirements for a functional, incisive business report and, doggone it, he was proud of what he'd written!

As he left the company's copy center with 12 fresh, multi-color copies of his masterpiece he bumped into Harold, his former mentor. Harold was nearing retirement age after a stellar career with the company, the last dozen years in the executive suite. Many people attributed his success to his ability to lead and motivate people in a low-key, friendly manner. He always had a friendly smile and a few moments for small talk with everyone he met.

"What do you have there?" he inquired of Rob.

"It's my report on the franchising option, Hal. And, if I may say so myself, It's my best work ever," Rob replied, his smile meeting Harold's.

"Good for you. I'm betting that's some writing you can be proud of," said Harold. "You're a good writer. What did your editorial staff have to say about it?"

"Editorial staff?" The old boy must be having a senior moment. I don't have an editorial staff, thought Rob.

"Sure, you know, the folks who looked over your drafts and gave feedback. I don't know what I would have done over the years without the constructive feedback from my 'staff'—even if they didn't work for me. I sure hated asking sometimes, but I never regretted getting their input even if it was just to catch the typos. Well, there was the one time Lucile Stoddard ripped my work to pieces that wasn't so great, but, hey, she's dead now and I no longer hold a grudge." He laughed again. "Yup, feedback—love it or hate it, and most of us have those mixed feelings. But it saved me from looking even stupider than I am many times," he laughed as he walked toward his office.

Rob looked at the stack of reports and knew that he had missed a step. First thing tomorrow he would ask two or three people he trusted to give him the gift of feedback, perhaps before it was too late.

Understand the Feedback Process

The final step in the Straight Talk Writing Model is to evaluate feedback for continued success. This chapter focuses on why and how to apply a feedback process when producing written communication.

When we choose writing as the medium for delivering a message, we are aware that writing, by its nature, does not give immediate feedback. Using written media precludes getting non-verbal reactions such as we would from a speaking audience. Because of the nature of the medium, we need to make a special effort to get the feedback that will help us improve.

Writing does not lend itself to immediate feedback.

Two times when we can (and should) get feedback on our writing are:

1   While in the draft stages (first-stage feedback).
2   After the message is read (second-stage feedback).

Of course, if the feedback is negative and we have already sent the message, it becomes difficult to adjust or improve its effectiveness. Many writers find themselves backtracking or clarifying a document that failed to accomplish its big idea. This can be embarrassing and project an unprofessional image. Better to take the time and expend the effort for feedback before we deliver the message to its target audience.

For significant writing projects—those that are important to your organization or your personal success—or particularly for sensitive messages, the best time to get feedback is while your document is in draft form (first-stage feedback). Ask trusted colleagues to read your message to get their reactions to its content and tone. Read the message aloud yourself to see how it sounds and to catch sentence-structure problems or unintended implications. For routine emails or brief everyday messages, such feedback may be unnecessary.

Get first-stage feedback—review of the draft message—for significant or particularly sensitive documents.

To check message overall effectiveness (second-stage feedback), invite readers to respond to your message, and make it easy for them to do so. Phrase this request for feedback in conversational, sincere words. Avoid the cliché, "If you have any questions do not hesitate to call upon me." Instead, say something more conversational, such as, "I'd appreciate any comments you have about this idea" or "Please give me a call at extension 664 if you can provide any clarification or additional information."

Avoid clichéd phrases such as "If you have any questions do not hesitate to call upon me." Instead, ask more directly for feedback.

Self-Evaluation: Your Feedback-Receptiveness Attitudes

Think back to the last time someone criticized something you wrote. Recall a specific event or situation, and describe it in one sentence (for example: "My boss went through a letter I composed and edited it to sound more direct" or "My emailed request for information from sales staff got only a few responses and these didn't provide the data I needed").

Now, mentally review the situation with regard to your reaction and feelings. To what extent did you:

1   Hold back on defending or explaining yourself to the person who commented on your writing?
2   Work to understand the critique's point of view as best you could?
3   Ask for elaboration or clarification without being overly defensive?

4 Thank the person for giving you the feedback?

For most people, *giving* criticism (even in a constructive way) is risky. When people first offer such feedback, they watch closely to gauge the receiver's responses. The reaction they receive will usually determine whether they will offer feedback again. Reading something with a critical eye is not easy work. Be sure you avoid turning off future feedback be being defensive, dismissive, or argumentative.

Overall, how would you rate your feedback receptiveness in the above situation? What might you change, if anything?

No writer produces perfect writing every time. Writing improvement is an ongoing, iterative process. We can constantly tweak up something we have written. You are likely to look back at documents you wrote yesterday or last month and think of a dozen ways to improve them today. Getting feedback is an important part of the strategic communication approach we have been following throughout this book. Reach out for it. Be open to it. Learn from it.

All writing is draft writing. We can always improve it.

Feedback at a Writer's Workshop

Paul (one of your authors and a frustrated novelist) had been working on his novel for months. After many years of dreaming about writing the "great American Novel," he had finally completed a draft of *The Change Agent*, a story about a guardian angel who helped people make life changes. It was a labor of love—he enjoyed writing the multiple drafts of his story. At times, he faced the inevitable writer's block, of course, but overall it was a good way to spend a few hours in the evening after work—just playing with ideas and having his imaginary characters come to life within the theater of his mind.

In conversations with fellow aspiring writers, he had heard about the Summer Writer's Festival held at the University of Iowa[1] each year. Paul went online, got the details, and soon found himself driving across the country to attend a one-week session for beginning novelists in Iowa City. The format of the course was simple: it was all about feedback.

Each evening the 12 students would read the first 25 pages of the novels written by three students in the class. The discussion for the next day's workshop would talk through this writing sample in detail. Only two ground rules applied: (1) participants were to give honest and helpful reactions to the writing sample, and (2) everyone in the class was to participate—*except the writer whose work the group was discussing.* His or her job was to listen. Not to defend, not to explain, not even to react (if possible). Just listen.

"The course was one of the best experiences I have ever had," said Paul. "I got so many great ideas and such a fresh perspective on what I was doing, that it took me months to digest it all. And my novel is much better than it could ever have been without the input of my new friends at Iowa." Feedback is the writer's friend.

We simply cannot make positive changes without negative feedback. By "negative" feedback, we do not mean hurtful or damaging. Quite the contrary, we mean corrective ideas or fresh insights that make us see the message from another point of view. In a moment, we will discuss where you can get such valuable feedback.

> **Good feedback gives corrective ideas or fresh insights that make us see the message from another point of view.**

Feedback may take the form of a direct criticism or complaint ("Your email really angered me"), but often is subtler, such as negative reactions, edited comments on a written document, rejection of an idea we have presented, or, worst of all, simple failure to respond to your communication. Indeed, the worst feedback may be no feedback—when nothing happens after we send a written message.

> **The worst feedback may be no feedback.**

Feedback comes from two sources, external and internal. External feedback comes from your target audience—your primary readers—and from trusted colleagues. Internal feedback comes from a systematic process of self-evaluation. Both types of feedback form the basis for any improvement in writing skills.

You will build your communication skills by applying four aspects of the feedback process:

- Giving it to others.
- Soliciting it from others.

- Receiving and processing it.
- Evaluating yourself with the "Credibility Checklist."

The remainder of this chapter looks at these processes and shows how to make the most of each.

Give Constructive Feedback

Most people enjoy giving feedback if it is positive and complimentary. People like to get compliments, and you are probably glad to dispense positive comments that make others feel good. However, if you only offer positive feedback and ignore or dilute any negative comments, you are cheating everyone. The writer will miss the opportunity to learn something about the way the message came across to you. You, as an evaluator, will miss the opportunity to learn from recognizing your own shortcomings that you may see in someone else's work. Without this information, writers will never know if what the readers read mirrors what the writers meant to say.

Responding to others' work can help you recognize your own shortcomings.

The most useful feedback points out a need for improvement and offers suggestions for how to make that improvement without discouraging the writer. How this feedback is given will largely determine whether the writer will use the feedback. Obviously, tact and clarity are helpful. Truly useful feedback is that which first acknowledges the positive, then points out a need for improvement, and finally offers a suggestion for how to make that improvement without de-motivating the receiver of the feedback. A general pattern for giving good feedback looks like this:

- Describe something positive (such as, "Your report made a lot of good points ...").
- Express constructive criticism in terms of "I" (such as, "I got lost when you were talking about ..." or "I had difficulty understanding your information about ...").
- Give a specific example (such as, "For example, I couldn't see the connection between your description of the market and your solution ..." or "I didn't understand what you meant by ...").
- Offer an option for a solution (such as, "Perhaps if you could show me that information on a chart ..." or "It would help me if you'd define some key terms such as ...").

- Close with another positive statement (such as, "Your writing style is conversational and, if you include a bit more backup data ..." or "With a bit more clarification of the budget, I think we'll be ready to make a decision").

Applying these guidelines might sound something like this:

Julie, your report's attention-grabber was really clever. That was a perfect story to introduce the need for improvement in the team. (*Positive opening*) However, (*Transition*) I had difficulty understanding the explanation of the cost projections for the recommended training. (*Constructive criticism in terms of "I"*) Maybe a graph or an illustration of some kind would have made it clearer for me. (*Option for solution*) Since you use stories so well to make your points, I know you could make the numbers simple and interesting for us non-numbers types. (*Positive, motivating close*)

Internalize this simple process and make it a part of your everyday communications with others.

How to Give Feedback Model

1 Describe a positive.
2 Express criticism in terms of "I."
3 Give example.
4 Suggest solution.
5 Close with positive comment.

Solicit Feedback from Others

To be effective communicators, we need to reach out for feedback. Feedback is our friend. Okay, sometimes it is a friend we would rather not hear from, but virtually any feedback can be useful. Below we will discuss ways to make the most of feedback by knowing who, when, and how to ask.

Identify Whom and When to Ask

Solicit useful feedback following these two simple guidelines:

- **Identify people you respect and trust—people who can provide you with the feedback you need.** Don't just ask friends you know will validate you. They may make you feel good but will be less likely to give you the beneficial information. Look for effective communicators who have some experience with the topic of your message—and who are straight talkers.

- **Ask people *in advance* to evaluate your writing.** Let people know that you will value their input. Respect that they are doing something for you and acknowledge that effort. Be sensitive to their time. Don't plop a big report on someone's already-loaded desk and assume he or she will jump to it.

Phrase your request respectfully. For example, "Terri, I would sure appreciate it if you would ...," "Let me run my report past you before I give it to the boss," "Read this letter to our unhappy client before I send it," or, "John, you've written some great proposals. Could I ask you to read through mine tomorrow before I finalize it?"

Customer Feedback Builds Stronger Businesses[2]

A complaining customer can be a company's best friend. Without complaints (feedback), organizations could not know how to improve. Without improvement, they would stagnate and eventually fail. Yet many companies make it difficult for customers to complain—to give needed feedback.

The best ways to get feedback are (1) let customers know that you are receptive to it and (2) provide ways for them to give it to you. Ask open-ended questions to give your customers opportunities to suggest ways they'd like to see you do business. Let them know that you really want their input. Really.

Why do we want to provide easy opportunities for customers to complain? Because 63 percent of unhappy customers who do not complain will *not* buy from you again. But, of those who *do* complain and *have their problems resolved*, only 5 percent will not come back. Put another way, you have a 95 percent chance of saving unhappy customers if you hear their complaints—if you get their feedback.

Ask customers for feedback, take it seriously, don't be overly defensive about "the ways we've always done it," and express appreciation to customers for pointing out problems.

This feedback principle applies well to written messages. The "customer" for your letter, report, or email will have valuable reactions for you. Getting those reactions can solidify relationships as well as improve your work.

Know How to Ask for Feedback

The way you ask will have considerable impact on the quality of the feedback you get. Closed-ended questions are rarely the best type for getting people to express their true feelings. If you ask a "yes–no" question such as, "So, how's this look?," you may hear "Great!" or "Fine" and feel better, but you won't get the information you need to improve your writing. Instead, ask open-ended questions that avoid single-word responses. The following are some possible open-ended questions you could use to get good feedback:

- How relevant was my material to my readers?
- How do you think my target readers will respond?
- How did you interpret what I wanted my receiver to do at the end of my message? What specific action step did you get from the memo?
- How can I improve this document?
- What techniques seemed to help my readers get the main objective of my message?
- What would you suggest for me to improve my writing style?
- I'm concerned that my tables, charts, graphs may not be very helpful. How could I improve them?

In addition to using open-ended questions, consider asking people to look at specific areas where you think you could improve. For example, you may say, "Rebecca, I have been trying to cut back on unnecessary wordiness in my writing. Would you look at this and suggest ways to edit it for a more direct tone?"

Ask specific but open-ended questions for best feedback.

Accept and Process Feedback

How you respond to feedback will largely determine whether you will continue to get it. People will not keep giving you feedback if you react emotionally (act offended or are quick to defend what you really meant to say), disregard (imply that the evaluator's idea is unimportant), or blame others ("Ted put together that crowded chart"). None of these reactions will help you improve as a writer.

Remember, the people giving you feedback are doing you a favor. Be appreciative, even when you may not agree with what they are saying. You need not (and probably should not) accept or use all the suggestions you get. Ultimately, you are the writer and have the right to make the final call about your messages.

Look closely at your attitudes. Hopefully, your ego is not so enlarged that you fail to recognize the value of good feedback. Apply the following positive attitudes and behaviors to receiving feedback:

- Develop feedback-receptiveness—be open to and verbally appreciative of good feedback.
- Listen carefully to comments, display non-verbal cues (eye contact, nodding, "uh huh") to indicate that you are listening. Perhaps take notes if appropriate. Let the person giving the feedback know that you are taking their input seriously.
- Ask for specifics and examples, then repeat these back to the person giving the feedback for clarification. Don't challenge or interrogate the person but do be sure you are clear about what they are describing.
- Accept responsibility for any needs and changes. Ultimately, you will sort out the valid and valuable feedback from all you receive. When you identify the best insights, accept the responsibility for applying suggestions to your future writing.
- Recognize that whatever your readers perceive, accurate or not, is very real to them—express appreciation for their point of view.

Evaluate Yourself with the Credibility Checklist

Giving, soliciting, and receiving external feedback from other people is critical to writing improvement. Without knowledge of how our readers react to us, we would be unaware of ways to improve our writing. (Sorry if this sounds repetitious, but it is important.) Another source of feedback, however, can be equally valuable: the internal feedback of honest self-evaluation. Self-evaluation looks inward at the most important element of your communication strategy: your ability to project *credibility*—the quality of being worthy of belief. A so-called "credibility gap" exists when readers see a message as lacking believability or as seeming manipulative.

Credibility: we know it's important. We would like to have it—lots of it, actually. However, exactly what is credibility, and how do you get it? Simply put, your credibility is your target reader's perception of you. The only *reality* is what that reader *perceives*. Your *intention* doesn't count. Credibility is in the eye of the beholder.

Arguably, the most important overall goal of your personal and professional communication strategy is the perception of credibility. If your audience perceives that you are credible—if they believe you, trust you, have confidence in you—you will be persuasive. Moreover, if you are persuasive, you will get what you want: you will achieve the objectives of your emails, reports, memos, and other documents.

Projecting credibility may be your most important communication task.

Your credibility is based on your reader's perception of four key characteristics—your goodwill, expertise, power, and confidence. These four characteristics make up the "Credibility Checklist," which we will show you later in the chapter. This checklist is your way of confirming your decisions throughout the Straight Talk Writing process.

- **Goodwill.** Your readers' perception of your focus on them and concern for them—their perception of *what you think of them.*

- **Expertise.** Your readers' perception of your education, knowledge, and experience—their perception of *the facts about you.*

- **Power.** Your readers' perception of your status, prestige, and success— their perception of *what other people think about you.*

- **Confidence.** Your readers' perception of how you present your writing, how sure you are of yourself—their perception of *what you think of yourself.*

Let's take these one at a time: each dimension is a step toward gaining the credibility you need for professional success.

Establish Goodwill

This one is not only first, but if you don't pull it off, you won't have a chance with the other three. Goodwill is your reader's perception of what you think of them. This dimension is about *them*, not about *you.* Goodwill is their perception of how much you care about them—how unique they are, how special they are, how important they are to you or your organization. No one cares how much you know until they know how much you care.

You will achieve the perception of goodwill from carefully selected information based on analysis of your target audience. So, obviously, if you haven't thought carefully about the people reading your document or receiving your email, you won't be successful on this dimension of credibility. You should consider personal and professional facts, cultural backgrounds, attitudes, and the consistent concerns that they have expressed to you. You may have to work with incomplete data, but make your best guesses based on what you know. This goes back to Step 1 of the Straight Talk Writing Model, context analysis.

Effective context analysis can help you project goodwill.

Demonstrate Expertise: Your Education, Knowledge, and Experience

This second dimension is your target reader's perception of the facts about what you know. Expertise, the second credibility element, is your readers' perceptions of your education, knowledge, and experience. This element evaluates how smart your readers think you are *with regard to the topic of your message*. You will achieve the perception of expertise through writing that shares the facts about yourself.

The good news, of course, is that facts are objective. The bad news is that *perception* of facts is often *subjective*. Use the information you learned in your context analysis to select the most relevant facts to share, based on each particular reader's interests and concerns. What impresses one reader might not work at all with someone else.

Show your expertise by tactfully describing your knowledge.

To project strong expertise, let your reader know that you have it, but avoid appearing arrogant or bragging about what you know. This can be tricky. You want to be seen as smart, but you do not want to lose goodwill points by acting superior or cocky.

You can best project expertise through illustrative examples that demonstrate your knowledge without boasting. Share your experiences with your readers but be careful not to directly take full credit for something you did as a part of a team. For example, you might include phrases such as:

- "Last year I led a group of employees in a project to overhaul the staff scheduling process, and we found that ..." (*Implies experience*)
- "The current research published in *Entrepreneur* magazine suggests ..." (*Implies current knowledge*)
- "In last week's training session we covered that process, and ..." (*Implies recent exposure*)
- Several laws have changed since I first learned about this ..." (*Implies relevant education*)

Look for ways to insert evidence of your credibility by projecting your expertise in appropriate ways.

Reveal Your Power: Your Status, Prestige, and Authority

Power, the third credibility element, is your readers' perception of what other people think about you—your status, prestige, and authority. You will achieve the perception of power with material that refers to your rank and illustrates your successes. An executive letterhead or perhaps just your organizational title can begin to reveal power. A reader's perception of what other people think about you is based on six sources:

- **Rank in your organization or formal positions.** Your job title may be sufficient to project this. Or, your writing could refer to a situation when you were president of an organization or leader of a team. You may need to explain your authority with examples in context, so that your target audience really understands how powerful (and credible) you are. (For example: "As division VP, I have had access to some big picture data that is guiding my recommendation.")

- **Awards or recognition you have received.** The recognition is best when it is relevant to the topic, of course. If the relevance is not obvious, you might have to make the connection for your reader. Be careful not to sound boastful when describing such recognition. (For example: "I was fortunate enough to earn a promotion based on my work with ...")

- **Personal power (your ability to control your own environment).** Illustrate this with examples of situations when you took charge of a problem relevant to you current message, such as producing a report, or newsletter write-up. (For example: "My staff won virtually every request for proposal we applied for last year.")

- **Interpersonal power (your ability to influence other people).** Use an example that demonstrates your reputation as a successful ad writer or refer to an incident when you persuaded someone to change his or her mind. Describe how that worked out. (For example: "I talked Giant Corp. into extending their contract based on the booklet we designed for their employees.")

- **Organizational power (your ability to mobilize resources).** Share examples of situations when you met deadlines or delivered on promises. (For example: "I pulled together the accounting and finance staff to update our projections ...")

- **Power by association with others who have power.** Without bragging, allude to your relationship with people in power (For example: you are the administrative assistant to a company leader, or you have connections in the industry).

From the perspective of a young manager, "power" may look like an attribute that you can only achieve when you are old or wealthy. Not necessarily. The power you achieve in other situations is often "transferable." This means that, although your current communication situation may be different from one in the past, you may still carry power credibility in the eyes of your reader. For example, the power of being president of a civic organization illustrates leadership ability that you can apply on the job. Being involved with a decision made by your boss on a manufacturing problem (association power) may be transferable to a recommendation you make in a document. Having authority as a squad leader for a National Guard unit may demonstrate your ability to lead a project on the job. All this is, of course, perceptual—in the eyes of your audience.

You need not overtly refer to these sources of power in every document you write, of course. Realistically, such references would be more appropriate in a report, recommendation letter, or proposal than in, say, a routine email or correspondence.

Express Confidence: The Way You Present Yourself and Your Writing

The fourth credibility element, confidence, has to do with your reader's perceptions of the way you present yourself with your writing. This dimension of credibility is the reader's perception of how your writing comes across— how sure you are of yourself and what you are communicating. Too many qualifiers or "weasel words," for example, will weaken your writing and the reader's confidence in you. Grammatical or other "detail" errors will damage this aspect of your credibility. Remember, this is their perception of what you think of *yourself*. Are you concerned about your professionalism?

Confidence may be the most important credibility dimension, and you may have the most control over it. Readers generally perceive confident communicators as having more goodwill, more expertise, and more power. Confidence arises especially from your success in applying the Straight Talk Writing Model's Step 3 (selecting and organizing information), Step 4 (delivering your written message), and Step 5 (evaluating your feedback).

You will best project confidence through excellent message preparation and writing skills. Careful proofreading and attention to detail about punctuation, syntax and the like will enhance this element of your credibility.

Finally, confidence stems from doing your homework and preparing messages tailored to your reader's needs and concerns. Once your material is right, it will be easier for you to feel confident. When you feel confident, readers see that confidence and responds positively.

> You can project confidence with wording that sounds confident. Too many qualifiers or "detail" errors can weaken this.

The Credibility Checklist

So, how is your credibility? Thoughtfully answer the questions on this checklist to find out.

The Credibility Checklist

> *Describe the Communication Situation:*
>
> **1 Goodwill: The readers' perceptions of my focus on them and my concern for them.**
> What did I do to show my target readers that I care about them?
>
> **2 Expertise: The readers' perception of my knowledge, education, and experience.**
> What knowledge, education, and experience do I have that might impress my readers?
> What have I accomplished that I am proud of?
>
> **3 Power: The readers' perception of my status, prestige, and power.**
> What is my rank in my current organization and how might this impress my readers?
> What awards or recognition have I received that might impress my readers?
> What is the source of my personal power (my ability to control my own environment)?
> What is the source of my interpersonal power (my ability to influence other people)?
> What are examples of my organizational power (my ability to mobilize resources)?
> What relationships give me "power by association?"
>
> **4 Confidence: The readers' perception of how I present myself—how sure I am of myself and my message.**
> What are some examples of how I exhibit confidence in my writing?

Get Internal Feedback

Consider completing a Credibility Checklist before you write a significant document and again after you have delivered it and received a response. The first use can help you anticipate reader reactions and can provide ideas for strengthening your message before people read it. Insights gained from reviewing what you did can provide a foundation for future improvement and continued success.

Performance Checklist

After completing this chapter, you should be better able to apply some principles for selecting and organizing information for your written messages. Specifically, you should now understand that:

- All writing is draft writing. You can always improved it by incorporating quality feedback.

- Writers can take advantage of opportunities for continuous improvement by applying four aspects of the feedback process—giving, soliciting, and receiving feedback, and evaluating themselves with the "Credibility Checklist."
- The way you ask for feedback will have considerable impact on the quality of the feedback you get. Open-ended, sincere questions generally elicit the most useful information.
- To improve writing, identify people you respect and trust who can provide you with the feedback you need.
- If your readers believe you, trust you, and have confidence in you, you will be more effective and persuasive as a writer. The success of any communication attempt depends heavily on the message receiver's perception of the sender's credibility.
- A credibility checklist reminds us to think about reader goodwill (their perceptions of what you think of them), expertise (their perceptions of your education, knowledge, and experience as these relate to the topic of your message), power (their perceptions of what other people think about you), and confidence (their perceptions of the way you present your written messages).
- Writing specific and full answers to each item on the Credibility Checklist can generate internal feedback and a realistic assessment of what your audience thinks of you and your message.

What Do You Know?

Activity 7.1: Get Internal Feedback with the Credibility Checklist

Consider an upcoming writing task you face. This may be an important letter, a detailed memo, a report, a proposal, a performance review, or some other writing project. Complete the checklist on page 191 in the context of that task.

Activity 7.2: Create an "Editorial Staff"

Harold in our opening story asked Rob if he had run this project past his editorial staff. That got Rob thinking about getting feedback. Do you have an informal editorial staff?

We all go to other people for advice and suggestions. For many people this is an occasional and haphazard process. However, many successful people are recognizing the important of a more formalized process of soliciting feedback and advice.

Identify the key people you would go to for each of the following topics—your editorial staff. Then describe briefly the characteristics of these people that make you interested in their advice. How do they measure up on the credibility checklist in your eyes?

Advice Topic	Who You Would Contact	Why? (Their Characteristics)
How to approach your boss with a written request		
How you should structure a proposal, report, or document you are in charge of writing		
How to better promote your career		

Add other topics and sources of feedback. Record your ideas about a board of such advisors. How could this be beneficial to you? What could you do to reciprocate? How might you contact them about "serving on your board?"

Reinforce With These Review Questions

1 True/False Feedback, although occasionally useful, is not absolutely necessary for improving one's communication skills.

2 Feedback comes from two sources: _____ and _____.

3 True/False The most useful feedback points out a need for improvement and offers suggestions for how to make that improvement without discouraging the writer.

4 Solicit useful feedback following these two simple guidelines: select people you _____ and ask _____ for their input.

5 True/False People who give you feedback are doing you a favor.

6 Careful context analysis and tailoring a message to a reader's needs is one way of building _____, one source of your credibility.

7 _____ credibility is established when readers perceive that you know a great deal about the topic of your document.

8 True/False Power you achieve in other situations is often transferable, causing readers to perceive you as credible.

9 True/False Asking a trusted associate to review the draft of your writing is almost always a good idea.

10 True/False The ultimate success of a functional document is determined by whether or not the reader does what the message asks.

Reference Tool for Straight Talk Writing

We conspicuously display our professionalism in our writing.

Because of their tangible nature, your messages live on, for better or for worse. The good ones accomplish their tasks while polishing our image. The bad ones ...? Well, we have all had the experience of writing something we should not have. We may have sent an email or letter in the heat of the moment that later embarrassed us. Or, we may have distributed an unedited (and grammatically unclear or misspelled) message.

This reference tool can help. Spend enough time to digest just six categories of writing errors and their remedies. Mastering these will greatly reduce the likelihood of "detail" errors that would otherwise diminish your credibility and communication effectiveness.

This material targets the most common grammar and usage mistakes, although it is not intended to be a substitute for a good style guide you can refer to for specific questions. We recommend that you keep a reference book handy or use an online guide for dealing with the less common rules and language conventions.

For now, and in the spirit of the ubiquitous 80/20 rule, we give you 20 percent of the guidelines that will fix 80 percent of any grammar or usage questions you face in workplace writing. Applying the information in this reference tool will allow you to avoid the vast majority of common language-use pitfalls. You will write with better confidence, will project professionalism, and will avoid credibility-damaging errors.

Avoiding Common Grammar, Punctuation, and Usage Mistakes[1]

In our quick review of common language problems, we will focus on the following six writing functions:

- Punctuation.
- Agreement (subject–verb and pronoun–antecedent).
- Pronoun case.
- Voice.
- Prepositions and connectives.
- Modifiers.

Common Punctuation Questions

Many writers get confused about the use of commas. The following sections present an easy-to-understand guide on using commas correctly.

Using Commas

1   Don't insert a comma in a sentence just because the sentence "sounds" like it "needs" a comma, and don't leave out commas just because you're afraid of using them incorrectly.
2   Learn the "names" or functions of the commas; then use the right commas to get your point across.

Below is a discussion of the names and functions of different types of commas.

The Conjunction Comma

Use the conjunction comma with a conjunction like "and," "but," or "so" to separate two main clauses. The choice of either "and" or "but," or another conjunction depends on the relationship you want to convey between two main clauses. However, be sure to include a conjunction—a conjunction comma without a conjunction cannot do its job properly. For example:

- The attorney filed the appeal today, but the judge will not make a decision on it until next week.
- The material used in our suit coats is the very best available, and we guarantee you will be satisfied with every coat you purchase from us.
- I scored 97 percent on my CPA exam, so I think I will probably get an excellent job offer.

The Series Comma

Use the series comma to separate items in a list of three or more items. Items in a list can be single words, phrases, or clauses. For example:

- We purchased books, papers, pencils, and erasers. (*Words in a list*)
- He studies for an hour in the morning, in the afternoon, and in the evening. (*Prepositional phrases in a list*)
- John typed the letter, Mary copied it, and I mailed it. (*Main clauses in a list*)

The Introductory Comma

Use the introductory comma to separate introductory words, phrases, and dependent clauses at the beginning of a sentence from the main clause. For example:

- Therefore, we signed the papers as he requested. (*Introductory word*)
- In addition, we agreed to re-write the contract next week. (*Introductory phrase*)
- When the check arrived, we were disappointed to learn that our refund was only $50. (*Introductory dependent clause*)

The Explanation Comma

Use the explanation comma to separate a clause or phrase of explanation or clarification at the end of a sentence from the main clause. The explanation comma is very much like the introductory comma, except that it *precedes* something that you added to the *end* of a sentence, while the introductory comma *follows* something added to the *front* of a sentence, as shown in the following examples:

- Hoping to be on time for the meeting, I ran up the stairs. (*Introductory phrase followed by an introductory comma*)
- I ran up the stairs, hoping to be on time for the meeting. (*Explanatory phrase preceded by an explanation comma*)

The "And"-Omitted Comma

Use the "and"-omitted comma to separate consecutive or independent adjectives that would otherwise be separated with the word "and." Thus, if you can insert the word "and" between two adjectives, you can use an "and"-omitted comma instead. For example:

- The report had a long, wordy conclusion. (*long* and *wordy*)
- The sharp-looking, expensive car was totally demolished in the accident. (*sharp-looking* and *expensive*)

The Parenthetical Comma

Use the parenthetical comma to enclose thoughts that could be enclosed in parentheses (as its name implies). Such thoughts are usually interjections or interruptions to a sentence, as in these examples:

- The man was, as you know, fired from his last four jobs.
- The equipment, in the meantime, sat idle and became rusty.
- We did not, however, forget that you were interested in taking over the project.

Notice that parenthetical commas may enclose interruptions that are single words (such as "however") and phrases (such as "in the meantime").

The Renaming Comma

Use the renaming comma to enclose a word or group of words that renames a person or thing already named in the sentence. For example:

- Bill Jefferson, the president of Interwest Health Services, will speak at the luncheon ("the president of Interwest Health Services" renames "Bill Jefferson").
- Pamela Adamski, a business education teacher in the Manchester School District, has received the district's "Teacher of the Year" award again this year ("a business education teacher in the Manchester School District" renames "Pamela Adamski").
- We sent the checks to the president, Marlow Marchant, and to the vice-president, Alan Kimball ("Marlow Marchant" renames "the president," and "Alan Kimball" renames "the vice-president").

The Dates and Addresses Comma

Use the dates and addresses comma to enclose information in dates and in addresses. For example:

- On Friday, December 22, we will hold the department Christmas party.
- On December 22, 2011, we will hold the department Christmas party.
- The King visited Buffalo, New York.
- Please send my package to 123 South Main, Denver, CO.

The "Hey, You!" Comma

Use the *"hey, you!" comma* (more formally called the "direct address" comma) to enclose interjections written to get the reader's attention—usually the person's name. For example:

- Thank you, Raul, for your time and effort on this project.
- Stacy, can I take half a day off today?
- I can understand your wanting the job, Kevin.

Using the Semicolon or "Super Comma"

The semicolon (;) is "stronger" or "more powerful" than a conjunction comma. We call it a "super comma." The "super comma" performs just two functions: that of joining (or separating) two independent clauses or that of clarifying items presented in a list (a series) when at least one of the items in the list has a comma in it. For example:

- We presented the sales seminar in Houston, Texas; Salt Lake City, Utah; Denver, Colorado; Reno, Nevada; and Los Angeles, California.

Do *not* use the semicolon to

- Separate dependent clauses (clauses that do not stand alone or convey a complete thought).
- Follow introductory phrases.
- Enclose parenthetical information.
- Introduce lists.

Using the Colon or "Super Period"

You can use the colon (:) to separate two main clauses in certain situations. When the second of two main clauses is the expected or natural explanation or result of the first clause, use a colon to introduce the second clause. For example:

- His prediction came true: we never did finish the manuscript.
- The sales impact would be dramatic: we had a 20 percent drop.

Use a colon *only* when you could use a period—after a *complete* thought (main clause); do not use a colon after only part of a sentence. For example:

- Please purchase the following items: a pen, a pencil, and an eraser.
- His talents are many: he paints, he writes, he acts, and he sings.
- His answer was simple: no.

One exception to the rule that a colon must come after a complete thought is this: when part of a sentence is used to introduce items that will be enumerated or listed beginning on a separate line from the introductory sentence fragment, you may use a colon to end the partial sentence. For example:

- He discussed several important principles in the communication seminar. They are:
  1   Context.
  2   Options.
  3   Organization.
  4   Delivery.

You should also use a colon in the salutation in letters. For example:

Dear Sarah:

Using the Dash

In most word-processing programs, a *dash* (—) is formed by typing two hyphens followed by the next word (no space). The software will automatically make it into a dash.

Use the dash—like the colon—to separate two main clauses when the second clause is the natural or expected result or explanation of the first clause. The dash acts somewhat as an arrow would—it alerts the reader to important or emphasized points of information. For example:

- He was right about one thing—we never did finish the manuscript.
- His answer was very clear—he wanted full price.

A dash can also be used in place of parenthetical, non-essential, or renaming commas as a way of emphasizing the enclosed part of the sentence. For example:

- His attempts to cover his error—attempts that were weak and poorly planned at best—were seen by us as being sufficient reason for his dismissal.
- We were—fortunately—able to finish the project before Christmas.

The difference in using dashes verses commas is that of emphasis—dashes tend to emphasize enclosed items, commas merely identify the enclosed items as being parenthetical or non-essential, and *parentheses* tend to de-emphasize the importance of enclosed items.

Using the Hyphen

Use the hyphen (-) to join two or more words that act together as a compound adjective to provide a single description of a noun that follows. For example:

- His below-par game was the cause of his depression Monday.
- The small-computer industry is one of the largest in America today.

Hyphens are also used in some nouns and adverbs. For example:

- Mother-in-law or father-in-law.
- Commander-in-chief (also commander in chief).
- Governor-elect.
- Co-worker.
- Full-time or part-time.

Also, "self-" words are always hyphenated (except *selfsame, selfish, selfless,* etc.). For example:

- Self-service.
- Self-examination.
- Self-evaluation.

Common Subject–Verb Agreement Questions

Subjects and verbs must agree (be consistent) in terms of *tense, number, person,* and *gender.*

Achieving Tense Agreement: Past, Present, and Future

"Tense" refers to *time,* be it past, present, or future. For example:

- Yesterday, I *wrote* several letters to our customers. (*Past tense*)
- I *write* to several customers each day. (*Present tense*)
- Tomorrow, I *will write* to several customers. (*Future tense*)

You must use the appropriate tense to reflect the correct time.

Using Progressive Forms of Verbs

In addition, each verb form has a "perfect" form, meaning that the action expressed by the verb has been *completed* (perfected) at a particular point in time, past, present, or future. Thus, we can choose from *past perfect, present perfect,* or *future perfect.*

We form perfect tenses by using what is called the "present participle" form of the verb along with a "helper"—*have, has,* or *had.* For example:

- At 4:00 yesterday afternoon, he *had written* four letters. (*Past perfect*)
- Today he *has written* only two letters. (*Present perfect*)
- By 2:00 tomorrow, he *will have written* all 15 letters. (*Future perfect*)

Recognizing Other Changes in Verb Form

Whether the verb has a singular or a plural subject and whether the subject is in the first-, second-, or third-person will usually affect the form of the verb. For example, notice the change in the verbs "do," "am," and "was" as the subject changes from first-person to second-person, from singular to plural, and so on:

Subject	"Do"	"Am"	"Was"
I	do	am	was
we	do	are	were
you	do	are	were
he/she/it	does	is	was
they	do	are	were

If you're a native English speaker, you've been using all these forms of verbs most of your life, and you use them correctly without much thought. The reason that this introduction to verbs is important to you is that it contains useful terms you should be familiar with before you study the guidelines that help you make proper choices of verb tense to fit each situation.

Following the Rules

In the next several pages we will describe some important rules for using verbs correctly.

Rule 1: Use the Correct Verb Form

Verbs have four basic forms:

1 Present (also called the "infinitive").
2 Past.
3 Past participle (the "have," "has," or "had" form).
4 Progressive or ongoing ("-ing" form).

We could arrange each verb on a chart like the one below to show its present, past, past participle, and progressive forms.

Infinitive or Present	Past	Past Participle	Present Participle or Progressive
run	ran	run	running
think	thought	thought	thinking
go	went	gone	going
do	did	done	doing
lay	laid	laid	laying
lie	lay	lain	lying
sit	sat	sat	sitting
set	set	set	setting
watch	watched	watched	watching

Present and past verbs are formed simply by choosing the present or past forms. Perfect tenses are formed by choosing the past participle form and using it with "have," "has," or "had" (*have* run, *has* run, *had* run). Progressive verbs are formed by choosing the present participle form and using it with a "being" verb (*was* running, *is* running, *will be* running). Perfect progressive verbs are formed by combining "have," "has," or "had" with a "being" verb and the progressive form of the verb (*had been* running, *has been* running, *will have been* running).

Rule 2: Express True Statements in Present Tense
Express statements that are *still or consistently true* in the present tense. Express statements that *used to be true* but that *are no longer true* because facts or circumstances have changed in the past tense. For example:

- Ancient people thought the world *was* flat. (*Not true*)
- Columbus knew the world *is* round. (*A truth*)
- I noticed that the report *had* many typographical errors. (*The errors have been corrected*)
- I noticed that the report *introduces* many new ideas. (*The report still does introduce many new ideas*)

Rule 3: Use Present Tense Infinitives After Past Tense Verbs
Whenever a past tense verb is followed by another verb, that second verb must be an infinitive or present tense verb. Often, the infinitive is accompanied by an "infinitive marker"—the word "to." For example:

- He didn't dare *to swim* after dark.
- I wanted him *to go* home early.
- I had hoped *to be* at the meeting.

When a past tense verb has not been used first, using "to have been" or a similar phrase is all right. For example:

- By this time tomorrow, I *want to have finished* the report.
- By the end of my career, I *hope to have been* recognized as an authority on the subject.

Rule 4: Make Subjects and Verbs Agree
"Agreement" is simply a matter of deciding whether you're talking

1   About one person (singular) or about more than one person (plural).
2   About ourselves ("first-person"—"I," "we," etc.), about the reader ("second-person"—"you," "your," etc.), or about someone or something else ("third-person"—"he," "she," "they," "it," etc.).

3   About a woman, about a man, or about people or things in general, regardless of gender.

Once you've decided exactly whom or what you're talking about in relation to these three characteristics (*number*, *person*, and *gender*), you must make sure all parts of each sentence "agree" with (are consistent with) all other parts of the sentence.

A verb changes form to sound right with its subject, depending on whether the subject is singular or plural, and on whether it is first-person, second-person, or third-person. For example, notice how the verb "write" changes in these sentences, depending on the subject of each sentence:

- I *write* a department management report every week.
- She *writes* a department management report every week.
- They *write* a department management report every week.

Subject–verb agreement (or lack of agreement) is usually very easy to hear, although it is sometimes tricky with the same kinds of subjects. The following rules will help you handle some potentially confusing agreement situations.

Rule 5: Separate Subjects Joined with "And" Need a Plural Verb Unless the Two "Subjects" Are Not Really Separate Subjects

Subjects joined with "and" can be singular or plural. The word "and" means about the same thing as a "+" in math—it means "both." Whenever you join two subjects with "and," you are obviously talking about more than one—about *both*—and have to use a plural verb. For example:

- Understanding English grammar *and* knowing how to use grammar effectively *are* important to a good communicator.
- The investment broker *and* her assistant *were* at the meeting yesterday.

The two subjects in each sentence could be split and used in two separate sentences (this time with singular verbs, of course) without modifying the wording of the subjects themselves, as shown here:

- Understanding English grammar *is* important to a good writer.

and

- Knowing how to use grammar effectively *is* important to a good writer.

Likewise:

- The investment broker *was* at the meeting yesterday.

and

- Her assistant *was* at the meeting yesterday.

Sometimes, a *single* subject happens to have the word "and" in it:

- My friend and associate (the same person).
- Ham and eggs (one menu item).
- The ability to type accurately and to proofread thoroughly (one set of related skills).

These are *singular* subjects (subjects that identify just one person or thing) that have the word "and" in them. Thus, we could construct the following sentences using singular verbs. For example:

- My friend and associate *is* attending the meeting. (We could not separate "my friend" and "associate" into separate sentences without adding another "my" before "associate.")
- Ham and eggs *is* my favorite breakfast. ("Ham and eggs" is one breakfast dish—one menu item. Thus, we would not communicate the same idea if we said, "Ham is my favorite breakfast" and "Eggs are my favorite breakfast.")
- The ability to type accurately and to proofread thoroughly *is* important to a typist. (The *real* subject in this sentence is "ability"—we could not separate "the ability to type accurately" and "to proofread carefully" into two sentences.)

Separate subjects joined with "and" need a plural verb. However, if the two "subjects" are not really separate subjects, we use a singular verb.

Rule 6: When Two or More Subjects Are Joined with "Or," the Subject Closest to the Verb Determines Whether the Verb Should Be Singular or Plural
When we join two *plural* subject with "or" (or "nor"), as in "the books *or* the tapes, the subject *closest to the verb* determines whether the verb should be singular or plural. For example,

- The *book* (singular) *or* the *tapes* (plural) *were* (plural) sent.
- The *books* (plural) *or* the *tapes* (plural) *were* (plural) sent.
- The *books* (plural) *or* the *tape* (singular) *was* (singular) sent.
- The *book* (singular) *or* the *tape* (singular) *was* (singular) sent.

When you join a singular subject and a plural subject with "or," put the plural subject last so that the sentence will have a plural verb. Doing so will make the sentence sound more natural. For example:

- The Smiths *or* John *is* coming. (*Sounds awkward although technically correct*)
- John *or* the Smiths *are* coming. (*Sounds more natural*)

Rule 7: Prepositional Phrases Do Not Affect Agreement Between the Subject of the Sentence and the Verb

We can mentally "block out" the entire prepositional phrase from the sentence while we decide whether to use a singular or a plural verb.

Often, a singular subject will be followed by a prepositional phrase that contains a plural word as the object of the preposition. For example, notice the plural words that are objects of the prepositions "of," "in," and "at" in the following sentence parts:

- An examination *of* the *records* ...
- The spectator *in* the *bleachers* ...
- The worker *at* the *controls* ...

When a verb follows such plural words, many of us understandably (but mistakenly) make the verb plural (as in "the worker at the controls *are* ..."). But the plural word ("controls") that follows the preposition is *not* the subject of the verb that follows—the singular subject that precedes the prepositional phrase is the subject ("*the worker* at the controls"). Thus, the sentence should read: "The worker at the controls *is* ...").

Rule 8: Singular Subjects Like "Each" and "Either" and Some Other Words Are Always Singular

Subjects like "each," "either," "neither," and "everyone," followed by prepositional phrases containing plural words ("each of the men," "either of the children") can be thought of as really meaning "each *one*" and "either *one*." These are *always singular.* For example:

anybody	anything	every	every one
anyone	each	everybody	everything
any one	either	everyone	neither
nobody	nothing	somebody	some one
no one	one	someone	something

Thus, we use singular verbs with them:

- *Each* of the men *is* applying for the promotion.
- *Either* of the children *sings* well.
- *Neither* of the applicants *was* qualified for the position.

- *Every one* of the secretaries *was* fired.
- *Something is* wrong here.

Rule 9: Collective Subjects Can Be Used with Either Singular Verbs or Plural Verbs Depending on the Meaning

Subjects that describe collections of people or things are called "collective subjects." For example:

committee	class	team
jury	group	staff
family	crowd	tribe

Such collective subjects can be used with either singular verbs or plural verbs depending on whether we want to tell the receiver that only one thing (a single "unit") is involved in the action or that at least two persons or things (individuals) are involved in the action. For example: if we wish to make an announcement on behalf of all our family members and want to show our readers or listeners that our announcement is really from *all* family members, we would say:

- The family *are* happy to announce Mom and Dad's fiftieth wedding anniversary.

But if the family is being talked about as a *single unit* instead of as individual family members, we write:

- The family *is* living in Lockport, New York.

Some verbs name actions that *require* only one performer; other verbs name actions that *must* be performed by more than one. For example: the action named by the verb "argue" requires more than one performer since it takes two to argue. Thus, we write or say:

- The team *are* arguing about who will be chosen for the award. (Although this is correct, most people would probably say, "The team members ..." because it sounds more natural.)

If the team members are united in arguing *with the coach*, we can talk about the team as a *single unit*:

- The team *is* arguing with the coach about who he should choose for the award.

Common Pronoun and Antecedent Agreement Questions

Pronouns are the generic words that we use to rename or replace other "brand name" nouns. Common pronouns include:

I	me	my	you	your
we	us	our	he	him
his	she	her	hers	who
they	them	their	theirs	that
whom	whose	it	its	those
which	there	this	these	

Antecedents describe the word (or group of words) that a pronoun refers to, replaces, or renames. A pronoun has meaning to the reader or listener only if it has an antecedent—a noun that the pronoun replaces—and only if it refers to the antecedent clearly. The underlying principles about the link between pronouns and their antecedents are these:

1   Every pronoun must refer clearly to one and only one specific noun in the same sentence or in a preceding sentence.
2   Every pronoun must "agree" with its antecedent in terms of number, person, and gender.

Following the Rules

The following section discusses rules for correct pronoun–antecedent reference and agreement.

Rule 1: Make Sure that Antecedent Reference Is Clear and Cannot Refer to Something Else
Good writers insure that the receiver cannot misunderstand pronoun–antecedent references. To avoid misunderstandings, be wary of these kinds of reference problems:

- Unclear reference.
- "Distant relatives" (relative pronouns like "who" and "which" that are placed too far from their antecedents).
- Meaningless pronouns.

AVOID UNCLEAR REFERENCE
Sometimes we are not sure what word writers are trying to replace or refer to when they use a pronoun. Examples of unclear pronoun reference include:

- When I received the letter and the check, I noticed that it did not have a signature on it.
- When the HR Department secretaries distribute copies of the new guidelines, let's take a good look at them.
- If the printer doesn't make a clear impression on the paper, I'll be glad to check it for you.

If a pronoun can refer to more than one possible antecedent, you'd better rework the sentence. You could correct the examples above as follows:

- When I received the letter and the check, I noticed that the check did not have a signature on it.
- Let's take a good look at the new guidelines when the secretaries distribute them.
- If the printer doesn't make a clear impression on the paper, I'll be glad to check the printer for you.

AVOID "DISTANT RELATIVES"
A "distant relative" is a relative pronoun or a relative clause that has been placed too far from its antecedent. People often mistakenly put a verb or some other part of the sentence between the relative pronoun and its antecedent, as shown in the following examples:

- The man was fired immediately *who did not complete* his report on time.
- Take the report to John *that has February's sales figures* in it.
- Information should be left off the resume *that does not relate* to your qualifications for the job.

We improve the sentences by placing the relative clause immediately after the antecedent in each sentence, as shown in the following examples:

- The man who did not complete his report on time was fired immediately.
- Take the report that has February's sales figures in it to John.
- Information that does not relate to your qualifications for the job should be left off the resume.

Rule 2: Avoid Meaningless Pronouns (also Known as "Expletives")
Pronouns without antecedents are also called "expletives." The most common expletives are probably "it" and "there," although other pronouns can also be expletives. For example, we often use "they" as a meaningless pronoun, as in "*They* say the grass is always greener on the other side." For example (the italicized pronouns do not refer to an antecedent at all):

- He said that *it* is very important to listen carefully.
- *They* claimed that *there* was nothing wrong with the new widget.
- *It* is essential to our project to have you on the committee.

Notice the difference in the examples below when we re-write them without expletives.

- He said that listening carefully is very important.
- The critics claimed that nothing was wrong with the new widget.
- Having you on the committee is essential to our project.

Rule 3: Be Certain that Pronouns Agree with their Antecedent in Number, Person, and Gender
Pronoun *agreement* refers to consistency between the pronoun and its antecedent in these areas:

- Number (singular or plural).
- Person (first-, second-, or third-person).
- Gender (male, female, or neutral).

In addition, relative pronouns must agree with their antecedents in one other way: "human" or "person" pronouns must be used to refer to people, and "non-person" or "thing" pronouns must be used to refer to things other than people.

CHECK FOR AGREEMENT IN NUMBER
Always refer to certain words by singular or plural pronouns, as in the following examples:

- We invite *everybody* to choose *his or her* own research topic. (*Singular*)
- *Some* of the managers need to bring *their* departmental reports to the meeting. (*Plural*)
- They have completed *much* of the work, but *it* has not been done well. (*Singular*)
- The *company* is selling *its* old equipment to interested employees. (*Singular*)
- As the *workers* punched in this morning, *they* heard about the strike plans. (*Plural*)

The most common problem with pronoun–antecedent agreement in number is the use of "they" or "their" to refer to a singular pronoun. Examples of misuse: "*Everybody* is invited to choose *their* own research topic" or "The *company* is selling *their* old equipment."

CHECK FOR AGREEMENT IN PERSON (VIEWPOINT)

We can confuse readers by writing illogical shifts within a sentence from one viewpoint (person) to another. For example, the following sentence begins in second-person (referring directly to the reader) and then shifts to third-person (referring to someone other than either the writer or the reader):

- When *you* choose a long-distance telephone company, *one* should consider the company's billing practices.

CHECK FOR AGREEMENT IN GENDER

The most obvious gender-agreement error would be to refer to a man as a "she" or to a woman as a "he." Few people make such obvious errors. The more subtle gender-agreement errors have to do with using all-masculine pronouns ("he," "him," "his") or all-feminine pronouns ("she," "her") to refer to antecedents such as "managers," "secretaries," "workers," "one," and so on—antecedents that are *neutral* in terms of gender.

Even if all secretaries in your organization happen to be female and all managers are male, use gender-neutral job titles that do not imply that such jobs must or should be confined to one gender.

Rule 4: Use "Who," to Refer to People, "That" to Introduce Essential Clauses, and "Which" to Introduce Non-essential Clauses

Pronouns and antecedents should agree in the proper use of the relative pronouns to:

- Refer either to persons or to things.
- Introduce either essential or non-essential clauses (although not strictly an *agreement* problem).

The principles governing the use of relative pronouns are as follows:

1 Use "who," "whom," and "whose" to refer to humans (although "whose" is also used to refer to things other than humans) and to introduce either essential or non-essential clauses.
2 Use "that" to refer to things other than humans and to introduce essential clauses.
3 Use "which" to refer to things other than humans and to introduce non-essential clauses.

For example, instead of saying, "The police officer *that* made the arrest," say, "The police officer *who* made the arrest." Instead of saying, "The company *who* bought the materials," say, "The company *that* bought the materials."

Knowing whether the clause you introduce is *essential* or *non-essential* is the key to choosing between "that" and "which." Essential clauses limit—or more narrowly define—the meaning of the antecedent and are necessary to the meaning of the sentence. Examples of essential clauses:

- The car *that I bought yesterday* is missing. (*The receiver needs to know* which *car*)
- The lake *that* we visited last year is now severely polluted. (*Identifies* which *lake is polluted*)
- The manager *who* wrote the proposal is Mr. Allen. (*Identifies* which *teacher*)

Non-essential clauses give additional or supplementary information about the antecedent. You could remove these from the sentence without changing the meaning of the sentence. Examples of non-essential clauses:

- My new car, *which I bought yesterday*, is missing ("which I bought yesterday" could be eliminated from the sentence without changing the meaning of the sentence).
- Snowflake Lake, *which* we visited last year, is now severely polluted (additional information only—is not needed to identify *which* Snowflake Lake).
- Our manager, *who* wrote the proposal, is Mr. Allen (additional information—"our manager" is not identified or differentiated by "who wrote the proposal").

Common Pronoun Case Agreement Questions

Pronoun case tells the reader or listener whether the pronoun is naming:

- The *performer* or *subject* of an action (called "nominative case").
- The *receiver* or *object* of an action (called "objective case").
- The *owner* of something in the sentence (called "possessive case").

Before studying the rules that help you to choose the correct form of a pronoun for particular sentences, take a minute to review Table A.1, which shows the various pronouns and their nominative, objective, and possessive forms. In reviewing Table A.1, remember these terms:

- "First-person" refers to the person speaking.
- "Second-person" refers to the person being spoken to by the "first" person.

- "Third-person" refers to the person being spoken about by the "first" and "second" persons.
- "Singular" means that just one person is involved.
- "Plural" means that more than one person is involved.

TABLE A.A. Pronoun Forms

	Nominative (Names the Performer or Subject)	Objective (Names the Receiver or Object)	Possessive (Shows Ownership)
First-person			
—Singular	I	me	my
—Plural	we	us	our
Second-person			
—Singular	you	you	your
—Plural	you	you	your
Third-person			
—Singular	he	him	his
—Singular	she	her	her
—Plural	they	them	their
Third-person/ unknown	who	whom	whose
—Singular	who	whom	whose
—Plural			
Third-person/ non-persons	it	it	its
—Singular	they	them	their
—Plural			

Following the Rules

The following discussion explains the rules for the correct use of pronouns.

Rule 1: Use Nominative Pronouns (I, We, You, He, She, They, and Who) to Complete the Meaning of "Being" Verbs (Is, Am, Was, Were, Be, Been, Are)
The following are correct uses of nominative (naming) pronouns:

- This is *he*.
- The project chairmen are *they*.
- The accountant who made the mistake is *she*.
- *Who* did you say that man is? (In this sentence, the "being" verb comes at the end of the sentence; but it is still completed by the pronoun *who*.)

Rule 2: Use Nominative Pronouns as Subjects of Verbs
Examples of correct use of nominative pronouns used as subjects:

- *He* and *I* are going to class (*he* and *I* are subjects of the verb "are going").

- *I* will give the assignment to *whoever* volunteers to work more hours this week (*I* is the subject of the verb "will give"; *whoever* is the subject of the verb "volunteers").

Rule 3: Use Objective Case to Name the Receiver of an Action (the Object of the Verb)
Examples of objective case pronoun use are:

- The manager agreed to show *us* the movie at no cost.
- Please introduce *him* to the group.
- I told *her* to be here at 8:00 this morning.

We can always locate the objective of the verb by saying the verb and then asking "who?" or "what?" For example: "please introduce him to the group," we can read the verb "introduce" and ask "who?" The answer is "him"—so "him" is the object.

Rule 4: Use Objective Pronouns to Complete a Preposition (Words Like "Among," "Under," "Over," "In," "At," "Beneath," "Beside," "Between," "Around," "Toward," "To," "On")
The following are examples of objective case pronouns:

- Send the book *to him* in the morning.
- The child stood *between him* and *her.*
- We must keep the secret *among us* workers.

Rule 5: To Use a Possessive Pronoun, Use the Possessive Form of the Pronoun—Do Not *Add an Apostrophe to the Pronoun*
Possessive case pronouns show ownership like this:

- The book had *its* cover torn off.
- Bob lost *his* report.
- Mary quit *her* job.

Important note: A very common mistake for writers is confusing *its* and *it's*. "It's" is never a possessive. "It's" (with the apostrophe) always means the contraction form of "it is."

Rule 6: To Use a Possessive Noun, Add an Apostrophe and Sometimes an "s" to the Noun
If the noun ends in "s" add just an apostrophe:

- The *boys'* bicycles were locked in the bicycle rack.

If the noun ends in "s" but the possessive form of the noun is pronounced with an extra "s" sound, add an apostrophe and an "s":

- This is *Chris's* book.

If the noun does *not* end in "s" add an apostrophe and an "s":

- The *boy's* bicycle was a Christmas gift.
- This is *Mary's* book.
- The *children's* department is on the fourth floor.

Rule 7: To Use the Possessive Form of a Plural Noun, Make the Noun Plural and Add the Apostrophe as with Singulars
First make the singular form of the noun into the plural form:

- *boy* is changed to *boys.*
- *man* is changed to *men.*
- *woman* is changed to *women.*
- *Jones* is changed to *Joneses.*

Then treat the plural noun as you would any other noun: if it ends in "s" add just the apostrophe; if it does not end in "s" add an apostrophe and an "s":

- The *boys'* toys were shared between themselves.
- The *men's* jackets were left in the front room.
- We walked through the *women's* department.
- This is the *Joneses'* car.

Rule 8: When Objects Are Separately Owned by Two or More Owners, Make the Name of Each Owner Clear
Examples of this rule:

- These are Betty's and Ramon's books (*Betty* owns some of the books, and *Ramon* owns some of them).
- These are Bob's and her reports (*Bob* owns some of the reports, and *she* owns some of the reports).

Rule 9: When One or More Objects Are Jointly Owned, Use the Possessive on Only the Last Owner Named
Examples of this rule:

- These are Betty and Ramon's books (because only "Ramon" is posses-sive, we know that Betty and Ramon *share* ownership of the books).

- Let's go to Grandma and Grandpa's house (the possessive is formed only on "Grandpa," so we know that Grandma and Grandpa *share* ownership of the house).

Rule 10: Use Possessive Nouns and Pronouns as Subjects of Gerunds (Gerunds are "-ing" Words that act as Subjects or Objects in a Sentence)
Examples of this rule:

- *His* coming to work late was very disruptive ("he" or "him" was not disruptive—his *coming late* was disruptive).
- I can understand *your* wanting the job (I'm not saying I understand "you"—I understand your *wanting*).

Some Tricky Situations in Correct Pronoun Case

Here are a few special pronoun usage situations, cases where we cannot always "hear" the correct way to use pronouns:

Using Pronouns after "Being" Verbs
"Being" verbs like "is," "was," and "are" can be seen as "equals" signs (=). Thus, saying

- The company president is he

means the same thing as saying

- The company president = he.

Likewise, we should be able to reverse the parts of a sentence that appear on both sides of a "being" verb and not change the meaning or correctness of the sentence. For example:

- The company president is (=) he

can be reversed without any problems:

- He is (=) the company president.

If you mistakenly use nominative pronouns after "being" verbs, the sentence may sound like this:

- The company president is (=) him.

This would sound strange when reversed to

- Him is (=) the company president.

So, whenever you see a "being" verb that is completed by a pronoun (that usually means that the pronoun comes right after the "being" verb), write an equals sign above the "being" verb:

$$=$$

- The keynote speaker was her

then read the sentence parts backward:

$$=$$

- Her was the keynote speaker.

If the sentence sounds right, the pronoun is correct. If it doesn't, change the pronoun:

$$=$$

- She was the keynote speaker

$$=$$

- The keynote speaker was she.

Getting "Who" and "Whom" Choices Correct

For some reason, we often can't "hear" whether "who" or "whom" should be used in most situations. We can hear "he" and "him," "I" and "me," and "they" and "them" quite easily, but "who" and "whom" are difficult. To solve the problem, rearrange a "who/whom" sentence and replace the "who" or "whom" with one of those words we *can* hear—"he/him," "they/them," "I/ me."

If we choose a word with an "m" in it ("hi*m*," "the*m*," "*m*e"), we know that "who*m*" is correct. If we choose a word without an "m" ("he," "they," "I"), we know that "who" is correct.

Here are the steps to this trick that we call the "M&M Rule" (because the "m" in the words we *can* hear gives away whether "who" or "who*m*" is correct):

1   Delete the part of the sentence that comes before the "who" or "whom":
    - ~~Send the report to~~ whoever/whomever asks for a copy of it.
2   Replace the "who/whom" or the "whoever/whomever" with "he" or "him," with "they" or "them," or with "I" or "me":
    - ... *he* asks for a copy of it.
3   Read the part of the sentence that you have not deleted (sometimes you'll have to rearrange it a bit before it makes sense as a sentence) and

see whether an "m" word or a "non-m" word sounds right. If an "m" word sounds right, use "whom" in your original sentence. If a "non-m" word sounds right, use "who" in your original sentence. For example, because

- ... *he* asks for a copy of it.

sounds good to us, we know our original sentence should say:

- Send the report to *whoever* asks for a copy of it.

Using Pronouns Joined with "And" Correctly
Correct case of a pronoun joined to another pronoun or to a noun is often difficult to hear, as in these sentences:

- Ted and *me* are going to the meeting.

The simple solution to this problem is to *separate the words that are joined with "and."* Then read the two words alone in separate sentences:

- Ted and me are going ...

becomes

- Ted is going ...
- *Me* is going ... (should be "*I* am going ...").

Therefore, the sentence should say:

- Ted and *I* are going to the meeting.

Our ears will tell us whether the pronoun has been used correctly.

Active and Passive Voice

Subjects that are *doing*—are the doers of the action—are called "active" subjects. In such cases, the subject and its verb are said to be in "active voice." Subjects that are being *done unto* by others or are receiving the action are called "passive" subjects—the subject and its verb are said to be in "passive voice."

Examples of active voice:

- East Coast Services conducted the opinion poll to determine the public's views toward the upcoming municipal election.
- The volunteers assigned to the project tabulated the survey results.

Examples of passive voice:

- The opinion poll was conducted by East Coast Services to determine the public's view toward the upcoming municipal election.
- The survey results were tabulated by the volunteers assigned to the project.

Choosing Between Active and Passive

Minimize the use of passive voice in workplace writing. We recommend this because passive voice is usually

- More wordy than active voice, because passive voice requires that a "being" verb be used with the verb itself.
- Less "lively" or vivid than active voice, because the subject of the sentence is not really doing anything.
- Less direct and sometimes less easily understandable than active voice.

Passive voice can be useful, however:

- When the performer of the action is unknown. For example: "The report was lost yesterday."
- When the performer of the action is unimportant to the writer's message. For example: "The typewriter was repaired quickly."
- When you want to emphasize the receiver of the action instead of the performer of the action. For example: "Jamie was fired immediately."
- When you want to be diplomatic and to avoid "pointing the guilty finger" at the performer. For example: "If the sales receipt had been returned with the merchandise, a refund could have been made."
- When you want to de-emphasize bad news to soften the blow. For example: "A job offer cannot be extended at this time."

Conversely, active voice places the *performer* of the action in the subject position in the sentence and thus emphasizes the performer while de-emphasizing the receiver of the action. For example: "Terrance gave the customer a full refund."

Maintaining Voice Consistency

A sentence should not shift from one voice to another. By maintaining the same voice in an entire paragraph, your message will usually read better. Examples of unnecessary changes in voice:

- When the meeting was adjourned by the chairperson (*passive*), the employees breathed a great sigh of relief (*active*).
- If the file has been misplaced by Wendy (*passive*), Chad will go to the main office for another copy (*active*).

Examples of all-active voice:

- When the chairperson adjourned the meeting, the employees breathed a great sigh of relief.
- If Wendy has misplaced a file, Chad will go to the main office for another copy.

Prepositions and Connectives: Putting Ideas Together

Prepositions and other connectives are the signals we use to show how parts of a sentence link together. *Connectives* in a sentence show whether we are stopping our discussion of one thought, turning to a new thought, or repeating or emphasizing thoughts we have already discussed.

Connectives include *prepositions* (words like "in," "by," "to," "among," and "between"); *conjunctions* (joining words like "and," "but," "so," and "because"); *relative pronouns* (including "that," "whether," "whichever," "whatever," "whoever," "who," "whom," and "which"); and *relative adverbs* (words like "where," "when," and "while").

Your writing can join words, phrases, and clauses in a sentence:

- To show that one idea continues or adds to the thought expressed in another part of the sentence. For example: "I learned the material, *and* I did well in the training sessions."
- To show that one idea presents a new or separate thought from what is presented in another part of that sentence. For example: "I learned the material *by* attending the training and *by* taking careful notes."
- To show that one idea is really a "subpart" of another part of the sentence. For example: "I learned the material *by* attending training and taking good notes."

Maintaining Parallelism

Effective use of connectives often centers on making sure that connected ideas or sentence parts are parallel. *Parallelism* is often a matter of simple consistency. More exactly, though, we can define parallelism this way: "equal grammatical structure for items that are of equal rank or importance."

Example of a sentence lacking parallelism: "Please send $10 *to* Alex and me."

Example of a sentence with parallelism: "Please send $10 *to* Alex and *to* me."

In "send $10 *to* Alex and *to* me," "Alex" and "me" are treated as separate, equally important parts of the sentence. That is, the writer expresses as *parallel* items in the sentence, because they have the same grammatical structure— "*to* Alex and *to* me." This second example also clarifies the ambiguity of the first example where it is unclear as to whether we *each* get $10 or just $10 to share. In the second example, we clearly each get $10.

Parallelism (or the lack of it) becomes very obvious when using bullet lists or enumeration. Check to be sure that each point begins with the same word form—verb, noun, adjective, adverb, etc. For example: "Job requirements call for *heavy* lifting, *extensive* carrying, and *prolonged* walking."

Example of a bullet list lacking parallelism:

"Employees interested in participating in the fitness challenge should

- Attend Monday's 10 a.m. orientation meeting.
- Already have gym clothes with them.
- You need to bring your medical waiver form."

Correct parallelism (starting each with a verb) would be:

"Employees interested in participating in the fitness challenge should

- Attend Monday's 10 a.m. orientation meeting.
- Bring gym clothes.
- Bring your medical waiver form."

Another example of enumerated list without correct parallelism:

"Assembling the coaxial coordinator requires just three steps:

1 Insert the freebish pin into slot 'A.'
2 The belt can then wrap around the grommet.
3 Having done this, pull the widget tight to secure it."

Correct this list with parallelism:

"Assembling the coaxial coordinator requires just three steps:

1 Insert the freebish pin into slot 'A.'
2 Wrap the belt around the grommet.
3 Pull the widget tight to secure it."

Following the Rules

The following rules will guide you in the use of prepositions and other connectives.

Rule 1: Use Simple Prepositions Instead of Wordy Prepositional Phrases
The wordy prepositional phrases in the left-hand column of the following listing can usually be replaced by the simple prepositions shown in the right-hand column.

Wordy Prepositional Phrase	Simple Preposition
inasmuch as	because, since
for the purpose of	to
in the event that	if
in order to	to
prior to	before
subsequent to	after
in regard to	about

In the following sentences, notice how we improve sentence readability by using a simple preposition in place of a wordy prepositional phrase.

Wordy Prepositional Phrase	Simple Preposition
Inasmuch as we were late for the meeting, we missed the new product announcement.	*Because* we were late for the meeting …
In the event that he attends the meeting, ask him for a copy of the report.	*If* he attends the meeting …
Subsequent to receiving your request for information *with regard to* the new store, we called the New Haven office.	*After* receiving your request for information *about* the new store …

Make a conscious effort to improve the "receiver friendliness" of your writing and speaking by eliminating wordy prepositional phrases whenever possible.

Rule 2: Use a Preposition at the End of a Sentence if the Preposition Sounds Natural and is Needed
Many an English teacher has taught that ending a sentence with a preposition is a situation "up with which we cannot put." But the fact is that when you force yourself to avoid ending a sentence with a preposition, you are often left with an awkward and unnatural-sounding sentence. On the other hand, some prepositions are not needed at the end of a sentence and can be

omitted. For example: "Where are you *at?*" or "I will type that *up.*" In deciding whether to end a sentence with a preposition, you should consider two important questions:

1   Does ending the sentence with a preposition sound natural? Would rewriting the sentence to avoid ending it with a preposition make the sentence sound awkward or artificial?
2   Is the preposition necessary, or can the preposition be omitted without any loss of meaning?

Rule 3: Omit Unneeded Prepositions
People often use prepositions that are not needed. Eliminating the italicized pronouns in the following examples does not change the meaning of the sentence.

- Let's try *out* the new procedure.
- Where did you sit *at* when you saw the concert?
- Add *up* the sales figures.
- Let us start *in on* the report in the morning.

Rule 4: Include All Needed Prepositions
Two kinds of sentence structures require prepositions that we often leave out: sentences with connected parallel elements (elements of equal importance) and sentences that include "split constructions."

CONNECTING PARALLEL ELEMENTS
As we mentioned earlier, because we should treat elements of equal rank or importance with equal grammatical structure, be sure to repeat the preposition before the second of two connected elements. For example:

- We told the job applicants *to* submit a completed application form and *to* call next week for an interview time. (Two elements of equal importance— "to submit" and "to call"—are separate actions.)
- The trainees prepared for the test *by* studying the workbook and *by* taking careful notes in the seminars. (Two elements of equal importance— "studying the textbook" and "taking notes"—are separate actions.)

If two connected elements are *not* of equal rank, do not repeat the preposition before the second element. For example:

- We told the job applicants *to* call next week and set an interview time with us. (Two elements, but not of equal importance—"call and set an interview time" is essentially *one* action.)

- The trainees prepared for the test *by* attending seminars and taking notes. (Two elements, but not of equal importance—"attending seminars and taking notes" is essentially *one* action.)

COMPLETING SPLIT CONSTRUCTIONS

When in one sentence you use two words that are completed by different prepositions, be sure to include *both* prepositions:

- She was interested *in* and prepared *for* the new job in the accounting department.
- The mayor was involved *with* and committed *to* the conservation program.
- The employees were active *in* and impressed *by* the social organization's activities.
- I was aware *of* but not excited *about* the proposal to build a new branch office.

Rule 5: Use Connective Pairs to Show Parallelism

Some conjunctions work in pairs to connect elements and to show the relationships between the elements. We call these pairs "connective pairs" or "correlative conjunctions." Connective pairs are:

- either–or
- neither–nor
- not–but
- both–and
- not only–but also.

To use connective pairs correctly, follow these two guidelines:

1   Do not mix the first half of one pair with the second half of another pair. "Either" must be used with "or"—it cannot be used with "nor." Likewise, "not only" must be used with "but also"—it cannot be used with "but."
2   Use the same parts of speech after each half of a pair. If "both" is followed by a phrase, "and" must also be followed by a phrase. If "neither" is followed by a noun, "nor" must also be followed by a noun.

The following sentences show correct parallel use of connective pairs:

- I said I would *either* go home *or* go to the office. (*either* verb *or* verb)
- *Neither* money *nor* fame could tempt him to sign the letter. (*neither* noun *nor* noun)

- The runner *not only* won the race *but also* broke the record. (*not only* verb *but also* verb)
- We decided *not* to send a letter *but* to make a phone call instead. (*not* infinitive *but* infinitive)

Repeating the verb after each half of the connective pair will achieve greater emphasis. For example: "He *not only runs* fast *but also jumps* high."

Rule 6: Use Conjunctive Adverbs to Show Relationships Between Complete Thoughts
We use "conjunctive adverbs" to join two complete thoughts (two independent clauses or two separate sentences) and to show the relationship between them. Conjunctive adverbs include words like "therefore," "however," "accordingly," "consequently," "nonetheless," "moreover," "furthermore," "nevertheless," "besides," and "still." In addition, you can use phrases like "on the contrary," "on the other hand," "in addition," "for example," and "at the same time" to connect complete thoughts in the same way a conjunctive adverb is used.

Because a conjunctive adverb introduces a complete thought, it must be followed by a comma. And because conjunctive adverbs have less "connecting power" than do conjunctions like "and" and "but," they must be preceded by either a period or a semicolon. For example: "We tried to finish the project before 5:00; *however*, we were unable to complete it." Or "The office can be staffed by just five employees. *Nevertheless*, it employs as many as ten people."

Rule 7: Repeat Relative Pronouns to Connect Parallel Clauses
Relative pronouns like "which," "who," and "that" can be used effectively to show parallelism between dependent clauses in a sentence. Just as we repeat a preposition like "to" or "by" before the second of two connected elements to show parallelism, we repeat the relative pronoun before each clause in a list of parallel clauses. For example:

- The weather forecaster said *that* it will rain today but *that* it will snow tomorrow evening.
- The laptop computer *that* was placed in Room 458 and *that* was stolen after only a week has been returned.
- Hideo Tada, *who* attended school here for a year and *who* wrote this report for us, is now living in Tokyo.
- We wanted to hire a secretary *whom* we could depend on and *whom* customers would feel comfortable working with.

Rule 8: Use the Connectives "Where," to Indicate Place, "When" to Indicate Time, and "While" to Indicate Duration
Commonly misused connectives are "where," "when," and "while." Here are some guidelines to help you use these connectives correctly:

USING "WHERE"

Use "where" to refer to a *place* or *location*. Do not use "where" to give a definition, as in, "Communication is *where* encoding and decoding take place successfully." Instead, say something like, "Communication is the successful encoding and decoding of a message."

"Where" is used correctly to refer to a place or a location in the following sentences:

- The New York Stock Exchange is *where* clients buy and sell stock shares.
- Las Vegas is *where* the largest gambling casinos in the world are located.
- Southern Arizona is the only place *where* these early Native American ruins exist in such good condition.

USING "WHEN"

Use "when" to refer to a period of *time*. Do not use "when" to give a definition. Instead of saying, "Free enterprise is *when* businesses are free to buy and sell in an unregulated market," say something like, "Free enterprise is the unregulated market in which businesses are free to buy and sell."

"When" is used correctly to refer to a period of time in these sentences:

- This is the year *when* we are going to achieve our $10 million sales goal.
- *When* he arrives with the pizza, pay him with cash from my desk.

USING "WHILE"

Use "while" to indicate *duration of time*. Do not use "while" to indicate contrast or comparison; use words like "although," "but," and "whereas" to show contrast or comparison. If you can replace "while" with a phrase like "during the time that," then you are using "while" correctly, as in these sentences:

- *While* the speaker made his last remarks, I began distributing the study packet.
- Alex operated the printing press *while* I stacked the printed copies on the paper cutter.

The following sentences correctly use "although," "but," and "whereas" instead of "while" to show contrast or comparison between two ideas:

- *Although* (not "while") I forgot to bring the graded papers to class, I did bring your new assignments.
- I cleaned the windows in the office on Friday, *but* (not "while") Bob cleaned the windows in the hallway on Saturday.

Modifiers: Saying it in Color with Adjectives and Adverbs

Adjectives and adverbs—the two kinds of modifiers or describing words—can be distinguished from each other by the kinds of things they describe. *Adjectives* describe (or modify the description of) *things*, and *adverbs* describe (or modify the description of) *action* or *other describing words*.

Using Adjectives

Adjectives are describing words that answer the questions, "What kind of [thing]?" or "Which [thing]?" Examples (the italicized words are adjectives):

- The *national* economy.
- The *friendly* neighbor.
- The *up-to-date* report.
- The *fully trained* technician.

Not all adjectives are just one word. Notice the multiple-word adjectives in the following sentences:

- The *half-done* report is on the desk.
- He gave us a *"get-lost-before-I-get-mad"* look.
- The manager *who wanted the report* came to my office.
- Reports *that detail expenses* are *printed on blue paper*.

Using Adverbs

Adverbs are words that describe verbs (action), adjectives, or other adverbs. Adverbs answer these questions: "Where?" "When?" "How?" "How much?" Examples (the italicized words are adverbs):

- Do the job *quickly*. (*Do the job* how?)
- It is good *enough*. (How *good?*)
- It was *very* expensive. (How *expensive?*)
- Read the letter *immediately*. (When?)
- Don't leave it *there*. (Where?)

Just as some adjectives are made from two or more words, many adverbs are *adverb phrases*. For example, in "He will work for an hour in the morning," the phrase "in the morning" answers the question "When?" And in "She works part-time for us," "part-time" answers the question "How?" or "How much?"

Following the Rules

The following are some key rules for using modifiers correctly.

Rule 1: Do Not Omit the "-ly" Ending from Adverbs

In conversation, many people drop the "-ly" ending from adverbs. For example, we incorrectly say things like "I was sure lucky" and "The work went real good" instead of "surely lucky" and "really well."

Especially in writing, use the correct adverb form to describe verbs and other describing words:

- He *surely* is lucky to get the prize money.
- I am *really* pleased to hear of your promotion.
- I think you did *well* yesterday.

Rule 2: Keep Related Words Together

Adjectives should be placed next to the *things* they describe, and adverbs should be placed next to the *action* or the *other modifiers* they describe.

The most common problem with keeping related words together is the simple misplacement of an adjective—especially adjectives like "only," "just," "about," or "almost." Examples of adjectives *not* placed next to the words they are meant to describe:

- I almost have enough money to start a new company.
- Please bring the speaker a cold glass of water.
- He only has $5 to spend at the store.
- Checks are only accepted with valid identification.

Notice how much more exact the sentences sound when the modifiers are placed close to the words they describe, in these examples:

- I have almost enough money to start a new company.
- Please bring the speaker a glass of cold water.
- He has only $5 to spend at the store.
- Checks are accepted only with valid identification.

Relative clauses are often mistakenly placed too far from the words they are intended to describe, but remembering to keep related words together will help you to avoid mistakes such as these:

- The man is here *who quit*.
- The report is very good *that he wrote at home yesterday afternoon.*

These sentences would have greater effect if they were rewritten like this:

- The man *who quit* is here.
- The report *that he wrote at home yesterday afternoon* is very good.

Rule 3: Avoid Dangling Modifiers

A *dangling modifier* is an adjective that does not refer clearly to a specific word or group of words in a sentence. In the following sentences, the adjective phrases dangle because they do not refer clearly to a particular word or group of words—or they are not next to the words they describe:

- *Having rotted in the cellar all winter*, my brother was unable to sell the apples.
- *To be sure the report would be delivered on time*, "URGENT" was written across the front of the envelope.

In the first sentence, the participle phrase "having rotted ..." is supposed to describe "the apples," but it is placed right in front of "my brother" instead. In the second sentence, the infinitive phrase "to be sure ..." is supposed to describe "we" or "I," or someone else not named in the sentence, but it is placed in front of "URGENT" instead.

To correct these dangling modifiers, we could re-write the sentences as shown here:

- Having rotted in the cellar all winter, *the apples* could not be sold by my brother.
- To be sure the report would be delivered on time, *we* wrote "URGENT" across the front of the envelope.

Rule 4: Avoid Overusing Modifiers

The use of too many modifiers—strings of adjectives or adverbs—detracts from the effect they are meant to have. For example:

- The lengthy, unorganized report describing last year's budgeted expenses in the personnel department was analyzed carefully and thoroughly by our very competent and willing auditors who work regularly in the accounting department.

The many modifiers make the sentence wordy and ineffective. Notice how the careful use of only two or three modifiers makes the sentence much easier to read:

- The auditors carefully analyzed the personnel department's expense report for last year.

Rule 5: Use "Comparative" Modifiers to Compare Two Things and "Superlative" Modifiers to Compare More Than Two Things

We use adjectives and adverbs to compare two or more things. When only two things are compared, the adjectives and adverbs should be *comparative* modifiers—modifiers used with words like "more" and "less" and adjectives with "-er" added to them (like "greater" and "smarter"). For example:

- This half is *better* than that half.
- Of the two, John is the *smarter* technician.
- Betty is a *faster* programmer than all the rest of our programmers.
- He is *more* capable than she is.

When more than two things are compared, the adjectives and adverbs should be *superlative* modifiers—modifiers used with words like "most" and "least" and adjectives with "-est" added to them (like "greatest" and "smartest"). For example:

- She is the *tallest* member of the team.
- He is the *smallest* quarterback to play in the NFL.
- She is the *most* qualified of all the applicants.

Rule 6: Make Complete, Logical Comparisons

Incomplete comparisons often make the reader guess at what you are comparing. For example:

- The Gilbreth diamond is far more beautiful—and costs less, too. (*More beautiful that what?*)
- You look much better today. (*Better than when?*)
- We have received more applications for clerical positions this year. (*Compared to another year or to non-clerical positions?*)

Be sure that your comparisons are logical. That is, don't compare apples to oranges, as has been done in these sentences:

- My duties were much more difficult than my brother.
- The houses and shops I saw in Japan were just like any town in America.

The first sentence compares "my duties" to "my brother" and the second sentence compares houses and shops in Japan to "any town in America." Restated to avoid the illogical comparisons, the sentences would say this:

- My duties were more difficult than *my brother's duties* were.
- The houses and shops I saw in Japan were just like *the houses and shops of any town in America.*

Rule 7: Use Hyphenated Compound Adjectives as Single Modifiers
A *compound adjective* is a group of words that provides a single description of a noun that follows. Hyphens are used between the words to make the words appear as a single unit. Thus, proper hyphenation of compound adjectives increases understanding and speeds the reader along. Notice the proper use of hyphens to form compound adjectives in the following sentences:

- The Small Business Administration approved a small-business loan for $2 million.
- He said that the large-appliance industry has been weakened by the recent economic depression.
- His "better-late-than-never" attitude kept him from hearing the opening remarks of many meetings.

Each compound adjective in these sentences provides a *single* description of the noun that follows it, regardless of whether the adjective has two, three, or more words in it.

The decision to place a hyphen between two words or to leave the hyphen out will often have a significant effect on the meaning of a sentence. For example:

- We need more qualified workers. (*We need what? Great numbers of qualified workers.*)
- We need more-qualified workers. (*We need what? Workers who are more qualified than the workers we have now.*)
- The large appliance industry is suffering. (*Which industry? The appliance industry, which is large.*)
- The large-appliance industry is suffering. (*Which industry? The industry that produces large appliances.*)

Hyphenated compound adjectives are used only *before* nouns. When they come after nouns, they are not hyphenated:

- The up-to-date report was submitted on time. (*Comes before the noun*)
- The report was up to date. (*Comes after the noun*)
- It was a well-written report. (*Comes before the noun*)
- The report was well written. (*Comes after the noun*)

Rule 8: Never Hyphenate After an "-ly" Adverb.
Although hyphens are often used after adverbs, as in "a well-written report," they are never used after "*-ly*" *adverbs* such as "carefully" and "quickly." Notice the absence of a hyphen after the "-ly" adverbs in the following sentences:

- He presented a *thoroughly* documented report to the city council members.
- The *easily* missed turnoff is just a mile from the main intersection.
- The *carelessly* typed report had to be returned to the word-processing center.

Rule 9: Separate Consecutive Adjectives with a Comma

As we mentioned earlier, if two or more adjectives provide *separate* descriptions of the noun or pronoun, they are called "consecutive" adjectives. Because they do not act as a single unit to provide just one description of the noun, they are not joined into a single unit with hyphens. Instead, they are separated with a comma. For example:

- It was a clear, sunny day. (*Two* descriptions of "day": "clear" and "sunny.")
- He submitted a long, poorly written report. (*Two* descriptions of "report": "long" and "poorly written.")

As you learned earlier, an easy way to decide whether you should put a comma between two adjectives is to separate the adjectives with the word "and." If the word "and" makes sense—and sounds right to you—put a comma between the adjectives. Of course, you can leave the "and" between them if you want; in that case, you should leave the comma out. Notice how we've used this trick to decide whether to put a comma between the adjectives in the following phrases:

- The new (,?) inexpensive information appliance . . .

"New *and* inexpensive information appliance" sounds right, so we should put a comma between "new" and "inexpensive":
- The new, inexpensive information appliance . . .

Or:

- His adjusted (,?) gross income . . .

"Adjusted *and* gross income" does not sound right, so we should *not* put a comma between "adjusted" and "gross."

A Final Thought

As we said at the beginning of this reference tool, the grammar and usage issues covered here are certainly not exhaustive but, rather, focus on commonly experienced questions. Consult a style guide or dictionary if in doubt about grammar or usage in your writing.

We also recommend that you set your word-processing software to signal grammatical errors. You can program Microsoft Word, for example, to underline (ours does it in green) questionable syntax as well as spelling errors (in red for us). These indicators are not 100 percent accurate depending on your intention as a writer, but they will help you avoid many, if not most, errors.

Finally, we remind you that not paying attention to correct grammar, syntax, and spelling will quickly undermine your credibility. Credibility is extremely important as you deliver your messages as a Straight Talk Writer.

Notes

1 Introduction to Straight Talk Writing

1 Peter F. Drucker, *Management Challenges for the 21st Century,* New York: Harper-Business, 1999, p. 170.
2 A classic book on NLP in business is Michael Brooks, *The Power of Business Rapport,* New York: HarperCollins, 1991.
3 Cynthia E. Griffin, "Bad Words," *Entrepreneur*, February 2000, 34.
4 L.E. Gant, *So People Don't Read?*, May 26, 2005, www.googobits.com/articles/p0-364-so-people-dont-read.html. Reprinted with permission.
5 *Uncle John's Absolutely Absorbing Bathroom Reader,* Ashland, OR: The Bathroom Reader's Institute, 1999, p. 103.
6 Of course, you may not have the luxury of having someone check every message you write, but solicit feedback for any mass-distributed documents and any writing that could have an impact on your career success. See Chapter 7 for more information on feedback options.

2 Define Context Before Writing

1 This story has been repeated many times as a classic communications foul-up. Neal Patterson sent the original email on March 13, 2001, but the story has had amazing "legs." If you Google the topic, you'll see dozens of references to the email and its impact. It is regularly cited by communication and management consultants.
2 Stephen P. Robbins, *Essentials of Organizational Behavior*, 9th ed., Upper Saddle River, NJ: Prentice-Hall, Inc., 2008, p. 248.
3 Adapted from G. Hofstede, "Cultural Constraints in Management Theories," *Academy of Management Executive*, February 1993, p. 91.
4 Interview by Robert C. Ford, "David Neeleman, CEO of JetBlue Airways, on People + Strategy = Growth," *The Academy of Management Executive*, 18, 2, May 2004, p. 141.

3 Consider Your Media, Source, and Timing Options

1 Reprinted with permission from *The Salt Lake Tribune*, September 6, September 8, 2009, pp. E-1, E-1.
2 This classic, early study is found in T.L. Dahle, "An Objective and Comparative Study of Five Methods of Transmitting Information to Business and Industrial Employees," *Speech Monographs*, 21, 1954, pp. 21–28.

3 D.A. Level, "Communication Effectiveness: Method and Situation," *Journal of Business Communication*, Fall 1972, pp. 19–25.

4 Review the credibility checklist in Chapter 1 if you are unsure about the factors that influence a writer's credibility with his or her readers.

4 Select and Organize Your Message Content

1 Originally developed in F.E. Fiedler, *A Theory of Leadership Effectiveness*, New York: McGraw-Hill, 1967.

2 We acknowledge our colleague and friend, Professor William H. Baker at the Marriott School of Management, Brigham Young University, who developed much of this approach.

3 This mind map found online is shown as an example. http://hello1071112024. files.wordpress.com/2009/03/retriement_speech_3.jpg.

5 Enhance Your Writing With Graphic Elements

1 Chip Heath and Dan Heath, *Made To Stick: Why Some Ideas Survive and Others Die*, New York: Random House, 2007.

2 Heath and Heath, p. 209.

3 Neither author is an attorney and this information does not purport to be legal advice. It is based on wide experience, however, and is intended to provide some commonsense guidelines.

4 See, for example, Scott Tambert, *How To Use Images Legally* (available online at www.pdimages.com/law/). Tambert is a specialist in public domain images research. He is not a lawyer, and you should always seek competent, professional counsel on legal matters. www.pdimages.com/web9.htm.

6 Delivering Effective Workplace Writing

1 The use of these conventions dates back many years and may be less mandatory than in the past. People used these phrases to convey professionalism in a time when commerce was more formal.

2 These convey a complete thought, remember?

3 This article coauthored with Gary C. Cornia, a respected public finance expert, appeared in *Exchange Magazine*, a publication of Brigham Young University in 1981. Funny how topics come back around after several decades!

4 In fairness, government agencies have come a long way in striving for plain English writing styles.

7 Evaluate Feedback for Continued Success

1 The University of Iowa Summer Writer's Festival workshops are renowned for launching successful writing careers. See their website at www.continuetolearn. uiowa.edu/iswfest/.

2 One of your authors has written extensively on customer service. His most recent book is Paul R. Timm, *Customer Service*, 5th Edition, Upper Saddle River: Pearson Prentice-Hall, 2011.

Reference Tool for Straight Talk Writing

1 The authors appreciate the help of our friend and colleague Ray L. Young in developing the material in this reference guide. Ray was an exceptional instructor at the Marriott School of Management, Brigham Young University.

Index